THE CASE FOR HILLARY CLINTON

THE CASE FOR

★ HILLARY CLINTON ★

SUSAN ESTRICH

ReganBooks
An Imprint of HarperCollinsPublishers

B
CLINTON

HarperCollins books may be purchased for educational, business, or sales promotional use. For information please write: Special Markets Department, HarperCollins Publishers Inc., 10 East 53rd Street, New York, NY 10022.

FIRST EDITION

Designed by Kris Tobiassen

Printed on acid-free paper

Library of Congress Cataloging-in-Publication Data

ISBN 13: 978-0-06-083988-8

ISBN 10: 0-06-083988-0

05 06 07 08 09 RRD 10 9 8 7 6 5 4 3 2 1

To Tom Oliphant
God Bless, and save me a seat.

ACKNOWLEDGMENTS

Many thanks to Judith Regan and Calvert Morgan, who literally make book, and to Amanda Urban and Melissa Lo, my agent and assistant, who do that too; to my many colleagues at Fox News, starting with the best bosses I've ever had, Roger Ailes and Bill Shine, for your support and your friendship; to my daughter, Isabel, for the melody, and my son, James, for the words, I love you both more than life; to Annie Gilbar, Katherine Reback, and Rose Sierra, for help on the hard days, to Bobby Grahm for perspective, to Maureen Gordon for wisdom, to Neil Geileghelm for instant response, and to Rose Shumow because she loves to see her name here and I love her; to Barbara and Bert (the real ones), Joan Buck, Lynne Wasserman, Pam Fleishchaker, Pam Morton, Larry Seigler, Patricia Peyser, Peter Ulikhanov, to my sister and brother for taking care of my mother; Joel Kaufman, Marc Gilbar, Hope Garcia, Kathleen Sullivan, and Judy Estrich—my best friend—thank you all.

CONTENTS

I.

IMAGINE

★

Imagine the moment when a news anchor will say, "Based on all our projections, we can now say that the United States of America has elected its first woman president . . ."

If you're old enough, think back to how you felt in 1984, when you heard that Walter Mondale had picked Geraldine Ferraro to be his running mate. Remember what it was like when she stood up to accept the nomination, and for a moment there were no limits to what was possible. Sally Ride was flying into space; Gerry Ferraro was running for vice president. All of a sudden it seemed true after all: Women could do anything.

Now, multiply that feeling by a thousand, and imagine how it will feel when a woman stands up to accept the Democratic presidential nomination—the first woman to be nominated for the presidency by either party.

And then multiply *that* by a thousand, and think of election night 2008. Imagine yourself turning to your daughter, or your mother or sister, or your niece or grandmother or granddaughter, and saying:

If she can do this, then the world really has changed.

And across the globe, in every language women speak, as the pictures travel and the word spreads, as those voices are heard, billions of girls and women will turn to each other and say the same thing, and the world *will* never be the same.

This is an argument for that night.

It is an argument for how we can get there.

For what all of us have to do to make it happen.

★ ★ ★

The following people are not real. (Although any resemblance to real people is entirely intentional.)

BERT: It's suicide. She'll win two states.

BARBARA: I hope Judith is paying you a fortune, Susan.

BERT: Maybe we should invite her for dinner?

BARBARA: After all those makeovers . . .

BERT: You want to imagine something? Imagine the Supreme Court with nothing but conservatives for the next fifty years, because we gambled wrong . . .

BARBARA: Bert says it's okay to make him a character as long as you don't tell people you've convinced him, because you haven't. And make sure you don't use our real names.

Remember Harry and Louise, the doubting-Thomas couple from those ads attacking Hillary Clinton's health care plan? Bert and Barbara are my Harry and Louise. If they were real, they might be my best friends.

You can't win, Bill Clinton said the other day, *talking just to people who agree with you.* You have to meet the arguments of people who start out on the other side.

That's music to the ears of a law professor.

When you're talking about Hillary, it's easy to find people to argue with. Most Democrats I know, even the ones who like her, are up in the air about Hillary. I've never been attacked like I have since I started telling people what I was writing about—and I live where it is very, very blue.

Bert and Barbara are actually more positive about Hillary than some other people I know. My friend Maureen thinks Hillary is about two years old, developmentally. Two is not a charming age. Two still has pieces missing. People are drawn to her, she says, but they're uncomfortable with her because they sense that there's literally something missing. Bill fills in the pieces. That's what keeps them together. That's why, whatever I write, Maureen is certain that people won't like it. There will be something missing.

My friend Neil thinks she is cold at the core. A phony. But he's impressed by her New York numbers. Maybe she can pull the same thing off, he reasons, if she can figure out what worked before Dick Morris beats her to it and finds a way to counterpunch. Neil thinks Dick is smart, but that he can't get over the fact that Hillary outsmarted him; and Dick's cross because he lost to a two-year-old, playing the same game over and over.

I think Senator Hillary Rodham Clinton, soon-to-be second-term senator from New York, centrist Democrat, strong on security, tough, moderate, family values, middle-aged, qualified, managed by Bill Clinton, is the next president of the United States. . . .

I have it in my head to try to convince my friends that I'm right and they're wrong.

★ ★ ★

Is Hillary running?

Yes.

Has she told me so? No, of course not. Ann Lewis, her chief political aide, will say only that "We're focused on the Senate campaign now." Of course, it's a necessary political ruse. Nobody's trying to convince us that Hillary's New York constituents are flocking to vacation in Minnesota and Wisconsin and Ohio, three states she has visited recently. Nobody really believes it's essential to have a state chair in Georgia when you're running for Senate in New York. She has the best possible guy in her California chair, and he told me only recently that he was vitally interested in the New York Senate race. Hillary made headlines in May by inviting her Iowa supporters to her Washington home for a fundraiser, an innovative step to take in a New York race.

In politics, there are steps you take when you're running for Senate, and steps you take when you're running for president. When you're running for president, you put together a presidential-caliber PAC run by a veteran presidential-caliber campaign chief like Ann Lewis; you start hiring national organizers; you amass a bigger war chest than any other senator who is up for reelection, even before you have an opponent; you put your people in place in the appropriate think tanks, media groups, state parties, and consulting firms so everybody is ready to go. All of which senatorial candidate Hillary Clinton has done.

Since election night 2004, Hillary Clinton has been leading in every poll for the Democratic nomination. Not only does she have the most money, the best organization, and the most loyal staff among all the potential players—she's also young enough, old enough, smart enough, bold enough, and for all those reasons beloved enough by the voters of the Democratic Party. And there's every reason to believe she's dreamed of it—more than two or three times, anyway. Why in the world wouldn't she be running?

Can you imagine any man in her position *not* running? They'd think he was nuts. His staff would kill him. They'd fill out the papers for him.

But can she win?

Can America elect its first woman president?

Can a woman who has been more vilified, humiliated, put down (and, yes, lied to), more than any of us—can she stand up, fight back, use her own intelligence and power, find her authentic voice, her real style, her center, grow into exactly who she was meant to be, and at the age of sixty—in her true prime—shatter the glass and change the world?

She can.

But it will take the help of a lot of people who have not been with her before. Women who "didn't quite get her," cringed at all the makeovers, found themselves more drawn to him than to her. Women who have even been critical in the past. Women like me.

BERT: People hate her. You know that. They think she's arrogant, self-righteous, crooked, conniving, cold, calculating, and ambitious. Personally, I think she's intelligent and charming, but she's unelectable.

BARBARA: They think she's a phony. And, Susan, she hates you— don't you remember?

I have not always been number one on Hillary's list . . .

(Alert to unsuspecting readers: What follows might be an old trick Evan Thomas of *Newsweek* tried to teach me in 1988: *Lead by saying something bad about your candidate.* Watch Jim Baker, he said. It's called showing the ball. *She must be telling me the truth if she's telling me this,* they'll think. And I am.)

★ ★ ★

At the 2004 convention, Madeleine Albright came up to me wagging her finger. "What you said about Hillary's speech last night was not helpful."

At first I thought she was kidding. It had been after midnight when I made those comments. Bill's speech, I had said, was terrific. But Hillary's remarks introducing him were no great shakes, especially given the big to-do that had been made about giving her time on the schedule. I gave it two asses, or something like that, on the one-to-four scale my friend Greta van Susteren was selling that night. I said what I thought.

"We need all the help we can get over here," she said, referring to the Fox News Channel, where I'm a political analyst. *Well,* I wanted to say, *I won't have any credibility if I lie.* But by then she had disappeared into the box. My friend, a senior Fox producer who was standing with me, couldn't believe the scene. Madeleine and I had known each other more than twenty years; we used to be excluded from all the same meetings together.

The Fox producer looked at me and shook her head. "Aren't these people your friends?" she asked me.

I don't blame Madeleine, of course. She was just carrying water.

I can remember the day I introduced Madeleine to the governor. Clinton, I mean. At least it was the first day he saw her in action, and I know he was totally impressed. It was 1988, a prep session before the first presidential debate, and Bill had come in to help Michael Dukakis get ready. I certainly remember the night we three ended up driving around Boston, along with the late, great political media man Bob Squier, Bruce Lindsey, and of course, a trusted Arkansas state trooper. I was at the wheel of the blue Chevy, looking for a bar that would let us in, certain that the next day would bring disaster.

We pulled up to the Four Seasons, and the valet was so full of himself at the sight of all the national media that he wouldn't even take the car. All he needed was one look at our dirty Chevrolet, with six people crammed in it, this big guy sitting in the middle seat carrying on, and he didn't even bother to look at our faces. *VIPs only,* he told us. Bill couldn't stop laughing. "What a sorry bunch," he guffawed, egging Squier on. "Couldn't even get into a bar . . ." Squier jumped out of the car, to find the captain. He was going to regret turning us away, I could hear him saying—because of all the people he's ever nixed, this time he chose the governor of Arkansas, who's going to be president some-day, and Madeleine Albright, who'll probably be secretary of state, just because they're packed into a dingy—but politically correct—midsize Chevrolet. (Of course I blamed myself for not washing the car.)

Like so much of what Squier said and did in his too-short life, it all turned out to be true. (Except for our premonitions of disaster the next day; on that score, we were just one debate off.)

Bill Clinton helped me get through the most difficult days of Dukakis's campaign, and the experience forged a deep friendship be-tween us. He used to call me at least twice a day during that campaign; I figured he had already decided he was going to run four years later, and he wanted to know every detail about everything. I had never met any-one with such a voracious appetite and such a stunning command of politics. Dukakis routinely rejected the great lines our communications guy, George Stephanopoulos, wrote for him; I sent them on to Clinton. The best intern in the place was Gene Sperling, hands down, and he sent Clinton stuff, too. Believe me, Bill took names. He studied the poll numbers more carefully than Dukakis himself, and knew every mistake the candidate made. He was also the first person who called to console me the morning after the election. He did everything he could to try to communicate with the candidate and defend me from criticisms I my-self couldn't answer.

So when Bill got in trouble—with Gennifer, and Paula, and all of that—I did my best to defend him. I did it because I thought the Re-publicans were going way too far, but mostly I did it because in Boston that's what's known as loyalty. When a friend is in the right, it isn't a matter of loyalty to support him. That's easy. That's just doing the right thing. *No* credit for that. It's when somebody screws up that they need their friends. That's when loyalty kicks in.

That's what I never could understand about Al Gore: why he couldn't just go out on the campaign trail and say, *The man picked me, I've served with him, I'm proud of what we accomplished together.* Why he couldn't show simple loyalty to the man. It's what he himself expected of Joe Lieberman—that he wouldn't run for president in 2004 if Gore did.

I thought the Republicans went way too far in their attacks on Clinton; I thought they were going after the Constitution. But I was also being a loyal friend. I knew the truth; I'd talked to him about it. But that's what loyalty is about—sticking with people not just when they're right, but when they need you.

I've never been as close with Hillary as with Bill. Though she's always been very pleasant to me, when I spent time at the White House during the Clinton presidency; I was talking with him, not her. When my family and I stayed overnight, she was out at a dinner; when she returned, she visited with us and then went to bed at a reasonable hour. He had dinner with my family, put my children to bed, and stayed up talking with me until two in the morning. When I attended dinners at the White House, I sat with him. I danced with him. He used to call me on the phone. We exchanged notes on a regular basis. When I would stop in Washington and visit the White House, he would sit with me in the Oval Office, talking about the press and the Republicans, and how he was doing. If you go looking for old quotes, you won't find many places where I criticized President Clinton.

But "President" Hillary? That's another matter. In the years leading up to the 2004 race, you can find me saying that she shouldn't run; how divisive she would be as a candidate; how the Clintons needed to move aside, stop dropping hints about Hillary, and give the real candidates a chance. Sean Hannity loves to remind me that I once lamented that the Clintons "suck all the oxygen out of the room." By "the room," I love to remind him, I meant the race for the 2004 nomination. If you were John Kerry, would you want to compete with Bill and Hill for attention? My point was that Kerry and Co. didn't stand a chance by comparison, and since I was certain she wasn't going to run, I didn't think they should play. But that line earned me a few calls from old friends asking what had happened to me, if Fox was making me say such things. I said I wanted the Democrats to win. (And for the record, I say whatever I want—on Fox or anywhere else.)

* * *

The right is very afraid of Senator Hillary Rodham Clinton. This is a different game. After a decade of being dismissed as the First Lady of Twelve Hairdos, or Saint Hillary of Big Health Care, she has transcended the rude comments and partisan character assassination attempts. Today she is the soon-to-be second-term senator from New York, widely respected by colleagues on both sides for her brains and her sense of humor. She is the best fund-raiser in the party, the most charismatic candidate, the front-runner, a centrist, and a woman.

For the first time since I've been watching, she also seems comfortable in her own skin. As one of her friends said to me, she has become the woman she would have been without Bill. She looks the way she would have looked, has the style she would have had, even the job she would've held, albeit from a different state. She has matured; it's not a makeover when you and your destiny unite, as they did for Hillary five years ago. She loves what she's doing, who she is; she is passionate about her work, surrounded by people who like and admire her; she is not at war with anyone. She is finding common ground, finding her groove, running the best office on Capitol Hill, and if she had any other name, we would be clamoring at the prospect of her running for president.

Is she still a polarizing figure? Perhaps, but the truly polarizing figure is the old public perception of Bill Clinton's first lady, not the woman she has become in her own right. The most fascinating numbers in all of these polling statistics are the numbers out of New York. Clearly, something very significant has happened there. You don't move up *thirty points*—that doesn't just happen.[1] And it isn't a matter of a makeover, the simplistic explanation my Republican friends are trying to trot out, for want of anything else. New York isn't that blue of a state; its departing three-term governor is, after all, a Republican, and Hillary started out with the same numbers there as everywhere else. If she can begin to do nationally what she has done in New York, the presidency will be hers—and there is polling evidence to suggest that she has. Not to mention the fact that polarizing doesn't disqualify you from winning, particularly if it allows you to energize your base. George W. Bush proved that.

Electing a woman president could literally change the world for women and girls, and boys and men. Stop and think about what it will be like to go to work in the days after the election, with every guy in your workplace feeling like the woman in the White House might be coming by to check things out—or at least that one of the women above or below him might. Imagine all the reshuffling that would begin, as the men (and women) started to realize the world was changing.

And when I say a woman president, it means Hillary. There is no pipeline full of other contenders. The Canadian-born governor of Michigan, Jennifer Granholm, is ineligible. (Arnold has no time these days to worry about his amendment.) And even the list of Democratic women considered for vice president has never grown larger than two: Gerry Ferraro and Dianne Feinstein. Pitiful, but just my point, I'm afraid.

I never had any doubt that, by every measure, Hillary would be the most qualified candidate in the 2008 race. But at first I had a lot of doubt about whether she could win. Hillary has never stopped being Target One in the world of political spin. Anyone who has grown up in that world, as I have, almost has to divorce herself from it to get something approaching a clear view of Hillary chances. Before I felt confident that I could support her, I needed to change my own mind about her chances—because there is no question that a defeat for Hillary would be seen as a loss for women. So I started reading the polls in earnest.

I saw one poll, of political insiders, that was full of smart insights.[2] But I was struck by how few of my colleagues identified gender *per se* as a factor in Hillary's prospects. Then I saw the category called "persona" that got the most votes among Democrats; most of the insiders queried thought she would win the nomination, but among those who didn't the top reason was "her persona," and the second was "her gender." I would argue that a persona of a cold, ambitious woman means a loss for women. As a woman who has spent a lifetime in these trenches, it seems to me that the battle lines are drawn, whether women would have chosen them or not. Which means that the net upside is huge, but you also are looking at a very real downside. It's not a fight you want to get into unless you have every belief that you can win.

And this time, I believe, Hillary can do it.

Why am I writing now? Because the reality is that Hillary isn't running yet, but her opponents are already running against her, some of them with their usual gusto, and they are having some success in the politics of intimidation. Fear tactics work. What we used to call "August" in presidential politics—the period before the campaign officially begins, when only insiders are supposed to be paying attention, except that the mud still sticks when it's slung, and the result can be an election lost before it has formally begun—comes earlier and earlier in every cycle. It is perfectly appropriate and necessary for Hillary and her team to be focusing on the Senate race, attuned to New York, *not* all the national talk shows. It's better that she avoid getting killed for not paying enough attention to her constituents. There will be time enough for Orlando and Ohio, starting a year or so from now.

But that doesn't mean that the rest of us should let the right launch their rockets while we sit on our hands. Electing a woman president is not going to be easy.

The conventional wisdom is that the Democratic nomination is Hillary's for the asking, as long as she can prove she can win. But the conventional wisdom is usually wrong in nomination politics, and proving electability isn't easy. Especially for a woman: Those of us who have toiled in the fields know that when you're talking about a "first woman," much less a "first woman president," you take nothing for granted. You should plan on fighting every step of the way; expect that nothing will be easy, and you're very unlikely to be disappointed. The idea that Hillary Clinton can be president is going to take some getting used to. The idea that women should—no, *must*—support her, that we owe it to ourselves and her, is not going to be an "easy sell," as one of my friends keeps telling me. If you hope to close the deal by November 2008, in other words, it's time to get started.

A few months ago, one of New York's new conservative publishing imprints released Ed Klein's outrageous hatchet job *The Truth About Hillary.* The book could not have been criticized more widely; even Sean Hannity and Dick Morris, two of Fox's most unreconstructed Hillary-bashers, disavowed it (winning themselves some credibility points in the process).[3] Nonetheless Klein has carried on, repeating his garbage stories of Hillary and Monica, a hash of ancient history, foolish rumors, and schoolyard innuendo. With luck, the controversy over Klein's book will help the media draw some lines as to what is acceptable criticism. In the meantime though, *The Truth About Hillary* is selling, debuting at number two on the *New York Times* bestseller list, and making news for the author's nonappearances on the TV talk shows.[4]

And what happens? Two weeks after it comes out the Democratic minority leader, Senator Harry Reid, responds to another new strong poll for Hillary by telling his hometown paper that she might not be the strongest nominee.[5] Matt Drudge, of course, headlined his comments on *The Drudge Report.* Now, why isn't she the strongest nominee? Presumably the likes of Harry Reid would respond that it's because she's polarizing. And what makes her polarizing? Well, how about all this trash talk from opportunistic writers, and politicians . . .

The talk among the women who don't "get" Hillary, or don't understand why she didn't leave Bill, feeds perfectly into what the right is doing. What's worse, it also gives the Harry Reids of the world a reason, or at least an excuse, to question her electability. The left doesn't get her;

the right answers that it's all just cold, hard ambition. The left doesn't understand; the right explains that there's nothing to understand if she's just a phony. They all feed at the same trough. And the hatred feeds on itself.

At its core, the challenge goes to her authenticity. Amy Sullivan, a wonderful writer at the *Washington Monthly*, professes to be a longtime and major Hillary fan, but there she is piling on with Ed Klein and Harry Reid.[6] Amy writes in the July/August 2005 issue that she has to be "the one" to beg Hillary not to run. *Why?* I think. Is there something new I have missed? I scan her column for reasons. Certainly, she can see through Ed Klein's garbage. What, then, is she afraid of? She's afraid the right will mount its usual campaign, based on hoary old complaints about endless makeovers and political expediency.

Of course they will. So what? Hell, compared to what Hillary's been through, that's kid stuff. Why should it scare us?

As I write this, there are countless Democrats who will someday stand with her, professing to be her friends, who are sitting back and wondering whether Sullivan might be right. Sorry, guys, but who do you think Harry Reid is really listening to? Klein is the chorus. These are the solos. This is what August is like.

No one on the Clinton team asked me to write this book, and no one who is currently working for Hillary helped me do it. This is my argument, not theirs, and they are certainly not responsible for anything I say. I would love to see Hillary win; I'd love to see the kind of people she attracts return to government. I have enormous respect for the talented people who are working for her right now, and who will certainly be working in the campaign—beginning with two spectacular women: Ann Lewis, who runs her PAC in Washington, and Tamera Luzzato, who heads her Senate office. Ann has been with her for fourteen years, which speaks volumes for Hillary. Tamera, a former chief of staff to Senator Jay Rockefeller, is one of the smartest and most mature women on Capitol Hill. Even conservatives concede—enviously, in their case—

that Hillary has one of the very best offices on Capitol Hill, a smoothly run operation full of first-rate people. This is a credit to both her and Tamera, whom I first worked with twenty-one years ago. But my friends are not responsible for what I say, nor can I hope to make them happy by everything I write.

Let me tell you something about Ann and Tamera before I go on, because it says something very important about Hillary, too. Both of these women, whom Hillary counts on as advisors and friends, have faced terrible crises in the last two years. For Ann, it was the death of her daughter at the hands of her estranged husband—a horrible act of domestic violence that left her other daughter raising Ann's grandchild. Then, in 2004, Tamera was diagnosed with a brain tumor, which initially appeared to be inoperable. Tamera, who had nursed her husband Frank when he was dying, cared for him with such grace and dignity, and later found happiness to her own surprise with David, was now facing what seemed to be a life-threatening illness of her own. It was too horrible for words. And what happened? As everybody always says, if you ever had one dime, Hillary would be the person you'd want to call. Hillary did everything short of move into the hospital room with Tamera. She was there every step of the way. Tamera was operated on at Johns Hopkins, and the doctors got the whole thing. The recovery took time, but Tamera's job was waiting for her when she returned. Though she was shaky, she went to the convention. And as soon as she was up to it, she went back to work.

Why? That's a good question. Neither Tamera nor Ann had to go back to work. Both of them have wonderful husbands. You cannot lose a child, or face a threat to your own life, without being reminded that there is more to life than work.

If working for Hillary were just another job, neither of them would be there today.

When my friend Tom had a sudden aneurysm in his brain last spring and was rushed into brain surgery, who were the first people on the phone to him and his daughter, a former Hillary staffer? Hillary and Tamera, reassuring them of the miracle of modern brain surgery, of how recovery works, of the need for patience. But the thing is, they didn't just call once. "She was all over both of us," Tom says with his great laugh. I'm embarrassed. Tom has been one of my best friends for thirty years, and Hillary called more than I did. It's not as if she has time on her hands. And mostly she was calling Wendy, to make sure she understood that her father would "come back," that it would just take time, and she shouldn't be scared.

Somehow, these stories never make it into those Hate-Hillary polemics. They certainly don't make it into the writing of Peggy Noonan, whom I happen to be very fond of as a fellow commentator, mother, and writer, and respect as a legendary speechwriter. Early in 2000, when conservatives were first gearing up to face Candidate Hillary, Peggy wrote an anti-Hillary polemic entitled *The Case Against Hillary Clinton*. Notwithstanding the similarity of our titles, I'm not trying to go argument-for-argument with her, any more than I'll be trying to speak for Hillary herself. The problem with polemics, in my view anyway, is they hide too much, papering over every interesting question instead of giving it a name and struggling with it. Polemics are for screamers, including those who do it stylishly with a pen, and for the chorus who came convinced. In my heart, I'm an academic, not a screamer. I envision my readers as people of good faith, open to argument. And I will try to wrestle with all the arguments in that same good faith.

When I was a young teacher, teaching labor law for the first time, I confided to a senior colleague that I was terrified to tell my students how little I knew about the subject. When I thought nothing of admitting total ignorance in the field, he said—that's when I'd know I'd gotten to be an old hand. He did it all the time, he told me wryly. It was a truly great man, Archibald Cox, who shared that wisdom—the man who wrote the book on labor law.

Today, I feel more and more like that old hand myself. I couldn't afford to be a judge, and I've slept in the Lincoln Bedroom. I have tenure at USC and job security at Fox, which means I'm lucky enough not to want anything from the next president, once she gets elected. In politics, that's as close as you get to being free, as Janis Joplin might say. I'm not afraid to say what I don't know; I've been teaching presidential politics since I stopped practicing it, and I believe I can best help Hillary Clinton get elected by telling the truth as I see it. Otherwise, I'm just one more shill in a silly screaming match.

★ ★ ★

A word about the title of this book: I can make my own arguments for why Hillary Clinton should be president, but ultimately it's Hillary who must make that case for herself. Every candidate ultimately does. It's her vision, not mine, you have to vote for—her soul you need ultimately to glimpse.

At an even more fundamental level, it's Hillary herself who will choose her own issues, domestic and foreign, and her message, her vision of the future. She'll start the process sometime around a year and a half from now, after doing exhaustive research on all kinds of things that haven't happened yet. Her team of unbelievably smart people will spend endless hours analyzing all kinds of decisions—about the economy, taxes, interest rates, progress on the war, who gets appointed to the Supreme Court, and how Americans are feeling about that—not to mention the threat of terrorism, and whether America feels as protected as it should. I'm not so foolish as to even try to guess what conclusions they'll reach, how events will play out or public opinion will react. I have too much respect for the professionalism of the people involved to do that. If you want a sneak preview, you'll get it on election night 2006—which will be a coming-out party of sorts, and an extremely important speech for Hillary.

The case *I* can make for her is the case for why *we* should support her, and why we should do it sooner, not later. It's the speech she won't be giving, the argument she won't be making, because she can't. They'd kill her. That's the truth of politics. She'll be talking about education and health care and armed services, about deficits and budgets and the environment. She'll be reaching out to moderate voters, wooing neoconservative pundits, finding the middle path through the polarized landscape of our politics, talking about prayer and values and video games. I hope she'll be talking in human terms, showing us that she understands the lives of real families, that she knows what women go through, that she will bring an extraordinary mind and an extraordinary sensitivity to the White House.

I can make the case that Amy Sullivan is wrong: that the right has already played all its heavy guns against Hillary Clinton, and that she has survived to see this much better day. Give in to them now, and they'll never stop crowing. Right now, the Republicans are on their weakest ground in years. It's time to take them on and win. They know what she can do—which is why they are fighting. And those who should be on Hillary's side have got to stop scratching their heads, with all due respect, and start fighting the real enemy. It's August, remember, and the right is thinking about November.

A recent CNN poll has found that Hillary can win.[7] She wins hands down as most passionate and best positioned on the issues, the most knowledgeable and most experienced in public policy. Despite all that, for the next three years, you can expect a loud chorus warning her not to run at all. These voices will have nothing to do with the policies she hasn't chosen yet, the issues that haven't emerged yet, the vision for our country she has yet to refine into a stump speech.

If you dare say that her candidacy is all about the "woman thing," you'll get eaten alive. If she said it, she'd be toast. But exactly what is it that makes Hillary—the Rock Star—the one candidate so many people say shouldn't even run?

How do you separate the fact that this race is about her being a woman, from the part that is about her being *this* woman—when she's the only woman there is?

★ ★ ★

I first heard of Hillary Rodham when I was in college. She was five years ahead of me at Wellesley, and we were on exactly the same track: stars of our political science department, Wellesley Washington interns, we both wrote our honors thesis for Professor Schecter, applied to the Harvard and Yale law schools, and then headed to Washington, D.C., to change the world. I went to Harvard; she went to Yale. I ended up clerking at the Supreme Court, then working for the chair of the Senate Judiciary Committee. She worked for the chair of the House Judiciary Committee. She worked for McGovern, I worked for Kennedy; she worked for Marian Wright Edelman, I worked for her husband, Peter Edelman. If there was one difference between us, it was that I could never figure out how to match my secure professional self with an equally secure personal self. Hillary, on the other hand, married Bill Clinton, the boy wonder of the Democratic Party. Where my personal life was nonexistent, she was a star in both areas of her life, personal and professional.

All the guys I worked for in the Kennedy for President campaign called her "Rodham." They also told these endless Bill Clinton stories, most of them about the things he was trying to do in Arkansas (which, unfortunately for him, included a much-needed tax hike), how he'd done the right thing by going back to his home state to run, first for Congress and then for attorney general. Several of these people had been in and out of Arkansas in his campaigns, and sometimes they told stories involving Bill Clinton and women. In those days, there were very few women in campaigns. That cycle, 1980, was the first one that included pro-choice language in the Democratic platform; as Senator Kennedy's representative, I was proud to work with Bella Abzug and Gloria Steinem and Ellie Smeal to put it there. We also worked with gay rights leaders (many of whom have been lost to AIDS) to include the first mention of sexual orientation in the platform that year. When President Carter secured the nomination after Kennedy's challenge, Ron Brown and I helped negotiate the terms of the convention with Carter's senior team; at twenty-six, I was the senior woman there, and he was the only African American, and it was a very big deal that Senator Kennedy sent us there. That's a long way of saying that I heard all these stories as the only woman in the room. I laughed at all the appropriate moments, and never objected or expressed shock.

There is one story from those days I'll always remember. Twenty-five years later, I won't get the details right. But the gist of it was that, after some hearing or another, then-governor Clinton raced out to have sex with a woman who was a witness or a lawyer in the hearing, while Hillary was participating in the hearing. He got back just as she was finishing, some laughed; that was the joke of it. She may have even been pregnant at the time, others joked.

I'd heard plenty of other stories, but this time I couldn't keep still. I just didn't get it.

What about Rodham, I asked?

Oh, they answered, she doesn't really care about that sort of thing.

Doesn't really care about that sort of thing? That made no sense to me. There is not a woman alive who doesn't care about her husband cheating right before her eyes, with every person in the room watching, with his friends joking about it . . .

★ ★ ★

A few years ago, I did a television taping with Esther Dyson, the technology wizard—the one woman in that crowd. Esther, who was running late, doesn't usually wear makeup, and one of her colleagues told the producer he was sure she'd go on without it. I looked at him like he was crazy. No woman wants to go on national television without makeup. I don't care what she wears to a party. Everyone disagreed with me. They were ready to start the minute she arrived.

Then Esther walked in . . . and asked for makeup. There was dead silence in the room.

She looked around. "What's so funny?" she asked.

What do you mean she doesn't care? I thought. *Is she still wearing bedspread dresses?* Whenever I had a moment of despair at Wellesley, with no idea of what to wear, how to look, who to be, I told myself I could always go back to the bedspread dresses I use to wear during my lowest moments in high school. My mother used to tell me how awful I looked. It was one of those times she was right, as it happened; at least I deserved it.

So what was the deal with Rodham? You really think she doesn't care?

Sort of, one of the guys said to me. She doesn't really care how she looks. But he's crazy about her, they all reassured me.

They're really happy together.

Here was this woman who was so cool and so smart—this star at Wellesley, who married the boy-wonder governor. Sounds like she's hit the jackpot, right? Except that people like me knew that her husband cheated on her right and left, and she couldn't even be bothered to worry about what she wears. In pictures of her from that time, she might as well have been wearing the bedspread dress; in fact, with her thick glasses and uncombed hair, it was really much worse. None of it seemed to add up. And there he was, with those big-haired women who looked like his mother.

In June 1992, after the Gennifer Flowers mess, I once teased him, "Look, I don't mind defending you, but I wish you had better taste."

"She used to be better looking," he joked about Flowers.

I don't know how women live that way, but Hillary is hardly the only one who has—and with men who had far, far less to offer. Am I the only one to wonder about the behavior of some of the very men who castigated the Clintons most harshly?

The discomfort millions of American women felt about Hillary after the Monica mess was something I felt twenty years earlier. When her husband called me in the summer of 2000 to talk about Hillary's problem with women voters, it was something I understood, as did she. Advertising helped; focusing on issues helped more. But the real solution was the Senate. It is there that she has found her footing, among men who appreciate her and enjoy parrying with her; where she has found her style, in the form of the power pantsuit and the short hair; where she has found the authority to make her own decisions and run things her way, and the freedom from public humiliation that has long been her due. It's in the Senate that she started earning a 69 percent approval rating in the process, with particularly high numbers among women.[8] Women are also among her strongest supporters at this point for a presidential bid.

I'm no shrink, but I can read a poll—and when the makeovers ended and she became the principal instead of the wife, the voters responded and her numbers climbed.

Voters are like that. They know.

I never thought I would run for office[9]. . . . But it began to grow on me, because people kept talking to me about it, so finally I decided to see whether it made any sense or not and I found that I really loved campaigning for myself.

Although it was very difficult to do it originally because no matter how much time you spend on the side of politics, on the side of advisor or supporter or kibitzer, to be the person standing in front of the microphone—to be the person being interviewed by Tim Russert, to be the person who's on the line—is an entirely different experience. I worked really hard at trying to become a better candidate and trying to persuade the people of New York to take a chance on me, which they did and for which I am very grateful.

I just love being in the Senate. It's a wonderful experience and opportunity. I think especially now, with all the issues facing our country, it is a chance to participate in trying to help make decisions that will keep us safer and make us stronger and create more opportunity. So that's what I now spend all my time thinking about and trying to do. I never would have predicted that when I was here graduating all those years ago that I would end up being one of the United States Senators from New York. But I think that's the way life often is, you do the best you can every day, and doors open and doors close. You keep moving forward and try to have a life that you believe in and that you think is really worth living and worthy of the education, the opportunity, and blessings that we all received because we went here.

—SENATOR HILLARY CLINTON,
Wellesley Reunion, June 5, 2004

She is no longer in transition. She is no longer a self-made victim, a desperate housewife, half-Evita or half-Marie Antoinette, the ice queen. What a relief.

It used to be that you could only admire Hillary while cringing for her at the same time. It was like watching the best and worst fears of women collide; it was a choice between laughing with him or being considered one of her. What a terrible choice.

I think she's found her peace. No, not her peace; peace doesn't make you president. "Flow," as Mike Csikszentmihalyi, who invented the concept, would say. The time and place where she is at her best, where it all works.

If I'm right, she will be the next president of the United States.

★ ★ ★

I spent Election Day 2004 in New York, calling my friends in Boston every two hours from noon on. They kept reassuring me: President Kerry.

I should have been happy, but I was ready to kill somebody. Maybe it was because my mother was sick in Boston, no longer able to care for herself; my brother and sister and I were struggling with what to do next, my kids were mad at me in Los Angeles because I'd missed Halloween, and there I was in New York. Or maybe it was because I never quite convinced myself Kerry would win, hard as I tried.

That night, I walked into Fox and promptly started kvetching. Usually I'm known for being nice, and listening to everyone else's problems, and offering extensive and continuing advice, including free legal advice. At about seven o'clock that night, however, just before I went on the first time, I called Boston one more time. They had the same numbers I had; Ted Kennedy had called him President Kerry.

Then, while I was on the air, I was finally handed some raw numbers—the underlying tabulations, which we should have gotten earlier—and that's when it jumped right out. . . . The sample they were looking at, that purported to show Kerry well ahead, was 59 percent women.[10] "If the exit polls hold, Kerry will be president," I had just told my friend Brit Hume, when I looked down, saw that 59 percent, and realized this night was going to go to hell in a handbasket.

Fifty-nine percent: That figure meant that the poll was just wrong—it would inevitably be skewed to Kerry supporters. "What about fifty-nine percent women—doesn't that look a little high to you?" I found myself asking Brit. (My friends later told me I sounded rather hostile, which I did not mean to be. I have enormous respect for Brit, but it wasn't a happy moment.)

"I'm just looking at that myself, Susan," Brit says. "I think we have a problem, Houston."

Problem? A disaster. The funny thing is, even though I don't think I ever convinced myself that Kerry was going to win, I found myself deeply depressed after he lost.

I took a fair amount of abuse during the campaign for working for Fox News—in the movie *OutFoxed*, which I've happily still not seen, and from some of the lefties. I'm not one of those people who hates George Bush. I hate Osama bin Laden. George Bush I just disagree with. I'm afraid of cancer and earthquakes, not the religious right.

After working for three candidates who've lost in part because they were more liberal than the country (and me), I think there's a value to speaking to swing voters, and having credibility with them. Every time my friends attacked Fox News, the ratings went up. I would have fights with people from Hollywood, trying to show them that they were wasting their money paying for attacks on Fox, much less running ads of soldiers in swamps or even attacking George Bush's military record. Bush wasn't running on his military record. I don't know how many times I said Think Ohio, not Hollywood—think middle, not left.

After the election, I had no desire to go back and say I was right, much less to write about why. I just didn't want to deal with it. Like many Democrats, I found myself turned off by politics for the first time in my life—a dangerous aversion for someone who is paid to talk and write about it.

That's when my friend Judith Regan suggested turning my hand to fiction. I had tried writing a novel once before, after my experience running Dukakis's campaign, because I figured fiction was the only way to tell the truth about what you know. That draft centered on the relationship between the first woman major-party nominee for president and her woman campaign manager, whom she ultimately fires and replaces with a man; the candidate turns out to be just like the men, or so concludes the campaign manager she betrays. I dropped it after about a hundred pages, because I didn't really understand it then; I had the outline right, but I couldn't fill it in. The material was way too raw for me, and I was still too hurt, even for fiction. (Instead I ended up writing a major article on sexual harassment for the *Stanford Law Review*; "Sex at Work," as it happened, provided excellent intellectual preparation for my television work in the Clinton years, and excellent quotation fodder for the Republicans to use against me, and the president, during the Monica affair.)

Now, twelve years later, I went back to fiction—depressed but no longer raw. Make it as close to real life as you can, Judith said. Since I wasn't a fiction writer, that made it much easier.

I called my character Jerilyn, as in Jeb plus Hillary. I didn't make her perfect, not by a long shot. Actually, I figured I'd better take pains to make her unsympathetic, so it wouldn't look like a set-up. So even though she's smart and funny, Jerilyn had paid more than her share of dues. She cared passionately about making a difference, and about education in particular, but she could also be very cold, self-centered, and self-righteous. The people who worked for her loved her because there's no one you would rather have on your side in a fight; she had been there for each of them in special ways. Her passions were real. She had worked hard on herself. But there would always be something missing.

In my story, her brother was the governor, and then the president; her husband had become the CEO of the family real estate business. People called him the black Bill Clinton, and when the Senate seat opened up, they said he should run. She went nuts. She pulled out a list of women from his past, and that was the end of his candidacy. She appreciated him, and cared for him, but she would never totally forgive him, and their relationship lacked real trust and warmth; he wanted her to win, but he didn't hold her when she cried. He said the seat belonged to her.

And she won.

Having been a California senator for eight years, she was running for president.

Ten pages in, she was Hillary.

You have to come up with a story, Judith said. So I came up with a story.

The story had a smart television host (thinks like Greta, looks like Laurie Dhue) from Red News (guess!), who works for the brilliant and shrewd female Roger Ailes character (my part!), who will ultimately make Jerilyn president by saving her husband's ass . . .

And then they'll both owe her.

I had a number of variations. All involved a scandal about the husband supposedly sleeping with the Greta/Laurie Dhue-lookalike on the night of the third debate, and Mrs. Roger not using the information against them, to Greta/Laurie's relief and surprise. "Imagine what the liberals would do to us if we killed Jerilyn?" she says. "They'd destroy us." But that doesn't mean she can't play.

So Mrs. Roger (me) sits back and watches and leaves the dirty work to a wicked, wizened, woman-hating woman newspaper columnist (try saying that five times) who has hated Jerilyn and her husband and most everybody else since she was dumped by a big movie star. And there's a tape, of course—what would politics be without a tape?—that ends up on the front page. And then the networks go with the story. (Now, if every single element of this doesn't have a basis in reality . . . well, they say *Write what you know,* don't they?)

Jerilyn and Bill are righteously indignant. Bill claims he has been totally faithful to Jerilyn. Greta/Laurie is in Afghanistan for the weekend with the troops. Who's to say otherwise?

The shrew gets hers. Do I have to ask what network gets the first interview election night? Greta/Laurie makes it back just in time for the scoop on Red, White, and Blue News!

Over the credits, Mrs. Roger winks at the audience.

Or that would have been the closing shot in my mind's eye. The truth is, I never quite got that far. About halfway through, when I was busy trying to beat back a last-minute challenge from an "Anybody but Jerilyn" movement that was determined to stop her because she was a woman, I realized something: It really was possible for Hillary to win— the *real* Hillary, not just my concoction. If I could make it happen in my story, it could happen in real life. The details were beside the point; I'm not a screenwriter, but I know something about how campaigns work, and once I could divorce myself from the gloom and doom, and the screaming and yelling, and just think about it, with the exact same situation, the same people, just a different set of names, I could make it happen. I'd need a little luck, a few good breaks, but Hillary could be the strong, smart woman candidate I had envisioned, because she *was* that strong, smart woman candidate. And her opponent would be the

right-wing opponent they would nominate, because they would nominate a right-wing opponent. And the poll numbers I'd made up for her
to have in California turned out to be very similar to the real ones she
had in New York . . .

And what the heck was I doing writing purple prose, anyway?

To be honest, until then, I wouldn't have believed it myself.

And this was almost a year ago, when it seemed even more unlikely.
Even today, though, people still sit around and say she can't win. On one
of her recent trips to Los Angeles, one host of a major Hillary fund-
raising dinner told a reporter that he was sure she could win the nomination, but he didn't think she could win the general election. This was
the host of her own fund-raising dinner, mind you. He didn't mean to
be helping Ed Klein, but he was.

It was around the time of George W. Bush's second inauguration
that I found myself writing a column entitled "Four Years Till Hillary,"
which wasn't fiction at all. I sent it to Judith, and this book was born.
The column took me twenty minutes to write. All I did was take all
those reasons my character Jerilyn would and should win a presidential
race—and then replace the phony name with the one this candidate was
born with: Hillary.

She was already leading in every poll of Democratic voters, and she
was competitive with, or outright beating, every big-name Republican.[11]
She was moving smartly to the center. She was the best fundraiser in the
party. The deck was loaded in her favor. She was not polarizing among
Democratic primary voters; her strength among women and minorities,
among elected officials and party leaders, coupled with the structure of
the nominating system, made her the favorite to win the nomination,
the easy way or the hard way. The Republicans had their own mess to
deal with, and by the time they sorted it out she would have the Democratic nomination. Chances are, they would pick someone from the
right, which would improve her chances. She would turn out to be more
conservative and less strident, more Midwestern, more white-bread,

than people expected. Her strong showing in New York polls was the best evidence that, as the centrist senator in the black suit, a mature, independent woman, a passionate advocate for women and children, and a stronger military, with the help of the best strategist in the party, and her reputation for running the best office on the Hill, she just might be everything Democrats needed to win back the White House.

All of this wrapped up in a package named Hillary Clinton.

All we Americans needed to do was what New York voters had done: move beyond the old caricature and focus on the woman she had become. One of the extraordinary things about presidential politics, for better and for worse, is that it offers a true window into the candidates.

What's more, the possibility of electing Hillary Clinton offers something that no other candidate, no other campaign, does: the promise of real change. What had depressed me so on Election Night 2004, and in the weeks that followed, was not that John Kerry himself had lost, but that all the things I'd once taken for granted as hard-won first steps to greater change, now seemed so fragile that they might not even survive to become our legacy. How could it be that I was now fighting about whether equality really was a good thing? I have been pointing out the same injustices, arguing the same issues, running in place, for thirty years. Why haven't we all moved on?

For better or for worse, Hillary's campaign would be seen as a test of women. I have friends who fight this idea, to this day. They want a different test, a different representative. But it doesn't work that way. The one who comes first *becomes* the test. That there is no one right behind her, no one in sight behind her, is why it is a test that matters so much. The idea that we could actually win it was the most positive thought I'd had in years.

Women are in a terrible slump. For the last few years, this is what we've all been talking about when we get together—older and younger women alike. The researchers are finally catching on, too: A new study headlines the fact that even a short period out of the workforce will reduce lifetime salary potential by as much as 40 percent.[12] And who is taking the time out? Women, of course. According to a 2005 article in the *Harvard Business Review*, it turns out that the penalty they pay is huge. We knew that. It turns out that most of the very few women who reach the top, and who still don't get paid as much as men, don't have children. We knew that, too. The rules didn't change, we just work harder. Most of the women I started out with gave up on that a long time ago. Who can blame them? My students don't try. Those of us who are still at it push people to participate in the political system, and many of them look away in disgust. I thought 9/11 would shake everyone up, once again bring out the best in us, but in terms of our politics, it hasn't.

According to the pollster Mark Penn, women who seek office start with a ten-point public perception deficit in the critical factors of leadership and decisiveness.[13] Every woman politician I have ever talked to believes that women are at a disadvantage in seeking office, particularly if it is an executive position. When they went looking for potential choices for their book *Madam President,* Eleanor Clift and her husband, journalist Tom Brazaitis, clearly had to stretch to fill an entire volume.[14] No one I know complained that there weren't any women on John Kerry's VP list, because no one knew who to put there.

"Is Carly Fiorina's firing from Hewlett-Packard a setback for women?" a reporter asks me. What can I say? Male CEOs get fired every day. But there are 493 of them in the Fortune 500, not the eight there are without Carly.[15] When I started counting twenty years ago, I think there were three or four. The number of women in top corporate jobs has increased—by a few percent. The number of women being promoted to tenured positions at Harvard, where I used to teach, has gone down. So has the percent of women going to business school, and the percent of women becoming partners in major law firms (they don't stick it out, my friends bemoan), and the number of women serving in state legislatures.[16] No woman other than Hillary is running from either party, nor will any woman be on either party's vice presidential list.

Last spring, my students and I took on the op-ed page of the *Los Angeles Times* for not including a representative number of women authors.[17] We'd been counting for years: Three-quarters of the articles were routinely written by men; local women couldn't get in the door; three men were now heading the department, and the top guy ignored repeated requests for meetings. I took a lot of heat for going on the attack, but that's not the point: No one ever disputed our numbers. Yes, women were underrepresented, they said, but look, the other papers were even worse. And they were. The *New York Times* had one woman columnist out of seven, the *Washington Post* one out of five. Consider this: when you pick up the *New York Times,* the most important "bulletin board" in the world, nearly half the time (43 percent)—just over four days out of ten—there isn't a single piece on the op-ed page by a woman. This isn't a matter of equality; we're talking total exclusion. Four or five men to zero women, nearly half the time, and the one woman they've let in the door says it's just fine that she's the only one. The perfect token. (And, by the way, isn't that Hillary awful?) At Harvard, President Larry Summers suggested that women may not have what it takes to be scientists, even as the university's numbers on promotion and tenure were declining. And then everyone else says, we're no worse than Harvard. Had he not made the verbal slip, no one would have even focused on the fact that Harvard's numbers were going in the wrong direction.

Writing about Jerilyn in the aftermath of John Kerry was my escape. In the real world, I was surrounded by the voices of defeat and doom—women, progressives, pro-choicers, environmentalists, mothers, every tired Democrat I heard moaning and groaning, weeping and whining. Of course, they all had reason. Nonetheless, we were all counting our steps backward, looking for ways to stall, marveling at how much could be lost.

I tried to make my Jerilyn unappealing, but no matter what I did, I couldn't believe the garbage she'd had to put up with. And she was still out there fighting, for what we both believed in. Never any doubt about that. And along the way, she had finally found her own voice. The joke was that she got kicked around more than her brother, which was good, so they'd let up on him. I knew that joke. I'd heard it before. In 1992.

And this was, finally, her moment. It was her turn. She was about to turn sixty, she was thinking big, and she was going for the gold. And dammit, by hook or by crook, I was going to make her win. Because if she could win, we could all win. It wasn't just that she deserved it, and she did, many times over.

It was the right answer for all of us. If she was ready, we should be ready. The case for a woman president had never been stronger. We had our candidate, if we would only open our eyes and see. We had the most qualified candidate in the race, the candidate of our lifetime.

We had a woman who would make a difference for all of us—a real, dare I say revolutionary, difference for girls and women and families all around the world.

Could the stakes be higher?

What were we waiting for?

★　★　★

If you are a woman, please answer the following questions:

How many black jackets do you own?

How many pairs of black pants do you own?

How many pairs of black shoes?

If the total exceeds ten, you have a stake in this election. You are being judged, whether you like it or not. Look in the mirror. Name the last nominee who looked, dressed, or thought this much like you, had this much in common with you, whose election other people might see as a triumph of "people like you" . . .

If that's how other people see it, why don't you?

And, if you're a man: This isn't just for women. If you're a man who's wondering why so little has changed, you can look in the mirror too . . .

2.

IF NOT NOW, WHEN?

★

Would it matter if the voice of authority in America were a woman's?

Would it matter if the woman who stood up in Beijing for women's rights as human rights, and traveled the world to meet with women and children, became the most powerful person in the world?

Would it matter, realistically and symbolically, if the Cabinet were appointed by Hillary Clinton? If the justices of the Supreme Court were appointed by Hillary Clinton? If the most powerful person in the world were a woman with a lifelong passion about women and children, a lifelong commitment to improving the lot of families, a lifelong mission to achieve equality for women?

Would it matter for America? Is the sky blue? Is the Pope Catholic?

We would never have to worry about *Roe v. Wade* again. Let's start there.

★ ★ ★

In 1984, a group of women got together to promote the idea of a woman on the presidential ticket. At the time, there were no women in the United States Senate, and perhaps one woman governor. One of the women on their list was New York congresswoman Geraldine Ferraro, who had just been selected to chair the Democratic Platform Committee. The Mondale campaign, then considered unbeatable, installed me in January 1984 to run that committee for Gerry. The idea was that the nomination battle would be over in a matter of weeks, literally, and then they would come back and tell us what to do. That was the last I heard from them for months: The idea of "inevitability" led the Mondale camp to near-total disaster in New Hampshire, and a long and arduous road back—which proves that even front-runners who probably should lose sometimes don't.

While Mondale was slogging it out with his rivals for the nomination, Gerry and I were on our own, with the "A team" in the background pushing the idea of a woman on the ticket. We trekked around the country showing off her considerable skills, forging strong alliances with various wings of the party, covering our bases with the Hart and Jackson camps, and having a very good time with everybody working together. The people who participated in that process still remember it as one of their best experiences in politics; Gerry made her reputation and so did I.

When Mondale finally secured the nomination, the boys came back and the focus turned to vice presidential selection. At first I assumed Mondale wasn't going to pick a woman, and that if he did it wouldn't be Gerry. Dianne Feinstein, then the mayor of San Francisco, was the favorite within his circle. But all of a sudden I realized that, as a Mondale plant—not one of Gerry's own people—my position there truly mattered. Where Gerry could only get info on the selection process from the newspaper, I was getting the straight story from people I knew on the inside.

Before Gerry had really become a serious contender, she was invited to go to Minnesota to perform a "platform briefing" charade for the Mondale people. Word leaked out about the upcoming meeting, from where no one knew, and when it did Gerry concluded that the leak was intentional—that she was being used. It was totally unfair to her. I accompanied her on the trip, but it was an awkward visit; I couldn't figure out how to be on both sides. Then, during the briefing, Gerry referred a few of the questions to me. A newspaper story followed in short order: *Mondale unimpressed with Ferraro at briefing.* She was furious. I called my friend Paul Tully, who was on the Mondale team. If they didn't want her, I told him, that was fine. But could they please stop destroying her? It was worse to have a woman out there and to knock her down, than not to consider her at all.

When Gerry went out again for her official interview, it went somewhat better. But on the Fourth of July, during a trip to Minnesota for a "women's meeting" where NOW was pushing for a woman on the ticket, I had a conversation with Mondale himself—and I got nowhere pushing for Gerry. I'd been told that Mike Berman, Mondale's vetter (the chief of checking everything), was deep into the process of vetting Dianne Feinstein.

And then something changed. I got another phone call, this time from Jim Johnson: The thinking had changed. Dianne was out, and they were taking another look at Gerry. (Despite rampant speculation then and since, the problem had nothing to do with Dianne's husband's finances; Mondale himself later told me he was concerned about the liberal slant of the "San Francisco Democrats.") Now it was between Gerry and Michael Dukakis. Mondale got on the phone with me to talk about Gerry. We talked about her law school grades, of all things. Given how well Gerry had done at law school, he asked, and how well she'd done with me in the platform process, did I think she could get up to speed on foreign policy? No problem, I said. I hung up, and that was it.

I called Gerry and told her she'd better get ready for the vetting process, but she was skeptical. She'd planned to run some errands that day, she said, and she was going to go ahead with them anyway. Okay, I said, but Dianne's out and I think you're about to be invaded. Within an hour, Berman was on her doorstep, ready to do her taxes. My then-boyfriend,

Marty, Mondale's speechwriter, started writing the announcement speech; they put Gerry on a plane; and suddenly the thing we'd spent months dreaming about—and weeks pulling our hair out about—was happening.

Be careful what you wish for, some people say. The campaign was filled with moments both spectacular and painful, and some of them outlasted the election season. Gerry's husband, John, was put through the wringer, investigated and ultimately acquitted of criminal charges. Her son was arrested on drug charges. Would any of it have happened if she hadn't been picked? But Gerry doesn't regret it. Her family did fine, supported by their strong roots. She is proud of making history. Their kids turned out great. All three of them ended up successful, happily married, with beautiful children.

The whole thing was audacious, more so than even I was able to appreciate at the time. A woman vice president, when our best hope until then was a congresswoman who was only starting her third term. Absurd. But it happened. Without a single woman in the Senate, without a woman governor on the list, a group of women had this big dream, and for a golden moment it happened. And if that time it wasn't meant to go all the way . . . well, this time we have a woman who isn't waiting to see if a man will pick her.

In 1984, the choice was utterly beyond our control. The selection process was discomfiting, until the very last moment, and I worried every day that my relationship with Gerry was going to be destroyed by the careless way the campaign was treating her. The triumph came with her selection, but the process leading up to it, including the parading up and down the driveway, was humiliating to everybody. The sense that she was being paraded one extra time because she was a two-fer—a woman who came with a platform—just added insult to injury. There were no more women at the table than usual; there was no sense that this was truly a different kind of campaign, that things had really changed.

It was constantly confusing. After the choice was announced, the tension ebbed for no more than five minutes before it started again. I got out of the line of fire, and sat right behind Vice President Mondale on his plane—it was my first time on a presidential plane of any kind—and listened to every word I could. I had the best seat in the house. But I never knew for sure how much Gerry's status as a woman affected the conversation on the plane. Four years later, when I worked with Michael Dukakis, we were determined to do it differently—but then Lloyd Bentsen was such a different person from Gerry. On one hand, he was formally much more deferential; he is an extraordinary gentleman, who would always ask *me* permission to do or say something, as if I would ever say no. On the other, we were far more respectful to him than any-body ever was toward Gerry. In truth, that may have been in part be-cause he knew much more about almost everything than any of us. When I got to travel with him and his wife, B.A., or spend a week do-ing debate prep with him, I used to say I'd died and gone to heaven. Peo-ple used to compete for the chance to travel with Bentsen. With Bentsen's permission, I had asked Tad Devine, now one of the top Democratic consultants in the country, to run Bentsen's camp, and there was never a single problem. Had Bentsen been at the top of the ticket, people always said, we would have won. But Bentsen was a conservative Democrat who could never have won the nomination; when he himself ran for president, he got nowhere.

In general, nobody covers vice presidential campaigns. Gerry's was an exception.[1] But the coverage was mixed at best. Even when she got past the financial questions, a good chunk of the coverage was always about her clothes and hair and shoes. Every time she misspoke, on the other hand, it became a federal case. The guys on our plane would go nuts. By the end, most of us who had worked so hard to get Gerry on the ticket were counting the days until it would be over.

Even so, the Ferraro effect was clear. It wasn't just the moment—the convention, the bounce, the only bright spot in a dismal campaign. No, the impact lasted long after the election was over. To this day, Gerry meets people whose lives she changed. She is a truly amazing woman who continues to inspire. And the cultural impact is supported by objective evidence: The years that followed saw a dramatic increase in the number of women elected to office in America. It was absolutely measurable. PACs were formed. EMILY's List was created two years later, when Ellen Malcolm stepped up to the table. Barbara Lee stepped up, too, creating a foundation that has done pioneering work in illuminating the obstacles to women in executive positions, and promoting greater activism by women. Abortion stopped being a dirty word, and started being a positive issue. Candidates stopped being afraid of gay rights. Barriers were breaking down. We began having "Years of the Woman" in politics on a regular basis; 1992 was the biggest, with six new women elected to the Senate and nineteen to the House.[2]

But women's progress has slowed down in politics in recent years, as it has in corporate America.[3] In 1999 the percentage of women serving in state legislatures went flat at 22 percent, and recently it has even dropped slightly. Women have done better getting elected to legislative positions than as governors or big city mayors, a dichotomy that mirrors the split you see in corporate America.[4] Academics complain that they can't do good enough studies of women in executive positions, because there aren't enough to constitute a valid survey.

Women in State Legislatures 2005

In 2005, 1,663, or 22.5% of the 7,382 state legislators in the United States are women. Women currently hold 399, or 20.2%, of the 1,971 state senate seats and 1,264, or 23.4%, of the 5,411 state house or assembly seats. Since 1971, the number of women serving in state legislatures has increased more than four-fold.

Women in State Legislatures 2005

Year	Women Legislators	% of Total Legislators	Year	Women Legislators	% of Total Legislators	Year	Women Legislators	% of Total Legislators
1971	344	4.5	1985	1,103	14.8	1998	1,617	21.8
1973	424	5.6	1987	1,170	15.7	1999	1,664	22.4
1975	604	8.0	1989	1,270	17.0	2000	1,670	22.5
1977	688	9.1	1991	1,369	18.3	2001	1,666	22.4
1979	770	10.3	1993	1,524	20.5	2002	1,682	22.7
1981	908	12.1	1995	1,532	20.6	2003	1,664	22.4
1983	991	13.3	1997	1,605	21.6	2004	1,659	22.5
						2005	1,663	22.5

Municipal   As of January 2005, among the 100 largest cities in the
Officials   United States, 13 had women majors.

One is African American (Shirley Franklin, Atlanta)
and one is Latina (Heather Fargo, Sacramento). In order of city population, the mayors were:

City	Mayor	Rank
Dallas, TX	Laura Maer	9
Cleveland, OH	Jane Campbell	35
Long Beach, CA	Beverly O'Neill	36
Kansas City, MO	Kay Barnes	38
Virginia Beach, VA	Meyera E. Oberndorf	40
Atlanta, GA	Shirley Franklin	42
Sacramento, CA	Heather Fargo	43
Tampa, FL	Pam Iorio	60
Lexington, KY	Teresa Isaac	67
Lincoln, NE	Coleon Seng	78
Plano, TX	Pat Evans	80
Glendale, AZ	Elaine M. Scruggs	82
Scottsdale, AZ	Mary Manross	89

As of January 2005, of the 243 mayors of U.S. cities with populations
over 100,000, 38 or 15.6% were women, including three African Americans and six Latinas. Of the 1,135 mayors of U.S. cities with populations over 30,000, 160, or 15.9%, were women.

Source: Center for American Women and Politics, Eagleton Institute of Politics, Rutgers University.

Let her tell it herself:

These are some of the statistics that create that context.[5] Women make up
51 percent of the adult population in our country, but only 14 percent of
the Cabinet, the United States Senate, and the United States House. . . .

14 percent of the Congress in both Houses. It is true, however, that we are 22 percent of the United States Supreme Court, 21 percent of federal judges, 16 percent of governors, 21 percent of state senators, 23 percent of state representatives, 9 percent of state judges, 21 percent of big city mayors. In corporate America, women hold 13.6 percent of the Fortune 500 company board seeds. In academia, except for Wellesley of course, women account for only 3 to 15 percent of full professors in engineering and science departments. And even in sociology, which is the best of the best in terms of female representation, on average 35.8 percent of that faculty is female.

The first woman in the Cabinet was, of course, Francis Perkins, appointed by President Franklin Roosevelt as Secretary of Labor in 1933. Since then only twenty-eight women have served in the Cabinet, so Madeleine [Albright]'s accomplishment is even more extraordinary. Nineteen states have no women serving in the 108th Congress, and five states have never sent a woman to the United States Congress—in case you're interested, Delaware, Iowa, Mississippi, New Hampshire, and Vermont. By January 2004, only twenty-five women, seventeen Democrats, and eight Republicans will have served as governors of twenty-one states; Texas and Arizona are the only states to have elected two women.

—SENATOR HILLARY CLINTON,
Wellesley College, June 5, 2004

As Sue Tolleson-Rinehart and Jeanie Stanley smartly point out, "the new acceptance of women in office emanated from old gender-role stereotypes about what women and men do."[6] A 1999 survey by Deloitte & Touche found more Americans ready to accept women in office, yet continued to find men scoring more highly on the top-rated issue of crime.[7] To quote Tolleson-Rinehart and Stanley: "The readiness to accept women's political leadership is new; the belief that women will be different is not."

The idea that women are different from men was enforced as a matter of law in this country until 1971.[8] (Every time I type that fact, I stop in disbelief and double-check it—and I've been teaching gender discrimination for almost twenty years.) I was in college then. Hillary had already graduated. It wasn't until then that the Supreme Court—which in 1954 had overturned the concept of separate-but-equal in matters of race—ruled that the unequal treatment of women under state law violated the equal protection clause of the Constitution.[9]

In 1971's *Reed v. Reed,* a woman had challenged an Idaho law that automatically preferred men over women as estate administrators in cases where both were equally close relations.[10] Even after the court struck down that automatic preference, male judges were easily convinced that men had superior business experience that better "qualified" them for the positions. The most women could hope for was to be judged by men according to the rules they had made for themselves—to best them at their own game. Back then, however, even that was a major step forward.

Ten years earlier, a woman had lost her challenge to Florida's jury system, which automatically included men in the jury pool unless they specifically sought an exemption, but automatically excluded women unless they specifically sought inclusion.[11] In what would today be considered a battered-woman case, one Mrs. Hoyt had killed her abusive husband, and was tried and convicted by an all-male jury. The state, in defending its obviously discriminatory system, specifically invoked a mother's role in preparing dinner for her family and applying Band-Aids to her children's injuries—dismissing the very idea that some women might fail to conform to maternal stereotypes. But *Hoyt* was even more devastating: In choosing to defer to the state judgment, the court affirmed the system in which women's voices, experiences, and work are seen as both distinct and secondary. Such a system of sexual asymmetry was the very reason that feminists, fully understanding that men and women aren't the same, were determined to seek equality under the law. Anything less would perpetuate the stereotypes that inevitably left women in the secondary position.

If you think of the public world as a sphere belonging to men, and the private world as belonging to women, then breaking down the legal prohibitions that bar women from entering the public world—and men from entering the private world—should give every individual the freedom to truly live as he or she chooses, free from gender-role stereotypes. As more men come into the private world, parenting will be more valued; as more women enter the public world, work will accommodate the needs of families; and the sexual asymmetry that values the public world more than the private will disappear.

Shortly after I joined the Harvard faculty, I met Shirley Abrahamson. I remember the moment well because there were so few women in the generation ahead of me, and she was positive and encouraging to me. But her message was also very troubling. Shirley was the first woman on the Wisconsin Supreme Court, and eventually became its Chief Justice. She had managed to do all that *and* have a family. When she asked me what was going on with my women classmates, though, I had to tell her that virtually all the married women I knew at school—which included many of my close friends—had pulled back or dropped out to raise kids. Shirley was horrified. She asked me how many of the men were already partners, and of course a whole bunch were; the disparity was already enormous. By that point, it was clear that the men I knew were going to end up running the world, as they have, and the women weren't, which has turned out to be 100 percent true.

For Shirley, that was incredibly disappointing news. Those women—women who today would be the CEOs, managing partners, Chief Justices—were the ones we needed to get to the top and change the rules, so that it wouldn't be so impossible for the next generation of women to get there. Instead, they were raising children. And my generation was more ambitious, and hard of hearing when it came to their biological clocks, than the young women I teach today.

Shirley was right to be concerned. Instead of changing the rules, my generation by and large played by theirs. The world of work has not yet been revolutionized: We don't job share, we penalize those who work part-time, and many women who take time off never recover. The only place where equality truly exists in the public world is at the bottom. For most middle-class women maternity is still destiny, and even a relatively short period out of the workforce corresponds to a permanent drop in earning potential. At the top, women are moving up extremely slowly, if at all. And while many women do opt out, those who try to fight it out as equals find themselves the victims of precisely the same unconscious stereotypes that are incorporated in the judgments we make about women politicians. I know some working mothers who simply don't tell anyone about their children, lest they be thought less ambitious or hard-working. The same assumptions still poison the workplace: When a man leaves work early for the day, it's assumed he has an appointment, whereas a mother who leaves early is assumed to have problems with her kids. When a man has a good year, the assumption is that it's the first of many; when a woman does, the assumption is that it's luck. Every university that has followed the lead of MIT and conducted a scientific study of itself has found a pattern of unconscious discrimination.[12] But most don't study themselves—unless someone like my friend Nancy Hopkins from MIT has the guts to force them to.

What's worse, we have become complacent about failure. So what if we only have eight female CEOs,[13] or if 88 percent of the board seats or 86 percent of Congress is male?[14] So what if twenty of twenty of the largest cities in America have men as mayors? So what if the decisions about the air you breathe, the food you eat, your health and your children's health, are made in rooms from which women are excluded? So what if you pick up your paper and read nothing but men's opinions? A generation has grown up believing that equality under law is enough, even if none of the goals in securing it has been met.

It isn't necessary that equal numbers of women and men want

power in the public world. It is certainly the case, as my eighty-two-year-old friend Rose says her mother told her, that a father is not a mother. And my kids only have one mother.

But there is absolutely no reason in the world that search firms can't find more than eight women in this country who could do better than some of the CEOs we've seen lately. There is no reason that the old boys' club continues to dominate corporate board membership in America, to the absolute detriment of stockholders—half of whom, by the way, happen to be female. There is absolutely no reason, in an economy in which almost no one stays at a single firm forever, and in which changing jobs and careers is common, that "taking time off to raise kids" should be the kiss of death it still is today, except that the people who make those judgments have never done it themselves. Ask me to find a qualified woman and I can always do it; ask the same old good ole boys, and they'll call the same old good ole boys. And if they have no reason to notice that their list comprises fifteen men and no women, that's just the way it'll be. "I never pay attention to gender," men proudly tell me all the time, until I point out that their policy of never paying attention to gender tends to result in one or no women per team. That's what feels normal to them.

If Hillary Clinton were president, that would no longer feel normal. In a stroke, there would be a new normal.

After Anita Hill placed the issue of sexual harassment at center stage, the nation focused on the issue—and then every man in America changed the way he behaved at work.[15] It was stunning. Language changed. Overnight, the atmosphere in workplaces across America was different. And it wasn't just the men who changed: women changed, too. They felt stronger. Imagine every boss in America looking, even for a moment, at his own workplace. Imagine every woman worker, even for a moment, understanding that she had a champion at the top—that *we* had won.

When universities pick women as presidents, departments discover literally for the first time that they have no women professors—and even then only because the president calls a meeting, and it becomes obvious that she will be the only woman in attendance. This often prompts hiring or promotions. Over the years, I've been brought on to a number of important cases because the judge was a woman and it was thought important that there be at least one woman on the team.

Electing a woman president would rock the boat in a way nothing else I can imagine could. It would force us to see where we stand, and where we are stuck; to notice when there are no women in the room. It would force a major reevaluation of where women are in America. It would change the voice of authority that comes into every home in the world every night.

At the most practical level, it would force the most powerful people in this country to deal with a government that looked very different— beginning with the Oval Office. All day long, groups of men go in and out of the Oval Office. I've sat in the lobby any number of times and seen them, and I can't imagine it's any different now. No one thinks twice about the fact that there are no women in the group. Why should they? No one thinks twice about the fact that there are no women on the Sunday political shows, bill signings, press conferences. It's what they— that is, *we*—are used to seeing, just like we're used to seeing white faces when we look around the table.

Once a woman is elected, every bigwig from corporate America will look around and say, "We better have some women on board." *But, sir, we don't have a woman. All our top executives are men!* And they are. Whether it's big companies or little companies we're talking about, the executive suites are like that. Ditto for all those news organizations that send their men to the White House. Oh my goodness, we better find a woman. And it better not be a token woman, either—that means we'll have to find more than one. Imagine, not just one woman, but two!

A hundred years ago, when I was a law student interviewing at law firms, most firms didn't have women partners. As the first woman president of the *Harvard Law Review*, I was the most sought-after law student in the country that year. And I always made it a point to ask if I could meet the woman partner. *But we don't have a woman partner,* some of them would say. *You don't?* I would reply in mock horror. One woman told me they had rushed her partnership through in time for my callback. (I was proud of that, and she was very grateful.) Wherever there were senior women associates, I was a very popular candidate. The only bad experience I had was the time they forced a sick woman to come in and meet me because she was the only woman partner.

So imagine what will happen to the staff, and the Cabinet and sub-Cabinet, when suddenly their ranks fill with a proper number of women—as always happens wherever Hillary is. Where you have women, eventually you have policies that will make it possible for people with families to work. Especially when the woman at the top has made that her top issue for thirty years. This isn't just any woman, after all.

And then, bit by bit, we'll get that old—I know I shouldn't say the word, but here it is—revolution started again. Nothing dangerous, just making it possible for people to contribute to society while having and raising children. *Real* family values for men and women, radical as that may sound. (We used to call it feminism in the twentieth century, but that's a dicey proposition these days.) And we might finally get those rules changed, just as Justice Abrahamson hoped.

And then not only will women benefit, and girls, but men and boys too, from the opportunities that real equality of opportunity offers. Equality doesn't mean everybody is the same, of course; it means you get to be yourself. Most women may still choose to take time off to raise kids, but there's no reason that such choices should be the kiss of career death they are today, and there's no reason men who want to take time off should be viewed as worse than mothers if they do. The reality is that far less has changed for men than for women; boys today are under as much pressure to succeed than their fathers were—if not more—in a world that is even more competitive and offers less security. The rewards of family, which momentarily were going to be offered to men as fathers, are something men should be demanding if they knew what they were missing in the lousy bargain they make. The promise of change should not be occasion for a gender war, but a joint effort, were it not so often displayed as a television entertainment instead of a continuing cause.

A successful campaign could change that. No person has ever been vilified as much as Hillary Clinton. In order to forgive her husband, we had to blame her. People still laugh at his infidelity. At an AARP lunch in Los Angeles recently, Liz Smith, the kindest gossip columnist on the planet, told a great joke about Bill "picking a bone with her for saying he didn't like older women"—the joke, of course, was that he was happy to count off a list of all those older women, to prove how much he liked them.[16] And everyone—a room full of older women who have every reason to support Hillary, who were given red wristbands on the way out for the fight on Social Security—roared.

Hillary's mistakes have been broadcast and rebroadcast, over and over. Her insecurities have played out a thousand times, in a dozen hairdos.

And yet her strength is a model to every girl and boy and man and woman who has ever put a pillow over his or her head and cowered in fear of what lay ahead. Her passion has held true throughout it all; her commitment to living a life that makes a difference is beyond question. Her brains, her faith, her dedication, her competence, her abilities— she has held on to all of that through the hardest trials, and triumphed. She has found herself and fought, and she and we are on the verge of literally changing the world.

Could electing Hillary Clinton really change the way you and I and this country conduct our government, think about politics, think about women and each other? Could it change what happens to women at work—whether people think twice, at least, when they walk into a room and see nothing but men, or put together a board that has no women?

Could it change the way our daughters grow up, and our sons—how they view their own power and potential, and that of the women around them?

Here's what Hillary herself says.

There's no way to predict substantively what if any difference would be made [by having more women in power], but I'd sure like to try to find the answer to that.[17] There's such a dearth of women leaders in so many parts of the world, and such an inequitable balance in the vast majority of countries, including our own, that there isn't any doubt, from all the work that's been done, that empowering women in poor countries—[and] in undemocratic countries, even if they're not poor—would make a significant difference in increasing the stability of those societies.

It is something that we worked on very hard, when Madeleine [Albright] became Secretary of State. She and I made a joint address about making women's rights much more of a central concern in American foreign policy. Again, not because we though it was a soft side of American diplomacy, [or] a nice thing to do but not necessarily a strategic objective—but, to the contrary, because having traveled the world, having studied what was going on elsewhere, we saw it as so much in American national interest, and in the future peace and stability of the entire world. I think you can look at so many of the places that are the most at risk to instability, violence, terrorism, and there is a direct correlation between how women are viewed and how women are treated and the likelihood of those nations having inimical interest to our own over the long term.

Secondly, I had an interesting interchange with someone who is not viewed as typically sympathetic to this kind of argument. Before the armed services committee a few weeks ago, Deputy Secretary Paul Wolfowitz was testifying, and he was taking a pretty severe beating over the 25 billion dollars that the administration had finally gotten around to request for Iraq, which they wanted originally to be basically a blank check. *Don't tell us how to spend it, just give us the money.* On both sides of the aisle, people were not having that. At one point I asked him, "What would you spend money on other than the defense budget in order to improve the chances of success in the war against terrorism and to undermine the legitimacy that the terrorists seem to have in certain societies around the world?" He said, "Well, if we had the money we would certainly invest it in global education." I told him I was glad to hear that, because I had just introduced a bill arguing for a global education fund that the United States would play a principal role in.

We've got to be *for* things. We can't just be *against* things. And one of the things we need to be for loudly and clearly is the empowerment of women and girls in societies around the world, in large ways and small. From education in health care, to encouraging that they be allowed to vote and drive cars and everything else that they are still deprived of, because I do think that it would make an enormous difference.

Finally, with respect to who holds these positions, Madeleine mentioned the parliamentary systems, [including] most of the rest of the democracies in the world. It is, based on my reading of both current events and history, a somewhat easier system for women to navigate—maybe just marginally easier, but easier because the constituency that you have to respond to, to be elected, is usually a self-selected one or a party-selected one. And then the constituency that you have to persuade to elevate you to a leadership position is your peers. So that people get to know you and can see you as a colleague, as opposed to token or a woman or whatever else they may be viewing you as.

Our system is about as hard as it can be for both men and women. It's incredibly difficult, and it's difficult at all levels, local to national. One thinks about that particularly in an election year for president because no matter who you are, you start at the same level. You have to raise enormous amounts of money. You have to travel the country. You have to overcome the media stereotypes that are imposed on you. So it's a very, very hard gauntlet to run. We need to recognize that, and encourage more women to run at all levels for elective office, and to be in positions to take appointed office such as secretary of state and federal judges. . . . We need to do more to create the pipeline for women from both the public and private sector to be able to have a greater increase to get to a critical mass . . . beyond the 14 to 20 percent that we seem to be stuck at.

—SENATOR HILLARY CLINTON,
Wellesley College, June 5, 2004

★ ★ ★

Try answering these few short questions. You might view them as simplistic—but that doesn't mean they're off the mark . . .

* Do you believe poor children, in America and the world, would be better off if Hillary Clinton were president?

* Do you believe public education would get more support in this country if Hillary Clinton were president?

* Do you believe more people would have access to better health care, at prices they could afford, if Hillary Clinton were president?

* Do you believe the air and water would be cleaner or dirtier if Hillary Clinton were president?

* Do you believe more women would hold positions of power, in both the private and public sector, if Hillary Clinton were president?

* Do you believe women would have greater access to birth control medicines if Hillary Clinton were president?

* Do you believe there would be fewer abortions in America if Hillary Clinton were president?

* Do you believe that the nominees to the United States Supreme Court would include more women if Hillary Clinton were elected president?

* What is the issue you care most about? Do you think your issue would be positively affected if Hillary were president? Do you think the people around her would be stronger advocates on your issue than the people who are currently advising George Bush? How does Hillary Clinton's record on your issue compare with that of John Edwards? Mark Warner? For that matter, does either of them actually have a record on the matter?

* And if all that is so, doesn't it follow that women who agree with those goals should support Hillary Clinton because she is a woman?

Gotcha. Right? Wrong.

Most women hate the idea that they should support a woman *because* she is a woman. Woman candidates know that Rule One is never, ever to ask for support based on gender. True enough.

But the bottom line is very simple. We don't live in a fair world. I would love to live in a world where women and men could run on equal terms, and be judged on equal terms—a world where the topic of Hillary, as opposed to anyone else, didn't require the wringing of hands and convening of panels it does today. Maybe my daughter and your daughter will, but not unless you and I—whatever sex you are—start fighting for it.

But let's not start by closing our eyes.

Were it not for her sex, would anyone be considering eliminating the front-runner as "unelectable" three years out?

Were it not for her sex, would the prospect of nominating a two-term centrist senator be considered suicide because that senator's marriage wasn't perfect?

If imperfect marriages were grounds for disqualification from high office, would there be anyone left to run?

★ ★ ★

In January 2005, Hillary Clinton gave to pro-choice advocates a speech in New York that was widely hailed as an important move to the center. Andrew Sullivan described it as a remarkable speech that drew gasps from the crowd.[18]

I am certain the press was guided to see the speech as an important move to find common ground on abortion, and to show respect for her political opponents. For me, however, it is first and foremost an example of why Hillary Clinton is different from any other candidate who has ever run for president.

Most men hate giving speeches about abortion. They read every word from the text. When I was working on the Democratic platform, I used to have to negotiate their language word for word with half of the Congress—something I did over and over, glutton for punishment that I was. "We support *Roe v. Wade* as the law of the land," we wrote. *As the law of the land:* I started adding that in 1979. I called it the "hide behind the Supreme Court line." I had another line that referred to opposing any effort to undermine the rule of law. All very clever stuff, designed to ensure we offended no one, and I gritted my teeth all the way.

In 1970 I started at Wellesley, the year after Hillary graduated. At that time not only was abortion illegal in Massachusetts, but so was birth control for unmarried women. As a result we didn't have a gynecologist on campus since the college didn't want to be responsible for breaking Massachusetts law. Girls were referred to town doctors; when necessary, collections were taken to send girls by bus to New York for abortions. And there were some horror stories along the way. In my sophomore year, for instance, a girl hemorrhaged on the way home, and we had to take her to the hospital, and the college inevitably found out. I have no doubt that's how things were handled in Hillary's dorm as well.

Hillary Clinton is also the mother of a much-wanted daughter. I am sure she loved her baby from the moment she knew she was growing inside of her, as all of us who have been so blessed do. As I found out, as so many of us find out, it can be difficult to do what we tried so hard not to; those of us who have lost babies know that's how we felt, too. But that has absolutely nothing to do with whether a fourteen-year-old rape victim should be forced to have a child, or whether a woman should be forced to carry to term a pregnancy that poses a serious threat to her life or her health.

Here is the paragraph in Hillary's speech that everyone focused on.

This decision, which is one of the most fundamental, difficult, and soul-searching decisions a woman and a family can make, is also one in which the government should have no role.[19] I believe we can all recognize that abortion in many ways represents a sad, even tragic choice to many, many women. Often, it's a failure of our system of education, health care, and preventive services. It's often a result of family dynamics. This decision is a profound and complicated one; a difficult one, often the most difficult that a woman will ever make. The fact is that the best way to reduce the number of abortions is to reduce the number of unwanted pregnancies in the first place.

The phrase that the neo-conservative pundits all left out, in describing the speech as remarkable, is that the abortion decision is "also one in which the government should have no role." Put that in, and the rest of her description is totally unremarkable. I don't know a soul from the pro-choice movement—other than the few screaming caricatures they always seem to put on TV—who doesn't agree with what she said, and I've been on the Planned Parenthood boards here in Southern California for sixteen years.

What the news stories and columns also left out was everything else in the speech. I don't blame them, exactly, but reading the entire speech makes clear just how deep Senator Clinton's understanding goes. As she pointed out, she had worked on these issues long before she entered the Senate, and she continues her work there. Is there anyone alive who doesn't know that she is the only almost sixty year-old who is still pilloried for writing a law review note that suggested—rightly, as it turned out—that there would turn out to be all too many occasions (albeit not precisely the ones she predicted) where children would need lawyers and courts to protect them from their own parents? Reaffirming her support for what used to be called teen celibacy (do you know anyone who's raised a girl through adolescence who doesn't support that idea, by the way?), Hillary reminded us that the point is to find out if it works. This is how Senator Clinton put it, in a paragraph I never saw quoted in the press.

> Research shows that the primary reason that teenage girls abstain is because of their religious and moral values.[20] We should embrace this—and support programs that reinforce the idea that abstinence at a young age is not just the smart thing to do, it is the right thing to do. But we should also recognize what works and what doesn't work, and to be fair, the jury is still out on the effectiveness of abstinence-only programs. I don't think this debate should be about ideology, it should be about facts and evidence—we have to deal with the choices young people make, not just the choice we wish they would make.

Here are some of the key points in the speech I read.

- ★ Thirty-four percent of teenage girls become pregnant at least once before their twentieth birthday.

- ★ The United States has the highest teen pregnancy rate of any industrialized country.

- ★ The 7 percent of women who don't use contraception account for 53 percent of our unwanted pregnancies. Getting contraception to women who need it—not blocking their access to information, or allowing employers not to provide equal access to contraception—is therefore key.

In another part of the speech you didn't hear about—the part where she appealed to all my Planned Parenthood Republican friends, though not to the religious-right types—she spoke about the importance of her legislative work on insurance reform, which would provide prescription coverage for contraceptives, and her efforts to support the FDA's calls to make Plan B emergency contraception available over-the-counter. All of these steps are directly related to reducing the number of abortions, precisely because they would reduce the number of unwanted pregnancies.

A few years ago, in an effort to understand why crime had dropped more than demographics might suggest, two distinguished and rather conservative criminologists suggested a correlation between the legalization of abortion and the drop in the birth of the most high-risk youngsters (the sons of single-mother teenage drug abusers), which in turn tended to produce a lower crime rate.[21] While the academics were not seeking to make any normative point, the conservatives were horrified at the seeming positive implication of abortion. Who did they think they were forcing to have unwanted children?

As it turns out, it's worse than that. In her speech, Hillary pointed out that in the 130-page Department of Justice handbook, there is not a line—*not one single line*—about providing emergency contraception for the victims of sexual assault. And yet according to the Alan Guttmacher Institute, fifteen thousand abortions per year are attributable to rape.[22] Hillary and twenty-one of her colleagues signed a letter to the Justice Department protesting the omission. Why didn't the other eighty-eight senators sign a letter? For that matter, why does the Justice Department need a group of Senators to send a letter in the first place before rectifying such an egregious flaw?

How many of those pregnancies could be prevented if the women in question were given swift, affordable access to emergency birth control? And how are those women ever to get access if the Justice Department regulations won't tell them about it, even though it is legal and safe, and the FDA's recommendation that it be made available over the counter isn't being allowed to go into effect, even though it might help that very small group—that 7 percent—that accounts for a disproportionate amount of the pregnancies.[23]

How many of us would not have taken the poisons we did, destroyed our bodies the way we did? How many of your wives and sisters and aunts and mothers does that apply to? Some day families should sit around and talk about what we did, and how we have paid, and what we think it will ultimately cost us—just so that everyone, and especially those who think there is no cost, will finally understand how wrong they are.

There is no other candidate, no other president, who will speak as this one does, to this issue and so many others. There is none other who will bring to the White House the voices of the women around the world, desperate for control over their bodies and health care for their children so they can have a chance at a life. Can you imagine the celebrations there will be in villages across the world when a woman they have spoken to, who truly understands their problems, becomes the most powerful person in the world?

And who will really care, by that point, whether she should have stayed with her husband?

★ ★ ★

So, am I for Hillary Clinton because she's a woman?

Of course. I am very much for a *strong woman president.*

It's hardly a secret. I have always believed women should support women.

I have always believed that there is a special place in hell for women who turn their backs on other women.

The first thing I did when I started teaching at Harvard—and found myself almost the only woman there, literally—was to make sure my colleague Martha Minow kept her promise to join me the next semester. The next thing was helping Kathleen Sullivan, who has since become the first woman dean of Stanford Law School, get hired at Harvard. I'm not saying this to blow my own horn. In these women, I found friends for life. And in turn Martha and Kathleen have helped hundreds of others. That's how it works.

There are always women who would rather be the only ones in the room than help another and find a friend. You know who they are. Everyone does. They think they get more attention by being the only one. The women they call friends are women who serve them. They walk into a room and talk to every man, and then they stand around as if there's no one left. Some of them even call themselves feminists.

I'm not saying that you should support Hillary if you don't agree with any of her stands. I'm not telling you that electing her is more important than all that. I'm not telling you that I know her like a sister, that I can vouch for her as a roommate, swear for her as a friend.

I'm not telling you that nothing else matters. But I am saying that *this matters.*

I'm speaking to women who got the chills when Sally Ride went up in space because they knew it mattered.

I'm speaking to moms and dads who don't know quite what to say when their daughters ask why there are no women in the picture, or no girls in the math group—who feel a choke in their throat when their own moms say *I'm so proud, because in my generation, we never had the chance to do that.*

I'm for Hillary Clinton for all the hundreds of times when we've all asked ourselves whether we were crazy, whether it was us or them—who've wondered, upon walking into a room, how it is that we've just stopped all the conversation. For all the times when we had no idea how to be, how to act, in a room whose tenor was determined entirely by men.

This race isn't just about Hillary. It's about any woman who has tried to get ahead anywhere, any woman who has supported an unpopular idea, taken a beating, and come back.

It's so our daughters will have a better chance than we did to balance work and family—a chance to have that be a real choice, and not a series of closing doors.

I'm for Hillary Clinton because so much of the antipathy toward her has been about everything *else*. And because the prospect of conquering it offers the greatest promise to women and to girls of our lifetimes.

I'm for Hillary Clinton for all the same reasons I have been fighting for women's rights for thirty years.

I am for Hillary Clinton because I believe in the promise of every individual, and in the possibility of a democracy like ours to afford the individual the opportunity to fulfill that promise, without regard to race or sex or creed or national origin.

That is what I believed fervently thirty years ago, when, as a scholarship student, I worked harder than anyone in my class and defeated the seven men who ran against me—sons of the wealthy and well connected—to win the most prestigious law student honor.

Let us in, I thought. *Let us play by your rules, and there's nothing women won't do, no height we won't reach.* That was the promise, the goal, all we were ever asking for, what we never got. And that is how Hillary will win, if she does.

Any woman who has ever been first at anything, been smarter than the guys around her, knows what I mean. And, yes, Hillary Clinton is fighting so that your daughter or your niece—or maybe you, next time—won't have to go through what you have in the past.

Hillary Clinton's election offers the opportunity for the rebirth of the best of the women's movement in America, the part that sought nothing more or less than the chance for a fair share of the dream. That dream, that promise, that positive potential, may have grown a little tattered in the past few years, but nothing less than that will launch it.

★ ★ ★

TIME OUT!

SO YOU MEAN IT'S JUST ABOUT WOMEN?

YOU MEAN THAT, JUST BECAUSE HILLARY IS A WOMAN . . .

AND YOU'RE A WOMAN . . .

THAT HILLARY WOULD BE GOOD FOR WOMEN.

AND WE SHOULD ALL BE FOR HILLARY?

No. NO. Every time you argue that having a woman president is important, that it will matter, that it will be good for everyone in this country—girls and boys alike—there's an easy answer lurking in the shadows, ready to undercut your passion:

SO THAT'S ALL IT IS,

IT'S JUST THE WOMAN THING!

To which we'd all better say,

NO.

ABSOLUTELY NOT.

It's fine to support Hillary because she's a woman. But never concede—or believe—that that's the *only* reason.

NEVER EVEN SUGGEST (except among close friends and relations) THAT IT'S THE ONLY REASON.

THIS CAMPAIGN IS NOT JUST ABOUT THE WOMAN THING.

IT'S ABOUT FINDING THE BEST-QUALIFIED CANDIDATE AND ELECTING HER PRESIDENT—AND NOT EXCLUDING HER BE-CAUSE SHE IS A WOMAN.

THIS IS ABOUT THE ULTIMATE PROMISE OF EQUALITY AND FAIRNESS.

Imagine if Hillary weren't a woman. She'd simply be the best-qualified candidate, with absolutely everything going for her, and she'd have a lock on the whole thing. I wouldn't be writing this book, because the outcome would hardly be in question. This candidate would be called the next Bill Clinton, only better. He'd be running the party already. And we'd all say out loud what everyone says quietly now—which is that when you look beyond this candidate, the rest of the field pales.

If she were a he—Harry Rodham, let's say—the Democratic Party would be thrilled. A well-positioned, brilliant, charismatic, well-financed, former high official from the Clinton Administration, now running 70 percent approval ratings in New York, about to be reelected to his second term . . .

He would be, as my son says, *hot*. He would not be facing charges of unelectability *or* overambition.

This campaign is about the best candidate being able to compete and win.

This campaign is about the most qualified candidate by any measure being judged according to the same standard as other candidates.

3.

BUT CAN SHE WIN?

★

"She projects strength and the capacity to run the country, to pick smart people, to know when to compromise. Those are things that the last few years have proven to me she can do. I don't see any of our guys who could beat her—at least not today."[1]

—HOUSE MAJORITY WHIP TOM COLE (R-OK),
on Hillary Clinton, National Journal, April 29, 2005

"I think she could win every state John Kerry won. And she'd probably be a better candidate in the swing states."[2]

—SENATOR LINDSEY GRAHAM (R-SC),
former Clinton impeachment prosecutor, New York, February 21, 2005

"She can't win, and she's an incredibly polarizing figure. And ambition is just not a good enough reason."[3]

—DAVID GEFFEN,
prominent Democrat and friend of the Clintons, speaking in New York City, 2005

Hillary Clinton will be the most qualified candidate in the race.

She is one of the most experienced candidates ever to run for president.

A second-term senator, respected by her colleagues, outspoken in her support of the military, a true believer in family values, a moderate Democrat whose pitch in the Senate has been perfect, a first lady who spent eight years by the president's side and expanded the role of first lady, a veteran of state visits to seventy-eight nations, an advocate who has spearheaded education reform since her days in Arkansas. Imagine. And a woman to boot.

A qualified woman—just what everyone is always saying they're looking for.

Any more excuses?

Don't take my word for it. Ask the Republicans. You can ask John McCain. Ask the guys who prosecuted her husband. Ask the American people.

The absolute easiest part of the case for Hillary Clinton is the part that for every other candidate takes the longest, and in many cases, is never completed successfully: meeting the competency bar. To meet it coming in, for a woman no less, at a time when toughness and security are key issues, is—well, a very good way to start the argument.

But this is politics, where qualifications involve the ability to get the job, at least as much as the ability to do it. For Hillary, that's when the fun really begins.

This is my argument: The national numbers, to the extent they prove anything at all, prove only that the election is wide open. A majority are at least willing to vote for Hillary.[4] That actually represents a positive improvement. Even more important, the numbers out of New York, which show dramatic improvement in key categories over the last five years since Hillary became a senator, and assumed her moderate public profile, suggest that the swing voters of New York, like swing voters across the country who will have to take a second look at her, are capable of doing just that. That doesn't even get into how much more appealing Hillary is than John Kerry, or how the electoral politics tilt in her favor. Given all that, and given everything else she has going for her, why in the world wouldn't she be able to win?

★ ★ ★

After senators Clinton and John McCain appeared on *Meet the Press* on Sunday, February 20, 2005, the conservative magazine *NewsMax* ran the following headline:[5]

MCCAIN: HILLARY WOULD BE GOOD PRESIDENT

Maverick Republican Sen. John McCain said Sunday that his New York colleague, Sen. Hillary Clinton, would do well if she becomes president of the United States.

"I am sure that Senator Clinton would make a good president," McCain told NBC's "Meet the Press," as both he and Clinton were being interviewed from Baghdad.

While noting that as a Republican, he'll be supporting the GOP nominee in 2008, McCain reiterated, "I have no doubt that Senator Clinton would make a good president."

Asked whether she thought McCain would make a good president, Sen. Clinton was somewhat less effusive, responding tersely, "Absolutely" before erupting in her familiar cackle.

At that, "Meet the Press" host Tim Russert quipped, "We may have a fusion ticket, right here."

Lee Atwater, Bush 41's brilliant but sometimes diabolical late campaign manager, used to say that there was a little boat, and on that boat were the people that Americans had decided were competent enough to be president. If you can't get on the boat, Atwater argued, you can't win.

When he told me that little story, he was making the point that in 1988 Michael Dukakis had never made that leap—and that, even if Lee himself had set up the obstacles, Dukakis had revealed himself in how he dealt with them.

Here's what we all must recognize today:

Hillary Clinton is already on the boat.

She is already considered capable of holding the presidency. She has already leaped the biggest hurdle—the one no other woman has ever crossed.

In a Fox News poll taken late last fall, 59 percent of the electorate considered her competent to be president.[6] The question was: Regardless of whether you would vote for Hillary Clinton or not, do you think she is qualified to be president of the United States?

	Yes	No	Not Sure
Total	59%	34%	7%
Men	53%	39%	8%
Women	64%	29%	8%
Democrats	84%	10%	6%
Republicans	33%	59%	8%
Independents	58%	33%	9%

Source: Fox News Channel poll, December 14–15, 2004.

Her numbers were particularly strong among Democrats, women, and African Americans, 70 percent of whom already think she is capable of being president. Isn't that fascinating? When it comes to the fundamental question of competence—could this woman do this job?—Hillary Clinton is not polarizing; her competence is accepted, a given. For any candidate—much less one who has never been vice president, much less a woman—to score numbers like that is nothing short of stunning.

Of course, qualifications in politics aren't measured the way they are for other jobs. It's not about how smart you are, or whether you know the names of all the leaders of all the countries, or whether your heart is in the right place. In other words, whether Hillary Clinton can do the job isn't really the issue. Among her enemies, the case against Hillary Clinton is that she's the worst kind of witch, and that she should lose. Among her so-called friends, the case is that she can't win. What that actually means, at this point, is not that they've done a real electoral analysis—but that too many people hate her.

In fact, as Dick Morris is warning Republicans in his effort to scare up a Draft Condi movement, the electoral analysis is pointing in Hillary's favor.[7] George Bush didn't leave many Republican votes on the ground in November; you'll never do a better job at squeezing every vote out than Rove and Mehlman and their team did. On the Democratic side, by contrast, the potential upside from both higher turnout and demographics is substantial. Not only can Hillary win the votes Kerry did, but she can do better among minority voters and married women, and that's where she picks up the votes to beat her Republican rival.

A Marist Poll conducted in February 2005 asked voters if they wanted Hillary to run for president in 2008.[8] Its results were variously headlined as proving that Democrats overwhelmingly favored a Clinton candidacy, and as proving that Hillary was still polarizing with the general electorate. Let's look at the raw results:

Do you want Hillary Clinton to run for president in 2008 or not?

Registered Voters	Yes, Run	No, Don't Run	Unsure
February 2005	46%	49%	5%
December 2004	38%	50%	12%

February 2005	Yes, Run	No, Don't Run	Unsure
Democrats	67%	29%	4%
Republicans	21%	74%	5%
Independents	48%	46%	6%
Men	44%	49%	7%
Women	48%	49%	3%
Younger than 45	62%	34%	4%
45 and older	38%	57%	5%

This is why I love polls. They never lie. They leave that to the people who read them.

If you're for Hillary, you'll see in this poll that the percentage of Americans who want her to run has increased; that there is no gender gap, which suggests enormous opportunity; and that where she really lags is with older voters, who are likely to end up on her side because of Social Security.

If you're against Hillary, you'll focus on the idea that half the country doesn't want her to run, including almost half of all women—suggesting that she has not solved her problem with women, even four years after leaving the White House.

Which interpretation is correct? Which way will the voters actually turn? Of course, no one can be proven right, until all the votes are cast and polls don't matter any more. So how do you decide? Look at another poll, of course.

If you look at the poll numbers in New York, they suggest that the real Hillary Clinton, the person she has become, is nowhere near as polarizing as the old idea of her. The very obvious, critical answer to the electability argument is Senator Clinton, the mature woman, not a madeover version, but a grown up, experienced woman.

In New York, she has already proven herself to be more appealing—

more conservative, more likable, less arrogant, more self-deprecating—than the people there started out believing.[9] She isn't just a better candidate; on every measure—caring about people, understanding their problems, leadership skills—Hillary Clinton now scores as much as thirty points higher than she did in her First Lady days. Voters haven't necessarily said they were wrong about her as first lady, but they are overwhelming in liking her as a senator. That doesn't mean she's Saint Hillary. You don't get to be perfect. You don't get to be right all the time if you want those kinds of numbers. But clearly the recipe has worked. If she can help voters see that they may have been right then, but that their instincts are still right now—that she will fight for them now—then she wins.

At this point, the question of electability is still Hillary's biggest problem. It is the sum of all her problems. It is what, or who, she is running against right now: herself, what people don't like about her, or think they don't like about her. People project on Hillary. You fill her in, usually for the worse. That makes it hard to define what you don't like, and hard for her to overcome it.

At a Q&A session in February 2005 at the 92nd St. Y in New York City, a major forum for speeches and for the gathering of the liberal elite, David Geffen, one third of the Dreamworks SKG team, a major donor and public buddy of Bill Clinton's, and one of Hollywood's true power brokers, had this to say about Senator Clinton's prospective presidential run: "She can't win, and she's an incredibly polarizing figure. And ambition is just not a good enough reason."[10]

And ambition is just not a good enough reason. Thank you, Mr. Shrinking Violet.

Lloyd Grove of the *Daily News* reported that the audience paused and then broke into hearty applause.

Can you name an unambitious president? Absence of ambition in a politician is a recipe for failure. Geffen himself has been described as many things, and ambitious is certainly one of the nicer ones. No one becomes as rich as he without plenty of it. The term is applied frequently to him, and even more so to his partner, Jeffrey Katzenberg (whom I know and like), and never critically. Ambition is a quality always found in Hollywood moguls; sometimes it's their most pronounced, and only attractive, quality.

Is it too obvious to point out that ambition is only critiqued as unattractive in women?

I remember being called an "ambitious chick" when I was running to be the first woman president of the Harvard Law Review in 1976. I bought the guy who called me that one of those posters that said "Women Are Not Chicks," with a note that said we never apologize for ambition. That was *thirty years ago,* guys. (Okay, twenty-nine.) This would be funny if it weren't real.

Is ambition the only reason Hillary Clinton would run for president? How absurd.

After spending thirty years in politics, fighting for the same issues; after fighting away in the minority party for eight years in the Senate—after spending more time traveling the world, seeing firsthand the worst struggles of humanity—is Hillary Rodham Clinton's commitment to public service, her passion for children and families, still open to question? Is David Geffen really suggesting that Hillary cares less about these issues than her husband did when he ran, that he was the morally superior candidate?

Is he suggesting that George W. Bush, or John Kerry, ran for better reasons than Hillary Clinton?

That the George Allen and Bill Frists of the Republican Party are men for whom burning issues have defined their lives, even as Hillary just collected badges?

Or how about guys like Evan Bayh or Mitt Romney or Jeb Bush, who inherited the family business—do they have a clearer claim than that ambitious Rodham chick?

Get serious. This is how the game is played.

★ First you say she stands for nothing. Then you say she's a left-wing ideologue.

★ When asked, *But how can she stand for nothing if she's a left-wing ideologue?* You say: *She carries too much baggage. Too much Clinton.*

★ When asked, *Doesn't everybody agree that Gore's big mistake was divorcing himself from Bill Clinton? That if he hadn't cut the cord, he would have won?* (Don't believe it? Just ask Professor Kathleen Hall Jamieson, one of the smartest women in the world, who has established in two books that Gore's mistake cost him roughly three points, and the election.)[11] You say *It's all about ambition.*

★ When asked, *But what about these boys calling her ambitious—these boys who have been in politics for twenty minutes, who've all lost races, who've never raised as much money as her, been abroad once, never been through a crisis?* You say *Let's just face facts. People don't like her.*

★ When asked, *What do you mean, they don't like her? How can that be true when she's ahead in every poll, they've already concluded she is competent to be president, she's the most qualified candidate, she has the most charisma, she can raise the most money, she's the rock star in the field?* You say, *But look at the polls, she's so polarizing, so many people start out hating her, she'll unite the other side, you just can't move numbers like that. . . .*

★ And when asked, *Have you seen what she's done in New York? Don't you know that when people in America get to see the grown-up, mature Senator Clinton, they too will realize that she is their best choice?*

. . . You will just walk away, muttering about New York being a blue state, and how there's something you just don't "get" about her. And if I dare even suggest that if she were a man you'd be doing cartwheels, you'll give me a long sermon saying that sexism has nothing to do with it . . .

After Geffen's comment, I asked a friend of mine about it. She told me that no one on the Clinton side had seen it coming. A few of them, including Hillary's personal assistant, apparently found out about it only because I kept asking everyone about it. Anyone who knows Bill knows that such a remark would absolutely infuriate him. Or at least that's what close friends of hers told me. "If you want to be a friend of his, you don't come between him and Hillary," she said. "This is not acceptable."

Oh, well. People who would never take shots at him fire at her with impunity; sometimes they barely seem to notice they're doing it. When I asked a friend of Geffen's if he was mad at Bill over something, he responded that Geffen is just really turned off to politics these days. You may also have heard that Geffen was recently forced to unlock a fence giving the public access to his beach. Bad time for him. Maybe that's why he decided to unload on Hillary. It doesn't matter. He's hardly the only one.

Hillary Clinton will run against a slew of men who have nearly all lost races, who can't hold a candle to her experience, who will argue that they should be elected instead of her because she:

1. Isn't electable—even though the only races Bill Clinton ever lost were the ones she wasn't involved with; even though she's the only one in the field who has never lost a race.

2. Isn't tough or experienced enough for the big time—even though she's routinely vilified for her toughness; even though, of all the likely candidates, she's the only one already considered capable of handling the job and has far more experience than any of them.

None of which anyone would dare argue if we were talking about a man.

And if she ever so much as leveled the same charges at them, she'd get killed.

Of course, David Geffen isn't the only one raising the question. Far from it. He is among the least self-interested, to be honest. He's just saving some money by getting out of politics.

"Southern Revolt on the Ascent of Hillary" read the headline on a *Times* of London story about an interview with Phil Bredesen, the Democratic governor of Tennessee.[12] (Of course no poll is cited to prove there's any such southern revolt, but who needs facts?)

Phil who? you might be asking. Exactly. Ever heard of him? Were you thinking he might be the next president of the United States? You probably weren't. But he was, mark my words.

What Governor Bredesen shared with the *Times* was a blockbuster: Voters, he felt, were "kind of dissatisfied" with the field of Democrats, and he thought Hillary would have an "uphill road," and "I sure hope there are other people who would step forward." The candidate "may well be someone that nobody has thought of. . . . The sense I get is that people are really hunting around and looking for something different."

Here's the delicious part: Governor Phil later told the local paper that he was apparently troubled that the news story made him sound unfriendly toward Hillary.[13] Imagine. Just because he suggested a "revolt" in the South against her, someone might think he didn't *like* her. How ridiculous. His press secretary told the press that the governor didn't take issue with any of the quotes, but didn't expect the context. "When you read this it seems full of malice, and that is not where this governor is at all with Senator Clinton," his spokesperson, Lydia Lendker, told *The Tennessean* on April 6.

Really?

The governor had himself been the earlier subject of a cover story in the *New Republic* as a possible presidential candidate, which would certainly put him right up there in the group of those you have never heard of.[14]

Hello, I'm President Whatshisname. Maybe no one's ever heard of me, but this is my chance. After all, she can't win. Nothing personal, of course.

Just for fun, I checked the governor's background, as if I were a negative researcher for one of his opponents. What did I learn? Among other things, that he made his money in the HMO business. Oh, when Gene Sperling was young, what he could have done with that was scary. Every HMO has made mistakes that have led to the death of somebody's mother. . . .

Gene grew up to run economic policy in the White House for President Clinton, first as Bob Rubin's deputy and then as his replacement when Bob became Secretary of the Treasury. But in 1988, he was the most amazing intern you can imagine. He worked about twenty hours a day, and even in those pre-Internet days there was no fact he couldn't find. One of the great things about politics, especially for young people, is that it offers a wide-open opportunity for those who are willing to work unbelievably hard and be absolutely flexible; from there, you can get anywhere. Somewhere out there today are dozens of young Gene Sperlings at work, doing books on candidates, finding out things about them that even they didn't know, figuring out how to use what they've learned, calculating what each candidate's votes might mean to the people of Iowa, New Hampshire, and the nation.

Back in 1982, Mike Ford, another legendary organizer, invited me out to Ohio to teach Jerry Springer's running mate to be a candidate. Jerry was running for governor, and his prospective lieutenant governor was a wealthy businessman who had never been in politics but was willing to contribute some obscene amount to the campaign. As we did our song and dance, the talk turned to his background in business. When I asked if he'd ever dealt with unions, his face started turning oh-so-slightly red. Then we got to lawsuits, and women, and judgments, and by that time this guy was screaming bloody murder at me. This was, needless to say, before Jerry went into TV, which he did after he lost that election. Going from business to politics, especially presidential politics, may look like an easy transition, but it can be more complicated than it looks. The level of scrutiny is altogether different. It can be particularly troublesome for Democrats who need the support of some of the very constituency groups—like labor, environmentalists, health and safety do-gooders—they tend to fight with on other occasions.

Charlie Cook, one of the most respected analysts in Washington, writes that Hillary Clinton's "obstacle boils down to this simple question: Can she win a general election?"[15] Primary voters, as Charlie points out, have generally tended to not vote strategically and appeals to who would do better in a general election have tended to fall on deaf ears. But 2004 marked a change in that regard. Howard Dean collapsed because he became obviously unelectable, and Kerry succeeded because he seemed the *most* electable. In a December AP poll cited by Charlie in his newsletter, a little over a month after the 2004 election, a survey of 399 Democratic primary voters, Hillary was well out front, but half of the voters were willing to change their allegiances if they became convinced their favorite wouldn't win.

★ ★ ★

So the question *Is she electable?* is urgent indeed.

My friends Bert and Barbara are typical Democrats who have nothing against Hillary personally. Quite the contrary, Bert liked her just fine when he met her during her Senate campaign. To him, there's no question that she's hugely intelligent, extremely hardworking, more disciplined than her husband. He understands exactly why Bill picked her out in law school and married her. (In fact, confides a mutual friend, Bill wasn't just taken with her intelligence. She was "beautiful. Really beautiful. He was smitten with her. Totally.")

BARBARA: Touching. If only it had lasted . . .

Actually, it has, in its way—the partnership, that is. Who do you think is going to run this campaign?

But is that enough?

BERT: Let's frame the issue: Why nominate someone who starts out at such a disadvantage with so many voters, who carries so much baggage into the election, who has no chance of convincing nearly half the voters in the country to vote for her? The point of a polarizing candidate is you're doing the other side's job for them. Now is that gender-based or gender-neutral?

Ask Nick Kristof, of the *New York Times*.[16] He is otherwise very favorable toward Hillary, and describes her as a role model for Democrats who want to win elections. He is also quite widely and rightly regarded as brilliant. He has both raised and answered these questions based on the reaction in the farming community where he grew up: "Ambitious, high-achieving women," he writes "are still a turnoff in many areas, particularly if they're liberal and feminist . . .

"In small towns like Yamhill, any candidate from New York carries a lot of baggage, and Mrs. Clinton more than most. Moreover, television magnifies her emotional reserve and turns her into a frost queen."

Washington consultant Michael Powell makes a similar point. Whether or not the Republican nominee can unify his own party and generate any enthusiasm for himself, there's a school of thought that says that once Hillary is nominated, she'll galvanize the GOP base against herself more effectively than any Republican could manage. Why shoot ourselves in the foot that way, some Democrats ask, when we could nominate a safe, moderate, white male, who would be far less offensive to the Republican base? Someone like Governor Whatshisname from Tennessee, whose picture was on the *New Republic*. . . . Or, perhaps, the governor of Virginia.

This is an argument you will hear constantly between now and 2007.

I call it the *Why not the Safe White Male?* argument. Safe white male presidential candidates are as hard to find as . . . well, you see where I'm headed. You'll never find anyone who's as safe as you hope, who can do as much as you need.

For instance, which of your *safe white men* are going to excite the base the way Hillary does, so they can spend all their time in the middle? I'll answer: None. There aren't any safe white males out there capable of exciting the base. Hillary holds 45–46 percent going in, and holds it solid. So whatever some of my liberal friends may say (or scream) about how the way to win elections is by throwing red meat, she can focus her efforts on the middle, which is where you ultimately win elections. The men, ironically, will have to run to her left, to beat her on her left, and will suffer for it. She doesn't have to spend the first half of the campaign—or, worse, the last—"securing her base."

She's been through more presidential campaigns than anyone else. She's been under more scrutiny than anyone on the planet. Of all the candidates, she has the fewest secrets, and is likely to make the fewest mistakes. Any safe white male we nominate can be counted on to make a hundred mistakes. In other words, chances are he won't be safe at all.

We know her problems. There's no such thing as a candidate without problems: there are only candidates with problems we don't know about yet, investments no one has investigated, a wife who has said things no one has been tracking (*Say what, Mrs. Vilsack?* Remember the week when he was the flavor of the month for VP and it turned out she had written a few things in the newspaper that were more than a little embarrassing?), a draft record that hasn't yet been vetted . . .

Moreover, even if you could find a safe guy who'd made no mistakes in business, with a wife who never said anything stupid, and perfect children, in-laws, brothers and sisters, something I don't think exists, the impact of electing him wouldn't be the same. Electing Hillary would make a bigger difference. So even if the risk of nominating Hillary is greater, which I'm not willing to concede—after all, you haven't got a safe white male, and I'm still betting that most hard core Hillary haters are ultimately Republican voters, the rewards are *certainly* greater, and therefore so must be the investment (we'll get to that later). If we win, we're looking at a chance for real change. If we lose, they'll say it's because we nominated a high-achieving woman who's a liberal and a feminist (I'm not disagreeing, Mr. Kristof).

★ ★ ★

In May, for the first time, a national poll found that a majority of Americans were either somewhat or very likely to vote for Hillary Clinton for president, a dramatic turnaround from 2003, when the same poll had found 57 percent saying that they were either not very likely or not at all likely to vote for Hillary.[17]

"If Hillary Rodham Clinton were to run for president in 2008, how likely would you be to vote for her: very likely, somewhat likely, not very likely, or not at all likely?"

	Very Likely	Somewhat Likely	Not Very Likely	Not At All Likely	Unsure
5/20–22/05	29%	24%	7%	39%	1%
6/9-10/03	20%	21%	12%	44%	2%

Gallup Poll. May 20–22, 2005. N=453 registered voters nationwide. MoE±5.

Poor Scott Rasmussen. Scott is a first-rate Republican pollster. But, in the words of my favorite blogger—a seemingly mild-mannered Englishman named Daniel Owen (www.ovaloffice2008.com)—he is developing what he calls an "unhealthy fixation" with Senator Clinton.[18] As Mr. Owen points out, Scott has created something called the "Hillary Meter" to measure how far off Hillary is from the political center.[19] His larger problem is that he can't find any Republicans who are any fun to follow—a problem that, to his credit, he's honest about. So instead he polls Hillary constantly—and then his clients (I assume it's them) mis-label the polls to hype up so-called changes that are actually within the margin of error.

If Hillary Rodham Clinton runs for president in 2008, would you vote for her?

	April 1–3	April 17–18	May 2–3	May 16–17
Definitely for her	32%	30%	29%	30%
Definitely against her	37%	40%	36%	37%
Depends on opponent	26%	23%	27%	27%

How likely is it that Senator Clinton will be the Democratic candidate for president in 2008?

	April 1–3	April 17–18	May 2–3	May 16–17
Very likely	27%	33%	31%	30%
Somewhat likely	36%	29%	30%	31%
Not very likely	20%	20%	20%	21%
Not at all likely	9%	8%	9%	10%

Methodology: Telephone interviews to 1,500 American adults. Margin of error = 3 percent.

Maybe it's the difference between giving people four categories and three. That's an old pollster trick. As you may have noticed, Scott conducts his polls at exactly the same time as CNN, and trying to spin precisely the opposite conclusion. I think the headline on this one from May was supposed to be that "Opposition to Hillary Grows" (from 36 to 37 percent, after all). I can laugh, but I'm not paying for it.

Hardcore Democrats love Hillary, hardcore Republicans don't, and enough people to make a substantial majority are open to voting for her depending on who she runs against, which is as good as it gets at this point. Her negative rating is about 40 percent—which also happens to be the Republican base vote.

Potentially more important, she has done as a senator exactly what she will have to do as a presidential candidate. She has overcome the stereotypes that traditionally plague women candidates, reversed the caricature of herself that defined her when she took office, and emerged as unbeatable.

What is the best evidence of what Candidate Clinton can accomplish? I would argue that it is the difference between the way New Yorkers viewed the woman who ran for Senate in 2000 and the senator who is seeking reelection today. Hillary's job approval ratings among New Yorkers are in the high 60s and low 70s, which is nothing short of stratospheric.[20]

> BERT: So are New York senior Senator Chuck Schumer's, and no one is suggesting he run for president . . .

But he didn't start where Hillary did. And don't forget, Bert, Hillary is running strong upstate—in the Red part, the part that looks like the rest of America.

Most people forget that the reason that the New York Democratic Party turned to Hillary Clinton six years ago was that they were facing what seemed to be a hopeless situation: Rudy Giuliani, the popular and successful mayor of New York, was planning a Senate run. But Hillary, at that point, wasn't in much better shape than the rest of her party. She began the campaign as a Monica victim, still emerging from her "right-wing conspiracy" mode and the impeachment inquiry. The first step in her campaign, a so-called listening tour, was much mocked by press and partisans alike. Many people were betting against her then. They said she would damage the cause of women, and make a fool of herself to boot.

Today, as conservative Thomas Galvin laments, "NYers love Honest

Hillary so much, she'd demolish Rudy Who in [the] 2006 Senate race."[21] He uses the old buzzword "makeover," trying to cast doubt on her authenticity. Dick Morris calls her successful transformation "branding." But this was no cynical shape-shifting exercise. Six years isn't overnight. You can fool some of the people some of the time, but the numbers demonstrate that her connection with the voters of New York is for real.

In October 2000, a month before election day in Hillary's race against Rick Lazio, a little-known congressman, 45 percent of New Yorkers thought Hillary Clinton was honest and trustworthy, and 44 percent didn't; her approval rating was 38 percent.[22] That is the definition of polarizing. After four years in the Senate, 64 percent found her honest and trustworthy; only 30 percent did not. That's a full twenty-point improvement. Her approval rating was up almost thirty points to 65 percent. In 2000, 62 percent had tagged her as a liberal; four years later, that number had dropped to 52 percent. In New York today, 74 percent of voters say that Hillary Clinton has strong leadership qualities; 65 percent say that she cares about the problems of people like them.

As you take a closer look at the numbers, remember that they come from Republicans as well as Democrats—that is, a general election sample:[23]

Question: Do you approve or disapprove of the way Hillary Rodham Clinton is handling her job as United States senator?

	Approve/Yes	Disapprove/No	Don't know/No answer
Feb. 9, 2005	65%	27%	8%
Feb. 12, 2003	56%	34%	9%
Feb. 14, 2001	38%	30%	33%

Question: Would you say that Hillary Rodham Clinton has strong leadership qualities or not?

	Approve/Yes	Disapprove/No	Don't know/No answer
Feb. 9, 2005	74%	22%	4%
Feb. 6, 2000	72%	21%	7%

Question: Would you say that Hillary Rodham Clinton cares about the needs and problems of people like you or not?

	Approve/Yes	Disapprove/No	Don't know/No answer
Feb. 9, 2005	65%	30%	5%
Feb. 6, 2000	52%	42%	6%

Question: Do you think of Hillary Rodham Clinton as a liberal, moderate, or conservative?

	Liberal	Moderate	Conservative	Don't Know/No Answer
Feb. 9, 2005	52%	31%	8%	9%
Sept. 27, 2000	62%	23%	8%	7%

NOTES: Most recent results are from Quinnipiac University survey of 1,218 New York State registered voters; margin of error of 2.8 percentage points.

There have been many other polls, and all of their results are in the same range. Her approval rating hovers in the very high sixties, a solid twenty points higher than it was five years ago. People see her as a consensus-builder, and a genuine leader.

If she can do nationally anything like what she's done in New York, she wins.

What she clearly seems to have done is *change* the way voters see her. As for the concerns of my friends, I would point out:

* New Yorkers don't hate her.

* They don't see her as a phony.

* They don't see her as a liberal ideologue.

* They don't see her as an ice queen.

* They see her as someone with strong leadership qualities, who cares about people like them, and gets things done.

And many of them are people who didn't always think that, who thought something entirely different. These numbers suggest that the cynics who claim people won't take a second look at her—that their opinions are so solidly entrenched and that their minds will never change—are wrong. That's critical, because if Hillary wins the nomination, as people are increasingly coming to believe, voters will be left with only two choices. There is no better opportunity for a second look than that: If there is any willingness to consider a candidate, a debate will be the place to make a judgment, and the New York numbers suggest that minds can be changed.

★ ★ ★

These numbers, of course, have been the subject of all kinds of speculation. Why is she drawing them? Are they real? Can they be expected to transfer to Iowa in the first instance, and rural Ohio later on?

One of the first and most important thinkers to weigh in on the subject was former *New Republic* editor Andrew Sullivan.[24] I can't even tell you how many people sent his column on the subject to me. The fact that it appeared in the *Sunday Times* of London just shows you how the game works; no one I know actually "gets" the London papers, but everyone reads Andrew Sullivan. The headline was worth years of work:

"*New York Warms to Hillary . . . Next It Could Be America.*"

"Something quite unusual is happening to Hillary Rodham Clinton," Sullivan wrote. "She's become popular." Quoting then-current poll numbers, he described the Democratic nomination as "Hillary's to lose"—which, whether true or not, only helped make it so.

Sullivan credited two factors: the fact that she has been elected in her own right, and her success in redefining herself toward the political center. "What many people disliked about her was what they perceived as her unreconstructed liberal politics and her use of her marriage to gain and wield political power. But in 2005 Hillary has recast herself in the public mind as a centrist and she has won election in her own right . . . it changes a lot."

He took special note of two political moves that bespoke a new maturity: a recent speech on abortion, and her vote for the war and tour of Afghanistan with John McCain. In a "remarkable speech to pro-choice activists," Sullivan noted, Hillary had "insisted that opponents of abortion were sincere in their religious faith and deserved a more respectful hearing from pro-choicers. She also declared that abortion itself was always an unfortunate event."

The gist: "We can all recognize that abortion in many ways represents a sad, even tragic choice to many, many women. The fact is that the best way to reduce the number of abortions is to reduce the number of unwanted pregnancies in the first place."

Or consider what Nick Kristof had to say in the *New York Times* in March, as he declared Mrs. Clinton the best guide for national Democrats as to how to win elections:[25]

"I've always been a praying person," Mrs. Clinton declared recently. Of course, this approach works in her case only because her religious faith is longstanding . . .

Democrats are usually more comfortable talking about sex than God. But that doesn't work in a country where 70 percent say that "presidents should have strong religious beliefs." . . .

The Democratic Party commits seppuku in the heartland by coming across as indifferent to people's doubts about abortions or even as pro-abortion. A *Times* poll in January found that 61 percent of Americans favor tighter restrictions on abortion, or even a ban, while only 36 percent agree with the Democratic Party position backing current abortion law.

That doesn't mean that there's no middle ground on abortion. In fact, most of America is standing, conflicted, on middle ground. Many people are deeply uncomfortable with abortions, but they also don't want women or doctors going to prison, and they don't want teenage girls dying because of coat-hanger abortions.

What has been lethal for Democrats has not been their pro-choice position as such, but the perception that they don't even share public qualms about abortion. Mrs. Clinton has helped turn the debate around by emerging as both pro-choice and anti-abortion.

That is potentially a winning position for Democrats. . . .

As Kristof noted, Hillary's new maturity and sharpening instincts have improved not only her policy positions, but her profile among those who know her best—her colleagues on the Senate floor. "Mrs. Clinton is also hard to dismiss as a screechy obstructionist," he wrote, "because she's gone out of her way to be collegial in the Senate and to work with Republicans from Trent Lott to Sam Brownback. Senator John Kerry never seemed much liked by his colleagues, while other senators seem to like Mrs. Clinton. Perhaps it's that, according to *New York* magazine, she surprises other senators by popping up during meetings and asking: Anybody want a coffee?"

Though in the same article Kristof questions Hillary's electability, he is impressed by her New York numbers: "Mrs. Clinton has an approval rating in the state of 69 percent, according to a *Times* poll published last month, and her negative ratings have tumbled to 21 percent. That puts her approval rating even higher than that of New York's popular senior senator, Charles Schumer."

No less an observer than Peggy Noonan describes her accomplishments this way, as part of her warning to Republicans to take Hillary seriously.[26]

> [I]t is good to be concerned about Mrs. Clinton, for she is coming down the pike. It is pointless to be afraid, but good to be concerned. Why? Because we live in a more or less 50–50 nation; because Mrs. Clinton is smarter than her husband and has become a better campaigner on the ground; because her warmth and humor seem less oily; because she has struck out a new rhetorically (though not legislatively) moderate course; because you don't play every card right the way she's been playing every card right the past five years unless you have real talent; because unlike her husband, she has found it possible to grow more emotionally mature; because the presidency is the bright sharp focus of everything she does each day; because she is not going to get seriously dinged in the 2008 primaries, but will likely face challengers who make her look even more moderate and stable; and because in 2008, we will have millions of 18- to 24-year-old voters who have no memory of her as the harridan of the East Wing and the nutty professor of HillaryCare.

That her worst critic acknowledges that Mrs. Clinton has grown more emotionally mature; that she has real talent; that her warmth and humor may actually be genuine; that she has a clear focus; that a good chunk of the country will see her with fresh eyes and that she has a clear shot through the primaries to a 50–50 electorate—all of that is a pretty good start in making the case that she is electable. She hardly sounds like the harridan Peggy herself described in her bestselling polemic.

As to how she moved those numbers in New York, maybe it's as simple as saying that messy, distorted, and noisy as it is, eventually, democracy works.

★ ★ ★

Of course, you still have to get those pesky electoral votes, where both Kerry and Gore fell short. There is the matter of the arithmetic. People are willing to skate over the Democratic primary process, probably too quickly. But no one skates over the Reds and the Blues.

At this stage, you can only be basic. You start with the Kerry states. If Hillary can carry the Kerry states, the Democratic base, she needs eighteen more electoral votes. The theory is that if she's strong enough to survive whatever the primary brings, boosted by the convention and a strong campaign, she should walk in with a strong hold on the Democratic base.

Then you consider the potential for growth, especially among minorities, women, and young people, who are more likely to be Democrats. As Dick Morris keeps pointing out, Democrats have much more room to grow than Republicans do.

2004 ELECTION RESULTS (Bush–286, Kerry–252)[27]

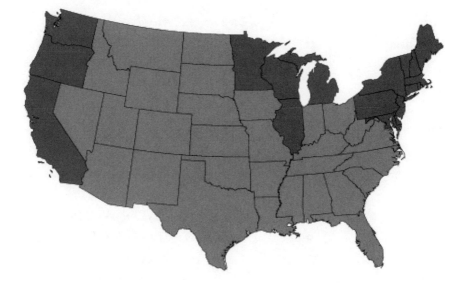

Here is the reality.

We live in a very red country, where pockets of blue contain major population centers. To think that Kerry could have won so little of the country, and yet come so close to winning, and he did it without any ardent support from anyone; his supporters basically agreed with him on the issues, and disagreed with his opponent. As a rich Boston liberal, he

wasn't someone people easily identified with, or who they would otherwise have expected to agree with them, share their values, understand
their lives. In every way but his status as a white man, Hillary Clinton is
far more moderate—and middle American—than Kerry. She has been
an unequivocal supporter of the war and the military; she supports the
death penalty, is a deficit hawk, and was an early supporter of welfare reform.

So, in theory, it shouldn't be that hard for her to pick up another
eighteen electoral votes. Where might they come from?

State	Electoral Votes	Candidate	Clinton-Gore (1992/1996)
Alabama	9	Bush	(LOST/LOST)
Alaska	3	Bush	(LOST/LOST)
Arizona	10	Bush	(LOST/WON)
Arkansas	**6**	**Bush**	**(WON/WON)**
California	55	Kerry	(WON/WON)
Colorado	9	Bush	(WON/LOST)
Connecticut	7	Kerry	(WON/WON)
Dist. of Columbia	3	Kerry	(WON/WON)
Delaware	3	Kerry	(WON/WON)
Florida	27	Bush	(LOST/WON)
Georgia	15	Bush	(WON/LOST)
Hawaii	4	Kerry	(WON/WON)
Idaho	4	Bush	(LOST/LOST)
Illinois	21	Kerry	(WON/WON)
Indiana	11	Bush	(LOST/LOST)
Iowa	**7**	**Bush**	**(WON/WON)**
Kansas	6	Bush	(LOST/LOST)
Kentucky	**8**	**Bush**	**(WON/WON)**
Louisiana	**9**	**Bush**	**(WON/WON)**
Maine	4	Kerry	(WON/WON)
Maryland	10	Kerry	(WON/WON)

State	Electoral Votes	Candidate	Clinton-Gore (1992/1996)
Massachusetts	12	Kerry	(WON/WON)
Michigan	17	Kerry	(WON/WON)
Minnesota	10	Kerry	(WON/WON)
Mississippi	6	Bush	(LOST/LOST)
Missouri	**11**	**Bush**	**(WON/WON)**
Montana	3	Bush	(WON/LOST)
Nebraska	5	Bush	(LOST/LOST)
Nevada	**5**	**Bush**	**(WON/WON)**
New Hampshire	4	Kerry	(WON/WON)
New Jersey	15	Kerry	(WON/WON)
New Mexico	**5**	**Bush**	**(WON/WON)**
New York	31	Kerry	(WON/WON)
North Carolina	15	Bush	(LOST/LOST)
North Dakota	3	Bush	(LOST/LOST)
Ohio	**20**	**Bush**	**(WON/WON)**
Oklahoma	7	Bush	(LOST/LOST)
Oregon	7	Kerry	(WON/WON)
Pennsylvania	21	Kerry	(WON/WON)
Rhode Island	4	Kerry	(WON/WON)
South Carolina	8	Bush	(LOST/LOST)
South Dakota	3	Bush	(LOST/LOST)
Tennessee	**11**	**Bush**	**(WON/WON)**
Texas	34	Bush	(LOST/LOST)
Utah	5	Bush	(LOST/LOST)
Vermont	3	Kerry	(WON/WON)
Virginia	13	Bush	(LOST/LOST)
Washington	11	Kerry	(WON/WON)
West Virginia	**5**	**Bush**	**(WON/WON)**
Wisconsin	10	Kerry	(WON/WON)
Wyoming	3	Bush	(LOST/LOST)

Ideologically, remember, we have a less liberal candidate than in the last go-round, running against a non-incumbent, with greater appeal, better organization, better turnout, and the best strategist in the world at the helm . . .

As I say, it's way too early to predict.

But I'm not trying to predict. I'm trying to persuade.

The question is not how she will win, but are there conceivable scenarios, sufficiently plausible, to support nominating her?

It's an extremely fair, smart question to ask.

Funny, this is the first time I can remember addressing it in this kind of detail at this stage of a campaign.

Now why could that possibly be?

POSSIBLE SCENARIOS TO GET THE EXTRA 18

1. Pick up one of the two big swing states . . .

Ohio (20) or Florida (27).

2. Pick up some of the South . . . for instance:

Arkansas (6), Tennessee (11), Louisiana (9).

3. Pick up some of the other states that Bill Clinton won in both '92 and '96, but John Kerry lost in '04 . . .

New Mexico (5), West Virginia (5), Missouri (11), Kentucky (8), Iowa (7), Nevada (5).

What makes these plausible scenarios? Hmm. Let's see:

In Florida, where Kerry lost and where a victory would have changed the result: Would Hillary do better than Kerry among African Americans? Yes.

Among Jews? Absolutely. Among Hispanics? I think so . . .

"Send her to the I-4 corridor between Orlando and St. Pete," suggests someone who knows about such things. "That's where she wins it. All she has to do is show herself as a traditional person who is balanced and thoughtful, and not some queen of liberal excess."

Another question: Who would encourage higher turnout, Kerry or Hillary?

It's not even close.

Same analysis in Ohio, certainly in the African American community. She's *got* to do better there than Kerry did. Remember, in the black community they call Bill Clinton America's first black president. That's where he will go, at the end, with a whole entourage, and he will bring out the vote all over the state of Ohio. . . . And that alone would make the difference.

Or let's consider what might be called the **5 Percent Approach**:

Look at the challenge in terms of the base and the swing vote. The challenge in any campaign is to secure your own base and then win the necessary share of the swing vote. The true base of each party is 40 percent (just look at the numbers for every election for the last thirty years), but unless you're in a landslide year or you have a third-party candidate, any Democrat who can say he's on your side gets to 46 percent. Old fashioned red-meat class warfare gets you that, and the pollsters tell me that no one has that base more strongly in hand than Hillary.

(Aside: Do I worry about that a little? Yes. Why? Because I think there's more work to be done among the same suburban women who have had to be reached everywhere; because the polls still show Democrats interested in a candidate other than Hillary in the race for the presidency at this point—and a certain amount of undecided voters, which means voters who aren't yet betting on Hillary.)

The excitement of a historic convention (Orlando? Cleveland?) putting Hillary's name in nomination could only affirm the love affair between Hillary and the base of the Democratic Party. For Hillary, not having to secure your base, but owning it—as Reagan did—should give her the advantage of being able to focus exclusively on her targets in the middle. So all Hillary has to do is find that 5 to 6 percent . . .

And where are they?

George Bush beat John Kerry by a margin of somewhere between eleven and fifteen points among married women, depending on whether you believe the networks or the *Los Angeles Times*. The numbers for white married women were obviously higher.[28] The DNC Women's Vote Center report concluded that "the biggest drop in Democratic votes between 2000 and 2004 was among white married working women."

Who can win these women back?

U.S. President National Pool Exit Polls[29]

	Percentage of All Voters	Voted for BUSH	Voted for KERRY
	%	%	%
ALL	100	51	48
Male	46	55	44
Female	54	48	51
Working woman	29	48	51
Not working Woman	71	53	46
18–29 years old	17	45	54
30–44 years old	29	53	46
45–64 years old	30	51	48
65 & older	24	54	46
Whites	77	58	41
White men	36	62	37
White women	41	55	44
Blacks	11	11	88
Latinos	8	44	53
Asians	2	44	56
Married	63	57	42
Not married	37	40	58

	Percentage of All Voters	Voted for BUSH	Voted for KERRY
Liberals	21	13	85
Moderates	45	45	54
Conservatives	34	84	15
Democrats	37	11	89
Independents	26	48	49
Republicans	37	93	6
Big cities	13	39	60
Small cities	19	49	49
Suburb	45	52	47
Small town	8	50	48
Rural	16	59	40

Fox News national exit poll. N=11,719 voters interviewed—using self-administered, confidential questionnaires—as they exited 250 polling places across the nation on November 2, 2004. Conducted by Edison/Mitofsky. All questionnaires were prepared by NEP (National Election Pool).

See? All you need are five points. Among married, white, working women. Among older women. Among women who think that issues of gender equity don't get enough attention in campaigns. Women who will never have a stronger champion on economic issues than Hillary Clinton. Women who for the first time will hear a presidential candidate speaking to them, and for them, in speeches. Will they hear that? How can they not? Will it matter? Why wouldn't it?

Kerry also did poorly among older voters. In the past, older voters have started off as some of the most resistant voters when it comes to supporting a woman candidate. I think Hillary will do much better. She will have two advantages. One is the Social Security issue. The Republicans have scared older voters; now the Democrats will. (Sorry, but I promised you I'd be honest, and they will, and it will work—because it *should* work. Because we *should* be scared.) The second is that a majority of older voters are women; wives outlive their husbands. Beyond social security, their largest concern is health care. No one knows that issue better than Hillary. As a result, older voters—who vote in higher percentages than any other group in the electorate—may up their votes for Democrats. You just need 5 percent . . . one point here, two points there.

Here's how it usually works: if you can win, you win. If Hillary can win Florida or Ohio, she can win New Mexico or Arkansas, and certainly Wisconsin; if she can win five points more among married white women, she can win Florida or Ohio. If she can win Florida or Ohio, then Arkansas, New Mexico, Iowa, Michigan, and every other battleground state will be in her corner, or at least in play.

And I've got news for her supporters: If she gets in trouble with her base—if she has to spend three years convincing people who should be her friends to like her—then it won't take a perfect storm to beat her.

4.

WHAT'S WRONG WITH HILLARY

★

Here is what I hear about Hillary from everybody: She is a real mother hen. The women—and they are mostly women—who work for her love her. She takes care of them. She gives them wedding showers and baby showers, fusses over them like a nice Midwestern adult Sunday school teacher, which is also what she is. She is in almost every way a very traditional woman. She has traditional tastes, likes traditional things.

She has a big laugh and a big sense of humor. She is very protective of Chelsea, who will be thirty, after all, when Hillary takes office. She has had to deal with her family, just like everybody: She moved her parents to Little Rock, took care of her brothers, included everybody in everything. She is, definitely, ambitious. But she's also tolerant. Women forgive Bill for his transgressions because he's attractive. What they don't get is why *she* puts up with them. When you ask people who might actually know, the answer you get is that she's made her peace, but that doesn't account for the public humiliation that came with the scandals.

After a certain point, someone explains to me, you don't care any more. After a certain point, I don't think anyone else does either.

An old friend of theirs—of his, really—describes staying over at the White House one night, when all three of them had gone out, and she and Hillary had come home first. They sat together outside the Lincoln Bedroom making small talk, waiting for Bill to get home.

What did you talk about? I asked her.

The usual, she said. Kids. She told me how proud she was about Chelsea; how getting that right was still the most important thing. You know, mother stuff.

And then, I can't believe what I said . . .

It was getting late, and she yawned, and I yawned. We'd done Chelsea and my kids, and her mother and my father. And I said . . .

If you were me, would you stay up and wait for him, or would you go to bed?

And she just rolled her head back and laughed, and said, "You're on your own there. I gave up trying to figure that out twenty years ago."

And we both laughed our heads off.

Then what did you do? I ask.

I went to sleep, she said. After all these years, who cares? I was tired.

When she announced her candidacy for Senate, Hillary found herself lagging among the very voters she most closely resembled. And the reason was not her positions; it was her husband. Women were more willing to forgive him than to forgive her for letting him off the hook. Forget about Bill; Hillary is the one who has had to deal most recently with a woman problem, and she still does, and no one understood it better than her husband.

The president himself called me about it in the summer of 2000. It was driving him slightly crazy. He put it to me simply: "Women are mad at Hillary because she didn't leave me. It's just not fair. What do we do?"

Bill Clinton has always felt that by dragging Hillary to Arkansas with him, she was sacrificing her career for his. He has said many times that he thought she had as much political talent as he did. That's why, during that summer of 2000, he recognized that her decision to stay with him was hurting her in New York. He pored over those numbers, and obsessed about how to move them. I was not the only one who spent hours on the phone with him discussing the problem.

I did my part. I wrote an article for *George* magazine about the time when he and I stayed up half the night talking about our frayed marriages, making the point that the Clintons—Monica notwithstanding— had an underlying partnership that a nine-night stand wasn't going to break up.[1] I don't think I ended up moving votes, but my ex-husband, I later learned, didn't much like the comparison. The point was that the Clintons, for all their problems, were still married.

An ad at the end of the campaign, by a breast cancer survivor named Marie Kaplan, told women to "Get over it," and vote for Hillary because she would be with women on key issues like breast cancer, reproductive freedom, and health care. In *Living History,* Hillary pronounced it the best ad of the campaign, the one that captured what she wanted women to be thinking about when they went into the voting booth.[2] It did not purport to answer their questions or explain her choices, but to refocus their attention. It worked well enough, for that place and time. But out there in the United States proper, there are still people who haven't gotten over their outrage at Bill and Hillary alike.

The most important new book about the Clinton presidency was initially mispromoted by conservatives who had high hopes for it.[3] The *Drudge Report* promised "NEW CLINTON BOOK: THE LIES, THE FIGHTS, THE INSULTS." In fact, *The Survivor,* by *Washington Post* reporter John F. Harris, does recount a few of the old, painful fights about health care.[4] But because it begins with the midterm elections in 1994, it leaves out much of the Hillary Haters' usual red meat: the events of the first two years, the stuff of the young, inexperienced Clintons—the kind of behavior that's most at odds with the qualified senator of today. There are some ironic moments, to be sure: After Dick Morris was fired in the summer of 1996, during the Democratic convention in Chicago, Hillary was apparently so worried about his mental state that she feared he might commit suicide, and both she and the president reportedly called him in Connecticut. There are also some old stories of Hillary as the tough fighter, and even Harris's descriptions of the tensions in the marriage are tempered by a realistic portrait of the deep respect the president has always had for his wife, and the intense partnership that the two of them have with each other and no one else.

But the real theme of *The Survivor* is how Bill Clinton—and, by extension, his team—evolved as a president and an administration, and eventually made the right decisions in the important crises, in particular Bosnia. It is a story of growth, proof of the value of experience, a testament to the fact that Clinton not only survived but also ultimately succeeded despite what Harris saw as a rocky and undisciplined decision-making process. As a first step in the writing of history, this should come as a sizable relief to both Clintons. Once it was actually published, to reviews that put the relationship issues with Hillary in the much larger context of the accomplishments of the Clinton presidency, conservatives quickly lost interest in such a balanced and ultimately favorable assessment; Drudge's only other mention of the book was a note of its plummeting numbers on Amazon. The point, for Hillary Haters, is that Harris offered no new incriminating evidence against Hillary. Rather, his contribution was to paint a much broader and ultimately generally positive picture of the Clinton administration—swear words and all—in which nothing was clearer than the value of experience in the development of a president.

"Don't forget," says one longtime Democratic hand, "there has never been anyone with the kind of experience she's had, living at the White House, by his side, partner, best friend, eight years of a sort of postgraduate course, the sort of education no one has ever had before assuming the job. Nobody, nobody, has that kind of experience." That is the experience that allows Bill Clinton to grow in *The Survivor.* "I think now she's at least as good as I was,"[5] President Clinton told a Japanese audience recently, adding that he would help her if she needed him, and you understand what that means after reading *The Survivor*. The job of the presidency is not one that is understood instantly; it requires skills and finesse to have the confidence to make those decisions, to wield that power. That's certainly not a story line conservatives are interested in, but it's an undeniable part of Hillary's resume.

Matt Drudge's attention quickly shifted from *The Survivor* to Ed Klein's *Truth About Hillary*. The pre-publication publicity was nothing short of sensational.[6] Klein, with credentials as a real journalist, claimed that he began the book with no axe to grind. But the book's publication as part of Penguin's new conservative imprint, Sentinel, was a giveaway. Sentinel famously promised that Klein's book would do to Hillary Clinton what the Swift Boat controversy had done to John Kerry. No one would ever look at her the same way.

As it happened, that was true of Klein, not Hillary.

Because, as it happened, he didn't have the goods, and they couldn't deliver on the hype. The attempt to do so made the whole Hate Hillary movement look bad. By stooping as low as they did, particularly with the pre-publication publicity, Klein invited others to wonder whether the statute of limitations on this kind of thing hadn't finally run out. After all, the Bill Clinton of today no longer looks like the fit, young Playboy President; instead he's obviously a distinguished former president who in the last year has survived two serious surgeries, pushed himself hard to help the tsunami victims, and even become the newly adopted "son" of Barbara Bush—a triumph over partisan politics if ever there was one. Tina Brown, Klein's former boss, nailed him as more huckster than journalist, and his new friends failed to back him up as conservatives sought to distance themselves from transparent trash.[7] But in doing so, they have now set themselves up: If Klein is trash, what does that make the rest of them? He tells the same stories all the other books do, quotes (or doesn't) the same sources or non-sources; beyond a few new stories—either tame or non-credible—what makes his book such a disappointment to most readers is that it's repetitive.

Klein's defense reveals his weaknesses. He says he interviewed a hundred sources, which isn't all that many for a biography of someone you don't know. He claimed to have learned what Hillary knew about Monica from an anonymous second-tier Democratic National Committee staffer. His account of tabloid rumors about the president's relationships in the last year simply reprinted tabloid reports. And the two biggest pre-publication leaks from the book—suggesting that he was charging that Chelsea was the product of a rape involving her parents, and that Hillary is or was a secret lesbian—deflated with the book's appearance.

The public was plainly disgusted, and conservatives really didn't have much choice but to condemn the book. But you can't separate out the same incidents and decide whether to condemn them or not based on which book they're in. Trash is trash, regardless of who is putting it out and collecting it. They could hardly say: *This one's bad, but stay tuned for the same stories told better in* American Evita, *coming soon in paperback, because that's not quite as trashy, and has somewhat better footnotes.*[8] Or: *We don't like Klein, but hey, wait till October, because then we'll be back with our friend Dick Morris, and don't forget, some of these stories we're calling trash here are his stories in the first place, and in the fall he'll be selling his little fantasy pitching Hillary against Condi Rice, who's never run for office, has no positions on domestic policy issues, has never gone through the tabloid wars much less gone door to door. But sure, the Republicans are going to nominate her for president . . .*[9]

Now, that doesn't mean the Klein book or others like it disappear. It debuted at number one on Amazon, and ended its first week at number five; there will always be a market for the Hillary trash, just as there is for hardcore porn.[10] If we're lucky, though, the Klein backlash may be the death knell for the Old Stuff.

However many books they write, however many trees they pulp, the simple fact is that the Haters have run out of material.

It's going to keep being the same old stuff, no matter who tells the story. Klein covers the same ground as Morris and Noonan, Tyrell and Davis, Anderson and Limbacher. Klein wasn't a member of the team, but he cited all the players. If Klein is trash, as even conservative John Podhoretz was forced to admit, in an effort to distance himself and other conservatives from the spreading stench, then so are all the others that Klein cites and relies on.[11] What's good for the goose is good for the gander.

Here is what all of this trash has in common:

None of it is about Senator Clinton—what she is doing, what she is working on, what she stands for.

None of the Hillary Haters' stuff has anything to do with her life now. All of that—almost to a word, even from the most conservative Republicans—is positive. They love her. She is a centrist. Everyone wants to travel with her. She's brilliant. They even flirt with her.

So what is there to carp about? Interviews she gave twelve or fifteen years ago. A land deal that's twenty-five years old. Her association with people long dead. A thirty-year-old law review article. A law firm she worked for in her twenties. A speech she gave *at college*.

To review some of their greatest hits:

- ★ **Travelgate:** A stupid decision to fire the people who arrange the most important matters for the very people who cover you—the press. Whatever the truth of it, Hillary's alleged role in the White House Travel Office firings occurred in 1993.

- ★ **Whitewater:** The land deal, involving the now-dead Jim McDougal. The deal occurred in the late 1970s. The investigation was officially closed in 2002.

- ★ **HillaryCare:** The health care effort—which, God forbid, would have allowed all Americans to buy into a health care plan if their company didn't provide it. This constitutes the right's favorite proof that Hillary was a big-government liberal—but as even Dick Morris tells us, Hillary learned her lesson, and moved to the middle ten years ago. The original plan dates to 1993.

* **Chocolate chip cookies, Tammy Wynette, and "stand by your man":** 1992. The headbands, the makeovers, Christophe and the Vogue covers, dancing on the beach with Bill. What does it all add up to? A woman who looked different, in a different time; who had both love and trouble in her marriage; who traveled a challenging road to get to where she is. Didn't we all?

That's it. That's all there is. Everything else is beyond trivial. Well, some of that is pretty trivial too, wouldn't you say?

Dick Morris has hinted at the notion that she's anti-Semitic.[12] What's the evidence? She asked him if he minded bacon—not once but twice! And she complained about his bill, and left a pregnant pause that Bill then filled by referring to how expensive political consultants are. That's it.

Others have turned her reaction, when it came to Monica, into her "big lie." Interesting. By that yardstick, how do we measure the performance of George W. Bush, who used evidence that was at best exaggerated to get us into a war he had no clue how to get us out of? Who confounded, intentionally or not, the connection between 9/11 and Saddam Hussein? Who still refuses to face the reality of an unnecessary war that is killing American soldiers on a daily basis and hasn't even bothered to present a plan for peace? Do they *make* yardsticks that big?

And you're taking this woman apart for not wanting to face that her husband was having an affair?

Hillary Clinton is a tough, smart politician. She believes in fighting back, even if it means using negative ads. She relied on her father and brothers to straighten her fiancé up before they married. Has she made some missteps along the way? Sure. She wanted her rich friends to give them pretty things when they left office, because she'd never had nice china and silver of her own. She also pretends she can cook, when she's really very bad at it.

Are you shocked?

She really wasn't named after Sir Edmund Hillary, a story Dick Morris has now told many, many more times than Hillary ever did.

Is this truly the worst that can be said of a woman whose life has been put under every magnifying glass every writer in America could find?

What do they really hate her for? Taking a job—*back in 1974!*—working for a left-leaning law firm that doesn't exist any more? What a ridiculous thing to hate someone for. Writing a law review article that even she doesn't agree with substantial chunks of anymore? What a foolish way to judge someone. Whitewater itself is going on thirty years old.

And no one actually disputes my description of Hillary the good mother, the mother hen.

Obviously, it is something else. Or someone else.

That someone else is their creation: Hillary the Icon. She is a Liberal Ideologue. A surrogate for Big Government. A Professional Victim, Corrupt to the Core. Her Power is Illegitimate, because it derives from her Husband, who she stays with because of her Outsized Ambition.

That is the Hillary whom they convince people is mocking them—Saint Hillary, the woman who thinks she is better than them; the woman who they sell as phony through and through. They need her for the obvious reasons that any movement needs villains, and enemies, and femiNazis and the like: to define the Club, to give it an identity, a spirit, a reason for being.

The fewer ideas you have, the more you need such a victim. For certain angry white men who have watched, with understandable fear, as the economy changed and stripped them of any security they expected, what better symbol than a powerful female victim?

Just one problem:

Every bit of evidence that supports the icon, from HillaryCare (Big Government/Liberal Ideologue) to Whitewater (Corrupt) to a few stories in George Stephanopoulos's *All Too Human* (Professional Victim) is not only entirely out of date, but also actually contradicted by what she has done as a United States senator.

What her critics have succeeded in doing is continuing to apply the labels as if there were facts underneath—while the factual base has grown positively ancient and decrepit, and the new facts are overwhelmingly positive.

And what her colleagues from both parties in the Senate have done—because they are, after all, a group of distinguished gentlemen— is say wonderful things about her. Heck, even the people who say terrible things about her can't help but say pretty terrific things about Senator Clinton. And once you've done that, it's hard to go back.

Convincing people that they should decide whether to support a sixty-year-old woman based not on her last eight years of work, but on what she did twenty years ago . . . doesn't that seem a little stupid?

The smaller point is: Hillary doesn't need to be defensive. It's actually dangerous for her to think that way, because it actually suggests that people were wrong when they felt she made mistakes in the past. Since they've already punished her and put those incidents behind them to the extent they ever cared, the best thing to do is take responsibility graciously, not try to prove you really were right.

One of the most important ideas in politics is to show people that you recognize that *they're right*. Give them a consistent story. That's much more important than trying to convince them that *you're* right. People will forgive almost anything, if you describe it to them in a way that validates their beliefs, and enough time to absorb it. In other words, with apologies to Mr. Dylan, I was so much younger then, I'm older than that now. You can even do it with your critics.

Laura Ingraham's first book, *The Hillary Trap*, is a serious look at issues of victimization, using Hillary as her icon.[13] At the end of the book, which was published before Hillary's Senate campaign, Laura calls on her to step beyond her role as a victim; *"From now on,"* Laura encourages Hillary to say, *"I'm going to act like the free and independent woman I am, and I won't ride on my husband's political coattails anymore."* Careful what you wish for, Laura. I'd say that is exactly what she has done. But it isn't that easy, as Laura herself has discovered. Since that book was published, Laura has deservedly become much more famous—but her success didn't come easily. Laura is the only woman who has made it as a major syndicated radio star who doesn't do advice. Although I obviously disagree with her politics, I think she is terrific on the radio. I don't think it's really even debatable. But before she joined the Talk Radio Network she was withering on the vine at Westwood One—and she used to tell me what a difficult time she was having, not only with her syndication, but also with the Republican White House radio office, which had her locked in a vicious circle because, they claimed, they didn't consider her important enough to be on their A list. When people say they're sick of hearing a bunch of liberal women whining about discrimination against women in the media, I tell them to go talk to Laura—who wrote the book on whining liberal women, and then found herself smack against not a glass ceiling but a brick wall, with no recourse but to complain to a liberal woman like me . . .

Peggy Noonan is the odds-on favorite in any game of I Hate Hillary.[14] She is a veritable genius at it, spinning gold from hay. In fairness to Peggy, who is not only a tremendously gifted writer but also fabulously charming, beautiful, and successful, she always advises her readers that she doesn't "hate" Mrs. Clinton; she wishes her "a long life with good health, much friendship, and many grandchildren." She just thinks that she is "disturbed," "borderline," "fake," and a "pathological narcissist." Other than that, Mrs. Lincoln . . .

For me, the most revealing scene in Peggy's 192-page magnum opus, *The Case Against Hillary Clinton,* is the last one, where Peggy reveals where she herself came from—from the town of Massapequa on Long Island, where the future Republican claims she didn't know any Goldwater girls like Hillary; where her crowd was bagging groceries at the A & P to make ends meet and going to state schools and not fancy places like Wellesley; and where they've always been jealous of girls like Hillary Rodham, who grew up "secure" (or, Peggy might have preferred to say, "privileged") in houses on corners in suburbs, and ended up at Yale Law School, not SUNY.

Peggy Noonan doesn't forgive her that.

But here's the truth: Hillary Rodham may have looked fancy from Massapequa—but not from Wellesley. My guess is that when Hillary got to Wellesley she was only one notch up on the pecking order from where I was. Above us were the girls from New York, from Chapin and Brearley, who ran the place. She was never a real Republican—a Bethlehem Steel, Jewel T, Fortune 500, Miss Porter's, Ethel Walker, black-dress-and-pearls, power elite, Tower Court kind of girl. She didn't play golf; she didn't know about clubs; she wasn't one of those well-traveled, well-dressed, positively scary girls who were impressive and worldly and went out with Edsel Ford and skied in Gstaad. If Peggy Noonan thinks Hillary Rodham, from some middling public school in Illinois in middling public school clothes, felt secure when she got to Wellesley, what can I tell you?

Hillary Clinton's father got dressed up in a suit every day and worked for himself. He ran a one-man drapery business; his daughter was just one step away from a Jewish scholarship girl like me. On my first day at Wellesley, one of the girls in my dorm showed me her twenty-five matching Lacoste golf shirts, and I looked at my shirts—all of them with tags torn out of the back because they'd been bought at discount stores—and I was embarrassed to unpack. Wellesley was like that. Hillary, I can promise you, did not have twenty-five matching Lacoste shirts. There was a special tea for girls whose mothers went to Wellesley. Neither Hillary's mother nor mine had gone to college. Her mother didn't come to her graduation. My father didn't come to mine. I had friends whose parents jetted in separately. When I arrived at Wellesley, I had been on an airplane once, to fly from Boston to New York and back. I had never been to Europe. Neither had Hillary. We both knew lots of girls who flew off to ski trips there as though it were New Hampshire.

The rich girls didn't run for student government. They didn't become orientation chairs, or Washington interns, like Hillary and me and Suzanne McTigue Magaziner, who was one of my cohorts, and went on to marry one of Hillary's and Bill's. Suzanne and I drove home together from our Washington internship summer. She was student government president my year, and we went to Harvard Law School together. Susanne's husband Ira Magaziner, is now running the Clinton AIDS program. We public school girls, who grew up in little houses with fathers in one-man offices, were the ones who raced a thousand miles an hour to get ahead—not so different from the girls in Peggy's A & P, except perhaps for the fact that Hillary's family was Protestant and had a little more money than the Noonans or the McTigues, who were Catholic, or the Estriches, who were Jewish. We were the high school valedictorians who somehow found our way to Wellesley, and then we got there and found these fancy blonde girls who were so far ahead of us in almost everything that we stuck to what we could beat them in—which was schoolwork, and running for things, and honors, and internships.

Peggy doesn't get that. She reads insecurity for arrogance. She probably dated a lot in high school. College, too. I bet she's always been beautiful and glamorous. It all comes down to what kind of chip you have on your shoulder.

Here is Peggy's detailed case against Hillary Clinton.

1) She's a Fake.

Why? In an imaginary scene from *The Case Against Hillary Clinton,* Hillary wins the election, thanks everybody, and dumps a call from her husband.

In another, real scene, she goes on Letterman during her Senate run, pretends to take a pop quiz on New York, and gets the answers right. Then—*horrors!*—it's revealed that she knew the answers in advance. News flash: *It was a comedy bit, folks.* It was dreamed up by Letterman's writers and Hillary's handlers. Do you think Richard Nixon called up *Laugh In* and said "Hey, I've got a great idea—how 'bout I come on your show and say, 'Sock it to me?'"

In a clever moment of appropriation, Peggy channels Eleanor Roosevelt ("I do not channel Mrs. Roosevelt," she promises), then tells us that if confronted with Hillary Clinton Mrs. Roosevelt would ask, "Tell me, what does she actually . . . stand for?"[15]

Come on, Peggy. You can like Hillary Clinton or dislike Hillary Clinton, but you know damn well that Hillary knows what she stands for—and you do too. If you want to say John Kerry is on both sides of too many issues, fine, but not Hillary. Since when is an appearance on Letterman the key to whether someone's stands in public life are authentic or not? After a lifetime of chiding her for not having the sense of humor to laugh at herself, you use a Letterman appearance as proof that she's a fake? Not fair.

Eleanor Roosevelt wouldn't have to wonder for a moment where Hillary stands. She'd know. She'd embrace her. And she'd work like hell to get her elected.

The only thing she'd wonder is where Democrats went wrong with you.

2) She's Nuts.

The lessons of the Clintons, as interpreted by Peggy Noonan:

"They can do anything."

"These people are not quite stable."

"The most interesting thing about her, and him, to me, is that they appear to be disturbed."

Disturbed how? She has a diagnosis. From an unnamed friend, who comes bearing a book. Pathological narcissism. Interesting.

I ask the smartest psychiatrist I know, armchair to armchair. *Bill's* the narcissist, she says. Hillary? Borderline at best.

I don't know any politicians, certainly none running for president, who aren't serious narcissists. You have to need the applause very, very badly, almost the way you need oxygen, to tolerate the abuse you must endure to reach the White House. I have no doubt that, most days, Hillary loves what she does. Just beneath the surface, however, she knows that people are trying to protect her from a tremendous amount of garbage—and more times than you can possibly imagine it explodes in her face. And while Hillary certainly generates more garbage than almost anyone, she also has more protection. If you're anyone else, running for president means facing more abuse than the average congressman does, and taking it means risking literally everything,

What's genuinely surprising in Peggy Noonan's treatment of Hillary is that she's not above going after her prey in the cattiest way possible. When Peggy first met Hillary in 1991 she had brown hair, wore glasses and a shawl, and was maternal; by 1997, she was chic, in a hot pink suit, short bright blonde hair, and sleek black heels. "The point is not that she had changed, people do," Peggy writes, "or that she's always trying to look better, people do that, too.[16] The point is that she changes so much and so often not only in her look but also in the image she is trying to project. . . . She will do whatever works and be whoever she has to be to achieve her objectives."

In fact, Hillary hasn't changed her look in years. She no longer wears pink suits or glasses or shawls. Like many women her age, she has found a uniform: black suit, short hair, brightly colored shirts, an occasional pastel for special events. I joked with the audience at a recent event at another women's college that she now looks like everyone in that room—no better and no worse, we all laughed.

3) She Has No Class.

"They are marked, too, by an absence of grace, a lack of personal humility that is actually jarring, perhaps because it threatens to lower both standard and expectations for our leaders."[17]

The evidence? A story from an unnamed Secret Service agent who supposedly worked for the Clintons early in the administration; a detailed rehash of the firing of White House press office staffers four months into the Clinton administration, complete with Maureen Dowd's conclusion that the First Lady's maternal image had taken a "Joan Crawford twist."[18]

Can you imagine an opponent standing there and asking Hillary what her role was in the firing of some press office employees fifteen years before? So many responses to choose from: *Shouldn't we be talking about Osama bin Laden? Or the deficit? Or our soldiers dying in Iraq?*

4) She Hasn't Used Her Political Capital.

Another imaginary scene: The first thing we're asked to imagine is that Peggy is friends with the head housekeeper at Michael Eisner's house in Bel Air. It's a strange premise: Does Peggy Noonan really make friends with other people's housekeepers? (My housekeeper is my friend, but believe me it's rare, and I feel certain that that's not Peggy's world.) Then, taxing our imagination further, Peggy asks us to envision that all the biggest Hollywood moguls—Jeffrey Katzenberg, Ron Meyer, Barry Diller—are there for lunch at Eisner's to hear the former first lady talk about the media. This is even less likely than Peggy knowing the housekeeper.

Harkening back to her days writing for Ronald Reagan and George H. W. Bush, Peggy pens an imaginary speech by Mrs. Clinton, scolding the media companies for making degrading movies, TV shows, and video games—and then Peggy snaps her fingers and says "It was all a dream." So the third thing we're asked to accept is that the real Hillary wouldn't make a speech upbraiding Hollywood for making poison. The fact is, she would; she has; she does. Just this past March, based on the Kaiser Family Foundation Report on "Generation M," in one of my favorites of her recent speeches, she took on the industry, just as she has for years:

> It is probably the single most commonly mentioned issue to me by young parents, almost no matter where I go, when we start talking about raising children.[19] We start talking about the challenges of parenting today, and all of a sudden people are exchanging their deep concerns about losing control over the raising of their own children, ceding the responsibility of implicating values and behaviors to a multi-dimensional media marketplace that they have no control over and most of us don't even really understand because it is moving so fast we can't keep up with it. And so I've spent more than thirty years advocating for children and worrying about the impact of media. I've read a lot of the research over the years about the significant effects that media has on children. And I've talked and advocated about the need to harness the positive impacts that media can have for the good of raising . . . healthy, productive children, who can make their own way in this rather complicated world. And I've particularly advocated for trying to find ways to re-empower parents, to put them back in the driver's seat so they feel they are first knowledgeable and secondly in some sense helping to shape the influences that affect their children.
>
> Almost a decade ago, we hosted the Children's Television Summit at the White House, and we worked for the passage of the Children's Television Act. That law led to the implementation of the V-Chip in every new television over thirteen inches, and mandated that broadcasters show at least three hours of educational and informational programming each week. More than five years ago, I urged parents to become more vigilant consumers of media—and I also urged them if they were concerned about

the constant exposure to violence or irresponsible sexual activity, that there was nothing standing in their way of coming together as parental groups and in effect producing a consumer's boycott against media which offended their values and sensibilities. . . . [M]any parents feel that way about video games, which were just coming into use in a rather large way and influencing how their children both spent their time and what they thought about. I also appealed to movie, music, and video game producers, and broadcasters to come together and develop one uniform ratings system—one that gave parents clear unequivocal information about the media products they and their children were consuming.

I think we've made progress, certainly since I started talking about this and certainly since we began focusing on it in the White House. But I still hear, as I said, from parents all over who just feel overwhelmed. . . . it's especially difficult for parents of young children who are trying to create some barriers to what their children are exposed to. Parents worry that their children will not grow up with the same values that they did or that they believe in because of the overwhelming presence of the media telling them to buy this and that, or conveying negative messages filled with explicit sex content and violence.

And parents who work long hours outside the home and single parents, whose time with their children is squeezed by economic pressures, are worried because they don't even know what their children are watching and listening to and playing. So what's a parent to do when at two o'clock in the afternoon, the children may be at home from school but the parents aren't home from work and they can turn on the TV and both on broadcast and cable stations see a lot of things which the parents wish they wouldn't or wish they were sitting there to try to mediate the meaning of for their children. And probably one of the biggest complaints I've heard is about some of the video games, particularly Grand Theft Auto, which has so many demeaning messages about women and so encourages violent imagination and activities and it scares parents. . . . They're playing a game that encourages them to have sex with prostitutes and then murder them—you know, that's kind of hard to digest, and to figure out what to say, and even to understand how you can shield your particular child from a media environment where all their peers are doing this.

And it is also now the case that more and more, parents are asking, not only do I wonder about the content, and what that's doing to my child's emotional psychological development, but what's the process doing? What's all this stimulation doing that is so hard to understand and keep track of?

So I think if we are going to make the health of children a priority, then we have to pay attention to the activities that children engage in every single day. And of course that includes exposure to and involvement with the media . . .

Generation M: Media in the Lives of 8 to 18 Year Olds shows us that media is omnipresent. It is, if not the most, it is it is certainly one of the most insistent, pervasive influences in a child's life. The study tells us, as you've heard, on average that kids between eight and eighteen are spending 6.5 hours a day absorbed in media. That adds to forty-five hours a week, which is more than a full-time job. Television alone occupies three to four hours a day of young people's time. And we all know, that in most homes, media consumption isn't limited to the living room, as it was when many of us were growing up. In two-thirds of kids' bedrooms you'll find a TV; in one-half you will find a VCR and/or video game console.

That's Hillary, not Peggy. If Peggy wants to write her another speech—a real one and not a fantasy—I'm sure she'd do a great job, too.

The problem is, the media companies don't care.

They know they make poison, or some of them do. And if they don't, they know that other game makers, other media companies, will make it instead.

You don't have to convince Hillary Clinton that it's poison, or that parents need help, or that the situation is out of control. But the industry has refused to do anything, no matter who gives the speech.

The other part of Peggy's imaginary speech is the part where Hillary condemns her husband's sexual conduct. I don't know what women want from Hillary. Do they really doubt that she disapproved, was mad, was honestly hurt by what he did? I don't think it's that.

So why is it so important to them that Hillary do the one thing that she can't do in her relationship, which is to denounce her own husband publicly? Why is that what Peggy and Laura ultimately define as "independence"? That's not about political capital or personal integrity. Come on, girls. That's not even fair.

If you're going to stay with the man, you don't denounce him. Even if you're going to leave him, why would it help Chelsea to hear her mother denounce her father? What good would that do? Besides, who are we, any of us, to say that she would be better off without Bill Clinton—that she could find someone else who could do whatever he does for her?

Finally, Peggy tries to warn her real-life friend, a prototypical married mother of two from that prototypical town on Long Island, not to vote to send Hillary Clinton to the Senate—because if she does, she is very likely to run for president down the road.

About that, she is certainly right.

Dick Morris's anti-Hillary book *Rewriting History* is a personal favorite of mine, for rather perverse reasons.[20] I am probably not the only person who has read it who's convinced that Dick thinks Hillary is going to be president—and is more than a little wistful because he knows exactly how to make it happen. If you spend a lifetime, as Dick has, thinking as if he were Bill and Hillary Clinton, it's awfully hard to stop on a dime. So, being too smart to leave all his clever thoughts completely unsaid, Dick writes his books—and among them *Rewriting History* is a little goldmine.

Oh, don't get me wrong. I read the whole thing, and Dick spends plenty of time in the book on the attack, too. As the president used to tell me after Dick had "officially" left the White House and gone to work as a Fox News analyst, where he regularly attacked his former boss,

"Dick has to earn a living." And he would laugh. It always struck me how forgiving the president was toward Dick, who was frankly out there trashing him, even as he was furious at George Stephanopoulos, whom I adored when he worked for me as a young man, and who I thought struggled to handle himself with integrity once he left the White House. But I learned quickly that Dick's name could be mentioned any time in Clinton's presence—but not George's. (That's how I also figured that Dick was still in the game, or at least that the president was still talking to him.)

Dick and I often do panels together on Fox News. We're sometimes called the "odd couple," because we disagree about so much. On the other hand, unlike the people who talk about them on some cable networks, we actually know the Clintons. That's television for you.

Indeed, Bill Clinton advised me to bring Dick in for help in the fall of 1987 after Dukakis fired my predecessor, John Sasso, for leaking a tape to Maureen Dowd that mocked Senator Joseph Biden, then one of our competitors, for copying the speech of an English politician. The only problem was that Dick had masterminded Dukakis's own earlier reelection defeat; that idea wouldn't have gone over very well with my candidate.

The trick, as the president himself says in his memoir, is to separate the wheat from the chaff. This is the case with most creative people—and the more creative, the more chaff you get. The best partnerships are between people who know how to edit each other; for a long time, Clinton and Morris clearly did. The same is true, in a way, of Morris's Hillary book.

For instance, consider this very fundamental question, perhaps as important as any that will be raised during this campaign: Is Hillary really a moderate? Is she still the Hillary of HillaryCare, or did she learn her lesson? Is her move to the center a product of 2005 politics, or might it perhaps have come as early as say, *1995?* Let's ask that well known Hillary-lover, Dick Morris, for the answer.

"The larger lesson of the 1994 defeat," Dick writes, "was not lost on

Hillary.[21] She and the president had to move to the center. They simply could not win re-election running as the liberal Democratic standard bearers. By 1995, Hillary was reinventing herself as a moderate, triangulating New Democrat. She provided crucial help in urging the president to back a balanced budget and to sign the welfare reform bill, the two acts that came to define his move to the center. Like Bill, she showed great dexterity in shifting in such a centrist direction, a move that appealed to the great mass of American voters. Her leftward tilt in the health care reform days was a thing of the past. She seemed to have learned her lesson."

Notably, Morris also points out that in her earlier work on educational reform in Arkansas "I never thought of Hillary as a liberal.[22] During this, her first foray into public policy, Hillary adopted a distinctly moderate tone, combining a liberal generosity toward education with an insistence on high standards—a foreshadowing of Clinton's New Covenant, coupling opportunity with responsibility. During her husband's second term as governor, Hillary was very much a 'New' Democrat."

The problem in health care, it seems, is that Hillary was unfamiliar with the substance and fell under the influence of Ira Magaziner, of whom Morris is more critical than he is of Hillary. Fortunately, Magaziner isn't running for president. On the deficit, she has always been a true believer. "Hillary was no stranger to the left, but in this case she went up the middle, taking the New Democrat tack and urging Bill to submit his own balanced budget plan to the Congress and the public. She also made known her opposition to the Gingrich budget priorities. To this day, Hillary is a vocal critic of the growing deficit, eager to cite the Clinton administration budget surplus at every opportunity as an eviscerated achievement of her husband's rule. On this issue, she was no liberal."[23]

Is she a good manager? According to Morris, she's better than her husband. "With clear lines of authority and strong discipline, Hillary runs a tight ship, never weakened by leaks or infighting. Such talent for management would be one of President Hillary's major assets, a welcome change from the floating chaos of her husband's administration. To date, Hillary Clinton has distinguished herself as a superb manager, political tactician, and hardnosed executive . . ."[24] She is also a tough politician who understood the need to go on the attack before her husband did. No Dukakis she.

And on the critical issue of whether she can win, well, Dick is both completely wrong, and ultimately right. That's what I mean by wheat and chaff—with Dick, you get lots of both. "Hillary's hold on a future Democratic presidential nomination stems from the control the Clinton organization has over the Democratic National Committee. Ever since 1992, the Clintons have run the Democratic Party the way a Mafia don runs his family."[25]

Alas, Dick, those days are over. Howard Dean, the current Democratic Party chairman, is hardly a Hillary guy or a Clinton "caporegime," as you called his predecessor. Harold Ickes, Hillary's caporegime, was about the last person of significance on the planet to endorse Dean. Hillary was in Afghanistan when Dean was elected, and she hasn't gotten much closer to him, metaphorically speaking, since then. No one has ever accused her of being color blind. Dean's appeal is largely limited to those whose favorite color is bright blue.

Nor would it take "The Perfect Storm," the title of Dick's chapter about what it would take for Hillary to win the nomination and the election. Perfect storms like the election of 2000 are once-in-a-lifetime events: Jack Corrigan, who was running all the legal challenges for Kerry, rightly predicted that whatever happened there would be a winner, because perfect storms have that name for a reason (or as Jack put it: "Tell them there'll be a winner, just don't tell them who it will be").

But those are just details. The larger point is that Dick sees no Democrat who can beat her, sees the growing number of African American and Hispanic voters as expanding her base, and—though he mentions them only once—cannot avoid recognizing the right's power over the choice of a Republican opponent. And for a guy who has just written 265 pages about how she has "rewritten history," he is hardly altogether downcast at the prospect: "But as the decade unfolds, in the quiet of her Senate seat, apart from the daily duels of political dialogue, Hillary will have the chance to become the person she still can become."[26] Exactly what New Yorkers decided, and her approval ratings have gone up thirty points. "Our current political landscape badly needs Hillary's perspective, her passionate idealism. Her willingness to fight for the underdog and her compass for issues are rare indeed in our male-dominated, profit-obsessed society . . ."

Imagine what he'd say if he still worked for her.

The rest of the books are all written by people who don't know Hillary at all. The attacks are all familiar. What's more interesting to me, and probably to you, are the positive things these folks have to say about Hillary.

Here's a brief sampling.

MADAME HILLARY:
THE DARK ROAD TO THE WHITE HOUSE

by R. Emmett Tyrrell, Jr., with Mark W. Davis

Give Bob Tyrrell (yes, that Bob Tyrrell, from the American Spectator, friend to the Arkansas Troopers, dogged pursuer of Clinton scandals), credit for this much: He concedes that Hillary runs a great Senate office, in which even the Capitol Police are happy to work for her (sorry, Peggy). "The praise for her staff is near universal"; they are, as Charles Cook says, "world class."[27] They quote a Senate staffer who says "She has demonstrated an extraordinary ability to establish herself within the Democratic caucus."[28] She understands "the mechanisms of influence." She has found power in the Senate, on the Armed Services Committee, and on the little known Steering and Coordination Committee. While Tyrell makes me look like Pollyanna, viewing Hillary's spectacular ac-

complishments in the Senate as well as the writing of her autobiography
as nothing more than the necessary groundwork for a presidential campaign, he's honest enough to recognize that not everything she says and
does is intended to help her politically. In fact, he goes on at some length
about those parts of her book that deal with issues such as Roger Clinton's drug arrest and Monica, which don't help her one bit. And while he
repeatedly chastises her for claiming that there is a right-wing conspiracy focused on the Clintons, suggesting that she is simply paranoid and
overreacting to legitimate concerns regarding her and Bill's behavior, the
point of the book is that she is conspiring, and has been all along, to get
herself into the White House. What's a coordinated plan to one person
can be a conspiracy to another. It all depends on the goal—becoming
president, or destroying a rival . . .

Hillary gets better marks from Tyrell, certainly, than the other way
around. "Hillary steers clear of the classic liberal agenda of defense—
arms control test bans and opposition to missile defense. From a quiet,
effective committee drudge, Hillary has emerged as the Democratic
Party's most persistent critic of President Bush, especially on homeland
security."[29] Tyrell and Davis quote Republican political consultant
Philip Kawior, who says Hillary that "'makes Bobby Fischer moves.[30]
It's only ten moves later that you begin to see the strategy unfold.'
Armed Services has been her most counterintuitive move in the Senate.
Visiting upstate New York's First Drum with President Bush to personally thank the 10th Mountain Division for its service in Afghanistan is
hardly what one expects of someone schooled on the ramparts of the
anti-war movement. It is less incongruous when you remember that as a
young woman who had just moved to Arkansas to begin her partnership
with Bill . . . Hillary had tried to join the U.S. Marine Corps, a killer
political credential in the era of so-called Chicken Hawk men. (This
alone is proof, if it was ever needed, that the young Hillary who wrote to
NASA to inquire about becoming an astronaut had her heart set early
on another sky high dream, the presidency.)"

Her critics, of course, ascribe a political motive to every move she makes. It must be that she is steering clear of the liberal agenda, rather than simply pursuing her own beliefs. It must be a calculated move to serve on Armed Services, rather than an expression of actual interest. It must be a reflection of outsized ambition to thank the troops, not a reflection of actual gratitude. But at the very least, there is grudging respect. Whatever her motives, she is good. Very good. The moves are the right ones, and she is well-positioned.

Tyrrell describes Hillary's appeal as "almost metaphysical;"[31] to him she represents the "transcendent dreams of the feminist,"[32] and as a gay rights advocate and eco-activist, she is able to connect with suburban women who secretly vote against their husbands and fathers. I sure hope so. According to Bob, her coalition is unprecedented, with links to "modern suburban women and left wing advocates."[33] He identifies her greatest strength as her connection with women and ability to grasp and communicate her concern for issues that the average male Republican is oblivious to, particularly the time-stressed life of the American family.

So much for those who say Hillary doesn't care about the concerns of average women in places like Massapequa, Long Island, where Peggy Noonan and her friends grew up. Thanks, Bob.

HILLARY'S SCHEME:
INSIDE THE NEXT CLINTON'S AGENDA
TO TAKE THE WHITE HOUSE

by Carl Limbacher

Limbacher begins his book, which he calls a "cautionary tale," with the "warning" that Hillary Clinton can win the presidency.[34] The funny thing is, smart Republicans were the first to see that Hillary could win—maybe because having elected two polarizing presidents (Reagan and Bush II), they understood that "polarizing" isn't necessarily a dirty word.

A polarizing president can count on an energized base, devote himself to courting the middle, and not waste his time trying to change the minds of people who won't vote for them anyway.

Limbacher's scheme involves Hillary cutting her Senate term short and challenging Bush in 2004. Sorry, Carl—no such luck. If she doesn't go for 2004, though, he observes that she could also do it in 2008. And Limbacher, being far more reliable a reporter than Klein, doesn't pretend to have anything to stop her. There isn't one serious new charge in the book: He has her rolling her eyes at a Bush speech, not attending enough funerals for 9/11 victims (shall we start down the funeral road with George W. Bush, who doesn't go to any?), apologizing to Dick Morris in case he was offended at all by being offered bacon (obvious proof of anti-Semitism?). He even blames her for Bill's supposed sexual abuse. (Don't ask me.) Limbacher is a good researcher. But what he ultimately proves is how quickly even a tabloid-style attack can grow boring. How many more of these can the market bear?

How many more times would you like to read about Hillary's summer job when she was twenty-four? Her job evaluation from her first boss?

Did you know that she represented a savings and loan that doesn't exist anymore, along with a fellow named Vince Foster who doesn't exist anymore either? Oh, you'd heard that too.

That's it.

Even if you drop the terms like Hillary Haters or "right-wing conspiracy," and just call them what they want to be called—researchers—it's still the same old stuff. If there were something to find, don't you think they'd have found it already? Madeleine and I used to talk about this, when we weren't trying to figure out how to solve the problems of the world. Pushing sixty, and they're still talking about her hairdos fifteen years ago. They can't even come up with a drunken fling, a wild night, embarrassing e-mails. How many of us would fare so well under their microscope?

"No George W. she." "Smart about defense." "Runs a great Senate staff." "Makes all the right moves politically." "A metaphysical appeal to women." And this is what her critics say.

It's so unfair, says someone who knows them both well. Bill can captivate you with his attention—it just comes to him naturally—but a minute later he can forget everything. With her, it doesn't come as naturally, but it's real when it does. It's authentic.

Al Gore used to have these note cards. Even with people who'd worked for him for years, he'd need the note cards to tell him how many kids they had and what their names were and that sort of thing. And this was for people close to him. No note card, no "How's Andrew?" or whatever . . .

Hillary doesn't need those note cards. I didn't even work for her, one Clinton staff guy tells me, and there wasn't a time that I ran into her that she wasn't all over me about the babies and what they were doing and how my wife was and did we need anything and could she help? And those of us who've spent a lot of time with politicians can tell when it's real.

Another story: Some time ago, this guy's father—a longtime Democrat who'd given a gazillion dollars to the Clintons—had a birthday coming up. He was going to be eighty-two; it looked as thought it might be his last birthday. What could be a better present than a call from the president? So the son put in a request for Clinton to call. I have no faith in anyone, so I e-mailed Tamera and Ann, and said "By the way, just in case, maybe you'll put this on Hillary's call sheet too." I was covering the bases. Maybe I knew too much. Guess who called? Guess who didn't? Ten points for Hillary for making an old man's birthday. Bill spoke at his funeral, but Hillary made his day.

Amy Sullivan, the Washington Monthly editor who wants to "beg" Hillary not to run, doesn't disagree with any of this.[35] She is certainly not a Hillary Hater. She's been a self-described Hillary fan, since the headband days. She understands that the old stories are old, and that the old routines have worn thin. She understands that women need a revolution, and that no one could lead it better than Hillary. But she's still afraid of what the right can do.

Conservatives won't trot out supposed lesbian lovers in 2008; they'll go after her more subtly. They know that 40 percent of the country can't stand Sen. Clinton, another 40 percent adores her, and the remaining 20 percent (which, according to those recent polls, seem to feel generally positive about her) is made up of fairly soft support. The best way to turn that support into opposition is to voice those age-old questions about the Clintons: She's inappropriately power-hungry and ambitious—remember that Tammy Wynette crack? He lacks moral character—do you really want him roaming the White House again? And don't forget health care—who elected her to that post anyway?

Another golden oldie—the charge that the Clintons will say anything to get ahead—is already being revived elliptically by conservatives. The day after Sen. Clinton's news-making abortion speech this past January, conservatives were all over the media, charging that she was undergoing a "makeover" of her political image. . . . In the six months since, the "makeover" charge has been repeated more than 100 times in the press. Give them another six, and "makeover" will be the new "flip-flop."

The target audience for these whispers and insinuations—and, let's not be naïve, occasional television commercials—is a familiar demographic: suburban women. Democrats lost ground in the 2004 elections among white, married, working women, and it's generally accepted that to win back the White House, the party needs a nominee who can appeal to these women. . . . No, Democrats, it's not fair. Hillary Clinton is smart, she's paving a promising new path for her party, she's a much better campaigner than anyone ever expected, and she's already survived more personal assaults than anyone should have to endure. But wishing the country would grow up and get over the 1990s already, that she could wage a campaign of issues and be evaluated on her political merit, won't make it so.

But don't despair, Ms. Sullivan. The Hillary haters and their tired ideas are fading as a threat. It's time to laugh in their faces. Call them the liars and failures that they are. Read those sorry quotes from the Klein book out in public. The jig is up: They're out of tricks. That's what they would do to us, isn't it? *What would a boy do in this situation?* we always used to ask ourselves. The Hillary Haters wish they had her hand; just imagine how Dick Morris feels every time he reads her numbers.

There was a time when they had better cards to play against her: special prosecutors, acts of impeachment, grand juries impaneled. It really was scary then. I remember one evening when I arrived at a Washington bar to meet someone, and spotted one of Ken Starr's deputies sitting with a friend at another table. I can't begin to tell you how embarrassed they were to see me. That was how things worked. I used to advise my students taking jobs in the White House Counsel's office to have their own lawyers on retainer. It broke my heart to see my students—many of them the smartest, most talented people I've ever taught—dragged up to Capitol Hill to raise their right hands in these phony scandals and investigations that cost God knows how many people their livelihood and potential.

Those days are over.

If you want to take their attacks as a reason to get involved, as a sign the campaign has begun, as an imperative to fight back, that's great.

But of course, that is not what Amy Sullivan's article is about. It ends by conceding that Hillary might have some chance of winning, but condemns Democratic "daydreams" of her candidacy that "cast a shadow over the Democratic field that makes it difficult for a potentially viable candidate to emerge:

> It's too early for anyone to say with certainty that Hillary Clinton can't win the White House. But it's far too early—and dangerous—to conclude that she's the best chance that Democrats have. . . .[36]

But her goal is precisely the same as Joe Klein's: to keep Hillary out of the race. "Someone has to say it," she writes, "so here goes: Please don't run, Senator."

But has she seen the field of alternatives?

5.

CAN SHE LOSE? THE ROCK STAR AND THE REST

★

"The Rock Star and the Rest," Jim Barnes of the *National Journal* called the field of potential candidates in his spring 2005 preview of the 2008 race. Republicans were contemplating jumping in left and right, openly acknowledging that their field looked lackluster compared to Hillary. "How do you stack the lesser-knowns and charisma-challenged up against the likes of Hillary, in spite of her negatives, or John Edwards, to name a couple of Democratic potentials?"[1] asked longtime GOP national committeeman Steve Roberts of Iowa, in Barnes's piece. "I am not saying all these folks are not capable, just that they are virtually unknown and don't tend to fire people up." So, despite columnist Ellen Goodman's plea that *everyone* wait until 2006 to start 2008, the permanent campaign envisioned by Hillary adviser Sidney Blumenthal has become the norm.[2] The shuttles to New Hampshire are already full. So many governors are contemplating presidential runs that the National Governors Association met this year in Iowa.

The conventional wisdom is that Hillary is the star of a dull field, that all the action will be on the Republican side, that the Republicans would never nominate a moderate like Giuliani or an outsider like McCain, and that Hillary will just clean house. That may be right. But if history is a guide, it usually isn't. This is no straightforward process. There's a reason all these men are crowding the planes to Des Moines and Boston. They understand that the nominating process may belittle you, but it also gives you the chance to topple whoever is that year's star.

I used to assign my undergraduate students a famous essay by Stephen Hess entitled "Why Great Men are Not Chosen Presidents: Lord Bryce Revisited."[3] Afterward, we would discuss all the things that would discourage a gifted person from going into politics: You lose all your privacy; your ego comes under assault; any fool can tell you off in public; sooner or later you're bound to suffer a humiliating public rejection; the pay stinks; working conditions are better in corporate America, as are the perks; a special prosecutor will investigate your friends; you could end up in jail for going to a football game or a golf trip; you travel better in the entertainment world; you have more security in law. *If you like television,* I told them, *get into television, not politics.* By the time we were done, the very idea that anyone with an ounce of talent would ever let his or her name appear on a ballot seemed shocking.

But they do. This is what I have noticed over the years: By and large, it's a group of very talented and impressive people who throw their hats into the ring. There is obviously a combination of factors at work: a desire to serve; ambition; adventure and challenge; competition; intelligence; patriotism even. If you met them before they ran, you would be impressed. But the minute they start playing presidential politics, they become buffoons. The Seven Dwarfs . . . The Musketeers . . . there are always names in the primary campaigns for the band of travelers who go by charter from place to place across Iowa and New Hampshire, hopping down to South Carolina, over to Minnesota, back to Iowa, Iowa, New Hampshire, Iowa, Iowa, for months on end, now years on end. They subject themselves to a process that feels small, that shapes everything, and that defines things on both sides.

Presidential campaigns, especially the early primaries, make dull clones out of potentially interesting and substantial men—and women. Elizabeth Dole and Pat Schroeder, very reputable women, never made it to the starting line. No matter who you are, it is hard to look very big standing in front of a group of twenty people early in the morning in Keokuk, Iowa, trying to convince them that you should be president, by repeating a collection of phrases you've uttered a hundred times before . . . and which are very similar to the phrases everyone else carries around with them. Hillary's Secret Service detail gives her at least one leg up, making her look more presidential, and she draws bigger crowds. When it comes to speechmaking, though, she has a way to go. The reality of Iowa is that even in the week before the caucus, the would-be nominee can be out there dragging celebrities around in the hope of attracting crowds bigger than fifty people. And these people—the ones looking bored in the back of the room—are the ones who will decide the country's fate.

Under such circumstances, discipline becomes essential. The campaign season amounts to an endless game of gotcha, in which giving the same boring and wretched answer over and over may preserve you, but misspeaking on any point just once in an endless day can bring you down once and for all. The first time any candidate makes such a mistake, and the press piles on, burning him or her in a way that's never happened before, is the moment when it finally comes clear that the press is an enemy, a free-floating crew paid to find excuses to criticize them. The same can be said, of course, for the other candidates, and indeed they work with the press—particularly in an era in which megaphones are on and blaring twenty-four hours a day. But this is no conspiracy: It's perfectly out in the open. It's all there, online. The other day, in a White House press conference, an ABC correspondent accused Fox News of being a friendly channel to the White House, citing the specific instance of Bill Kristol (who certainly has his own relationships) airing the details of one of Karl Rove's conversations on Fox.[4] I just shook my head when I heard the accusation—because I knew the same details, having read them online in an interview Rove's lawyer gave to the *National Review*.[5]

In 2008, on both sides of the aisle, we can expect to see a slew of governors running for president. None of these governors—save for Bill Richardson, who served at the UN—can claim bragging rights when it comes to foreign policy.[6] So it will be important for any of them who want to emerge as an "alternative"—whether to Hillary or to John or Rudy—to find some premise on which they can claim foreign policy credibility. Some governors have met the challenge—see Carter, Reagan, Clinton, Bush—by referring to the executive skills that led them to be tough and steeled their ability to make decisions; this, they said, prepared them to be commander-in-chief. But any governor is also prone to making a mistake on basic foreign policy questions—the kind of gaffe that can crush an incipient candidacy. This is the kind of mistake that happens when, having answered a question a certain way fifty or sixty times, you might say something different the sixty-first time and someone with a camera picks it up. Or when you get the words wrong on an Israel question, and don't clarify what you meant quickly enough, or smartly enough. Or when you say that you're for something you're not. Or, heaven forbid, when you start thinking out loud, speculating, inching toward those third-rail areas that make your handlers wish they'd stayed in law school.

The very idea of the Iowa caucuses, which are premised on this kind of early, free-floating conversation, has become an anachronism. Retail politics, trying out ideas at a one-on-one level, getting better as you do, thinking things through, hearing from voters. . . . Today, any of these things can get you in trouble. Everything is taped. It doesn't matter how private or informal a conversation may seem: It isn't small-d democracy when anything you say could be available to a million people in a minute if Matt Drudge thinks it makes you look stupid. Preparing a candidate these days is like preparing a witness facing a hostile deposition. Expect that someone is gunning for you every time you open your mouth. Partisans will track every word you say. Mistakes will be blogged. The minute I heard that Dean said something about being more "evenhanded" in the Middle East, I thought, *Oy vey*, he's toast.[7] If you knew that someone was recording every single word you said and fact-checking it in an effort to make a fool of you, how much would you say?

Politically speaking, we live in a no-slack zone.

Pandering, by contrast, is widely rewarded. Agriculture policy in America has been permanently distorted by the fact that Iowa comes first, and nobody on either side becomes president without selling their soul, and the country's shirt, to the farmers.[8] That's just one more reason they will never give up their first-place position.

The irony is that this process can transform one or two of the midgets into giants. If you slay a giant, you become one. You don't even need to do that much; in some cases, just finishing second, or coming from nowhere, convincing a few thousand more of these people than the person behind you does, can do the trick.

But that is also the absolutely terrifying part of the process for a front-runner. Inevitability can be the kiss of death. A few thousand votes can end a twenty-year rise to the top. For most of the people who enter the race for the presidency, the best day is the day you announce. Lyndon Johnson's presidency ended on the winter day in 1968 when he won the New Hampshire primary. Ed Muskie was the 1972 front runner until he stumbled in Iowa and fell on his face in New Hampshire, both of which he won. Even the guys who do well the first time around can't resist coming back and losing (think of Gary Hart).

In 1988, many people believed that if Lloyd Bentsen had been at the top of the Democratic ticket, the party would have won.[9] But when he did run, four years later, he got killed in Iowa and New Hampshire.[10] Which is at least better than winning the nomination and losing, as Mondale or Dukakis did, and being effectively banished from a party that once made you its star. Perhaps it says something that, when I moved to Hollywood after a losing presidential campaign, I was struck by how kind it is.

If you were trying to figure out who the most popular Democratic candidate in America was, you wouldn't come up with a process like this one.

If you were trying to figure out who had the best chance of winning from each party, you wouldn't come up with a process like this one.

If you were trying to come up with a process that represents all groups within the Democratic Party equally, would you give the lion's share of the power to two states with no black voters, big unions, big cities, or much history of voting Democratic, for that matter? Democrats have been trying for years to take the power away from Iowa and New Hampshire, but it's hopeless. The establishment Democrats aren't all that pleased by how completely the activists and ideologues control the nomination either, and there have been fights about that for years.

Imagine if we had a national primary for each of the two parties.

Would half the Republican wise-guys—or more—be telling you that there is just *no way* John McCain or Rudy Giuliani can win the nomination, and that these guys you've never heard of are more likely to win than the heroes of the Vietnam War and 9/11 respectively?

Would Hillary Clinton be anything other than a shoo-in? Who could even come close? If you wanted to find out who the most Democrats wanted, why not?

Why would nearly a dozen unknown governors be wasting their time?

Jim Barnes of *The Atlantic* recently polled his panel of political insiders as to whether they thought Hillary would get the nomination if she runs.[11] She may be running at 40 percent among voters, but among Washington insiders on the Republican side, she is above 80 percent. What I thought was interesting was that she was doing better among the Republican insiders than the Democrats, which may simply reflect the fact that the Democrats are out there pitching the other candidates (and thus making the case that she is beatable)—or it may suggest that they, like me, understand the peculiarities of the system we have created.

People talk about the Electoral College being unrepresentative.[12] That's nothing, compared to the primary process. Most of you will have no say in the nomination process, at least in a formal way, unless Hillary stumbles early. A very few of you will decide it. The nominating system was created to open up the party, to give a voice to those who didn't have one.[13] It was created to take power away from the bosses, and to make it possible for an insurgent to win the presidency. It was created to put a front-runner to a test, not to affirm his selection.

That, for better and worse, is the legacy we're working with.

★ ★ ★

How did it happen? First there wasn't President Muskie. Then there was Scoop Jackson.[14] Most of you have probably never heard of him, but he was a big contender who went nowhere in his day. Then there was Ronald Reagan, who almost lost the nomination in 1980 because he decided to skip Iowa.[15] As for the first George Bush, if John Sununu hadn't convinced the local station to open for George Bush on the weekend, Dole might have won the primary, and who knows where the "Big Mo" could have taken him.[16]

All of this is ancient history, I grant you—but it's history that everyone who does this nominating business understands. Each year follows a pattern; the trick is simply to figure out which pattern it is. It is as much an art as a science, but in truth it's more like a dance. If it turns into a marathon, you're more than likely to lose.

In politics, we used to joke, inevitability is the kiss of death. Because the measure of success is expectations, the bigger the gorilla, the higher the bar, the less the chance of meeting it. The current system encourages insurgents by beginning with two small states, Iowa and New Hampshire, where an unknown candidate who is willing to invest the time in retail politics can take on the five-hundred-pound gorilla, do better than expected, and then take off, raising enough money to support a solid effort later on. And "better than expected" doesn't have to mean winning. In 1972, George McGovern lost Iowa. In 1976, "Uncommitted" beat Carter in Iowa.[17] Yet in each case the result in effect was precisely the opposite because of expectations, and the candidates were able to capitalize on their success.

Inside the Democratic Party, there has been a steady effort to reverse the potential for a McGovern/Carter style insurgent phenomenon, and to date it has worked—sort of.[18] The longer and bloodier the fight, the less the nomination is worth. The last two nominees have been selected quickly and cleanly, relatively speaking, but they've still lost. In neither case could you look back and say that the party should have picked a more serious candidate. In both cases, the most establishment-ready candidate won. But with the advent of the Internet and instant communications, it seems almost certain that any modern insurgent who took off in the way Gary Hart did in 1984—on either side—could not as easily be stopped today.[19] What spurred Hart—what academics call the "media effects,"[20] including saturation publicity and public attention— would only be greater, and what slowed him down, moving money around and getting commercials on the air and papers filed, could now be done in an instant. You can't rely on front-loading to slow momentum the way you used to in the old paper age. Today you can take off faster and move money instantly. If anyone takes off, they can handle eighteen states.

The system that exists today came about through a series of reforms that began after the 1964 Democratic convention.[21] The Hughes Commission, the grandfather of all such efforts, was not "the cranky product of a bunch of sore losers," in the words of CBS Executive Political Director Marty Plissner, who may have been to more of these meetings than anyone on the planet. "It was a consolation prize won in Atlantic City in 1964 by (primarily) Fannie Lou Hamer, Aaron Henry, Walter Reuther, and Martin Luther King Jr. as a reward for not sullying the coronation of Lyndon Johnson with a floor fight over the seating of a 100 percent lily-white delegation from Mississippi."

The revolution in party rules and platforms in the 1960s and 1970s deserves some attention, because it set the standard for real-world breakthroughs in civil rights and women's rights.[22] The Hughes Commission was designed to deal with the exclusion of blacks from the Deep South delegations: even at the 1968 Democratic convention, there was only token representation of blacks in what was still the Democratic South, and men outnumbered women at the convention by a factor of seven to one. The McGovern Commission, created after the Chicago convention, called for "reasonable representation,"[23] but it wasn't until 1978 that the party resolved to require an "equal division"[24] between men and women for the 1980 convention—the only one, it turned out, in which men did not outnumber women.

Representation was only one of the recommendations of what came to be the McGovern Fraser Commission. Before 1968, most states didn't even have primaries; selection of the nominee rested largely in the hands of party leaders, who used the primaries as guides.[25] The "Call" to the 1972 convention required the states to open the process of selecting delegates to all "bona fide" Democrats, encouraged them to hold primaries or open caucuses, and provided for delegates to be apportioned between the candidates according to how well they did in the state contest.[26] The winner-take-all system was abolished at the state level, although individual counties could continue to award delegates as a block until 1988, leading some to worry that it would be too difficult for winners to win—and others to respond that that was the whole point.[27] Democrats insisted that every candidate who got above a certain threshold (for a long time it was 15 percent) should get convention delegates; this principle of proportionate representation—PR, as we called it— was bound to drag the process out, which, depending on your perspective, might be a good or a bad thing.

The idea, as political scientist William Mayer of Northeastern University has explained, was that a longer series of contests would allow candidates to secure early victories through the sort of retail campaigning that would truly judge a candidate's merit, and then build on that early momentum—instead of simply blitzing the populace with the kind of big ad campaign that could only be bought and paid for by rich candidates.[28] (Remember, campaign finance reform wouldn't come till years later.) The Democrats' approach was an attempt to ground the process in the principles of small-d democracy. Republicans continued, then and now, to allow winner-take-all systems, but most states require by law that Democrats and Republicans use the same method—primary or caucus—on the same day.

George McGovern resigned as the chairman of the 1972 commission when he decided to run for president, but in the primaries that year he was still the long-shot liberal.[29] The front-runner that year was Ed Muskie, the senator from Maine. Muskie was the party's establishment candidate; in those days, it was considered a sign of weakness to announce early, so Muskie waited until practically the eve of the caucuses— which turned out to be a huge mistake. In the meantime McGovern had been making inroads with the young, anti-war crowd, who were out organizing. Back then, Madeleine Albright was with the Muskie team; most of my other friends, including Hillary and Bill, and Paul Tully and Carl Wagner, who became my mentors, were with McGovern.

The first-in-the-nation status of the Iowa caucus came about through an accident in scheduling, not a conscious decision to embrace Iowa's particular brand of small-state participatory democracy. The rules said all the proceedings had to take place in the calendar year. In 1972, the state's Democratic Party could only get the hall it needed for its state convention on May 20. Because Iowa had established an extended, three-tiered process involving precinct, county, and then statewide caucuses, and because the process couldn't begin before the turn of the calendar year, they counted backward and set the date for the precinct caucuses earlier than ever before—on January 24. And so a phenomenon was born.

Muskie didn't even announce his candidacy until January 4, 1972. When the votes were counted in Iowa twenty days later, he had defeated McGovern—by a margin of 35.5 percent to 22.6 percent, with 35.8 percent uncommitted. That was closer than most expected—and the punditry declared that Muskie was no longer a foregone conclusion. For all intents and purposes he had failed, and the pressure was enormous to do better in New Hampshire, even as all the momentum was heading in the other direction.

Iowa isn't about delegates; that part doesn't even get addressed until May. It's about expectations, and whether you meet them, exceed them, or fall short. The results of Iowa have a tremendous impact on what happens next, creating positive momentum for the winner and, just as often, killing or crippling a weak campaign. It's possible to win in Iowa and lose at the same time—as Mondale did in 1984 when he defeated Gary Hart, but not by "enough," giving Hart the momentum to go on and beat Mondale in New Hampshire. Most people also forget that Lyndon Johnson won the New Hampshire primary in 1968, but was forced to withdraw from the race because he didn't win by enough.

Muskie's close finish in Iowa put him under enormous pressure to do better in New Hampshire. Weakened by his poor showing in the caucuses, exhausted from the extra campaigning that was then added to his schedule, Muskie made one of the most famous and costly mistakes in primary political history. Goaded by the tricksters of the Nixon White House into an unnecessary defense of his wife, Muskie appeared to shed tears during an appearance on the steps of New Hampshire's famously right-wing Manchester *Union Leader*. This was during the height of the Cold War, in those pre-Oprah days when signs of sensitivity were tantamount to surrender. Ed Muskie, that honorable man, was toast.

Muskie won New Hampshire by 46 to 37 percent. But even that margin was too small to count as a real victory. As a senator from neighboring Maine, and the front-runner, and the establishment candidate, he'd been expected to win by much more. His campaign fatally wounded, Muskie was out of the race by the end of April.

In the wake of his implosion, the party divided bitterly over the nomination of George McGovern (he's the one guy who falls below my magic base number of 40 percent, which is a measure of how deep that split was). The split over McGovern would take decades to heal. Many members of Congress and party leaders decided that the "Party" was a quadrennial gathering of the left-wing radicals who demonstrated in Chicago, nominated McGovern, and turned the South Republican, and they stopped coming to conventions. The organizers of midterm conventions clashed with those who thought getting together every four years was too often.

In 1974, a peanut farmer and former governor of Georgia appeared on the television show *What's My Line,* where contestants are asked a series of questions by celebrities who try to guess what they do. Jimmy Carter stumped the panel; no one knew who he was or what he did. By 1976, the same man who stumped the *What's My Line* contestants won the Democratic nomination.

A new commission, chaired by Morley Winograd, was meeting to make sure that the rules for the 1976 convention were even more fair and open than the rules that produced McGovern's nomination.[30] At least that was the goal of some of the people; others had started to think about how to prevent anyone like George McGovern from ever being nominated again, which became a recurrent theme among certain groups in the party. In the meantime, a political genius named Hamilton Jordan, not yet thirty, wrote a memo to Carter outlining a strategy for the unknown former governor to run for president. Carter, Jordan, and a press aide named Jody Powell headed to Iowa to test his theory.

The Iowa caucuses were held on January 19 that year. Senator Henry "Scoop" Jackson, the choice of much of the old Muskie crowd, had decided to skip Iowa and New Hampshire (where Muskie had run aground) and focus on winning Massachusetts, where many more delegates were at stake. The problem was that the press was staked out in Iowa, as they now are every four years. Mo Udall, another major candidate, never established a serious presence in Iowa, leaving only one candidate (Birch Bayh) as Carter's full-time opponent, along with that perennial candidate "Uncommitted." As it happened, Uncommitted beat Carter—but Carter beat everyone else, which was enough to earn him a rave from the most respected journalist there, the *New York Times*'s R.W. "Johnny" Apple:

> Former Governor Jimmy Carter of Georgia scored an impressive victory in yesterday's Iowa Democratic precinct caucuses, demonstrating strength among rural, blue-collar, black and suburban voters. Mr. Carter defeated his closest rival, Senator Birch Bayh of Indiana, by a margin of more than 2–1, and left his other four challengers far behind. The uncommitted vote, which many Iowa politicians had forecast at more than 50 percent, amounted to only about a third of the total, slightly more than that of Mr. Carter.[31]

Johnny Apple set the tone for the coverage by the networks, which in turn gave Carter the momentum for New Hampshire. By the time Massachusetts came along, it was way too late for poor Scoop Jackson. You'd think he would have learned from Muskie. (Some lessons don't come easy: Four years later in 1980, Ronald Reagan decided to skip Iowa—and almost lost the Republican nomination.)

Some observers—including Nelson Polsby and the late Aaron Wildavsky, authors of the classic *Presidential Elections: Strategies and Structures of American Politics*—believe that Johnny Apple gave Carter too much in that Iowa caucus rave. Now, I take a back seat to no one in my respect for Professors Polsby and Wildavsky, but I believe that what happened in 1976 was precisely what was supposed to happen. The insurgent did his retail politics, took off, proved himself, and won.

Hamilton Jordan's now famous strategy was three states deep: Iowa,

New Hampshire, and Florida. Back then you could work that way, be-cause the system George McGovern and his commission had designed gave outsiders with the time and talent for retail politics a chance to build on early momentum and capture the nomination. The system was a perfect breeding ground for an insurgent candidate with good ideas but no hope of raising a nine-figure war chest and running in fifty states, or even eighteen, at once—the kind of candidate who *needs* to start out smaller and build. That's why it used to be considered a sign of weakness to declare early. Only weak candidates *needed* to start early. If you were strong, you could afford to wait.

Because of those 1968 reforms, in 1972 and 1976 George McGov-ern and Jimmy Carter captured the Democratic nomination by running as insurgents in just this way. In 1980, however, the rules were changed again—and by 1984 the strategy that launched McGovern and Carter failed McGovern's former campaign manager, Gary Hart.

Why the changes? After the defeats of 1968, 1972, and 1980—broken only by Carter's anomalous victory in 1976—everyone was out to repair the damage, including the same people who'd started the primary-season ball rolling.[32] By then, the Democratic Leadership Caucus, known to some as the "White Boys Caucus," had begun its mission to move the party back to the center. Party chairman Chuck Manatt was taking on the crazies, by which he meant not only the ideologues but also the state parties in Iowa and New Hampshire. Chuck's initial position was to try to force those first-in-the-nation states into what we call the "window" (the four months within which every other state must hold its primary or caucus), in order to take away their power to control the process.

No such luck. The state chairs just did an end-run around the party and went to the candidates themselves, soliciting their agreement to come and campaign in the state's early contests regardless of whether their delegations would be officially seated—and that was that. For Iowa and New Hampshire, the quadrennial contests have become big business, and if they're going to happen, no candidate can afford to alienate the locals, so the candidates had to say yes. Despite all the predictable grumbling about how unrepresentative and unduly influential these two states are, they held on to their exemptions from the window requirement.

So Democrats took other steps to limit the ability of those states to ignite an insurgent to the point where he could overtake the system, adding party leaders, and redoing the post-New Hampshire schedule. Insisting on the maximum number of unpledged establishment delegates allowed Mondale to meet his promise to have his 50 percent plus 1 on June 3, 1984, after the last primary. The rules favoring the establishment front runner meant that even though all the momentum was with Gary Hart after he won New Hampshire that year, the system's advantages were in the hands of the former vice president, not George McGovern's former campaign manager. Hart didn't have time to take advantage of his victory before he was forced to compete in a major round of primaries; he wasn't fully slated in states down the road, which cost him delegates. Mondale's guys had to stay up all night dialing for delegates, and it took them till dawn to make their goal—and then only barely, but they did it.

Less dramatically, but no less significantly, the schedule saved Bob Dole from disaster in 1996.[33] After Dole failed to meet expectations in Iowa and then lost New Hampshire, he was able to come back and win in nine states at the same time two weeks later, in large part because he'd been in all nine of them organizing and advertising for months, a result of superior resources, endorsements, party organization, all that good stuff he had, that none of his opponents had. The schedule and his money advantage protected him from a long shot catching fire by giving the fire no time to catch.

To be sure, "unintended consequences," which even the best of the rule maestros can't predict, can still crop as a factor. The first beneficiary of Super Tuesday, the effort spearheaded by the moderate Democratic Leadership Council to get a group of Southern states to move their primaries up in unison in the hopes of influencing the party's selection, was the Reverend Jesse Jackson. In Democratic politics, in a multi-candidate field, black voters predominate in Southern primaries, which is why Hillary Clinton will look very strong in the South. How you look in a Democratic primary, much less a caucus, has precious little to do in many cases with how you will run in the state.

But the second beneficiary of Super Tuesday was Bill Clinton, which was precisely how it was supposed to work, and it helped him secure the nomination, just as an increasingly front-loaded system has led to increasingly tidy victories for Democratic front runners in each of the contests since. The rules have done just what they were supposed to. Since 1980, the candidates with the most money, the best organization—the ones who were supposed to win—have indeed won.

Mondale did beat Hart, Iowa and New Hampshire notwithstanding.

Dukakis? We had the most money. We had the best organization, and certainly the biggest, on the ground. Going through my files recently, I found a memo listing organizations in eighteen states as of the preceding December, going into the first caucus. We had New Hampshire wired. They used to call the field "the seven dwarves." As always, Cuomo didn't run. Clinton didn't run. Gore was barely forty years old. Gephardt, a fine man, faced the bias that a man of the House can't get elected president.

Bill Clinton? There's a romantic story people like to tell themselves about this figure named Bill Clinton, whom no one had ever heard of—that he simply emerged from nowhere to be the most talented man in American political life. The point of telling the story this way, obviously, is to reassure us that if we just look around one more corner, we may find his cousin, who is lurking as, say, a governor of some small unnamed state. And then we'll all turn and say, *Eureka! We have found him.*

Right? Wrong.

There are, of course, any number of problems with this story, as there are with any good fairy tale.

First of all, as I've mentioned, everyone in politics had known, or known of, Bill Clinton for twenty years before he ran for president. He was the boy wonder, for goodness' sakes, not an unknown.

Second, Bill Clinton was the front-runner from the start in 1992. That's why he was on the cover of *Time* the week before the Gennifer story broke—because the press corps had anointed him. He had totally charmed the guys who mattered most. Joe Klein, then of *Newsweek*,[34] and Michael Kramer of *Time*,[35] were crazy about him. *Time* put him on the cover in January—before the New Hampshire primary, which he was expected to win. Then he would go south and clean up on Super Tuesday. Done deal. I remember joking with him and Michael Kramer, who was doing the cover story, about the similar piece he had done on Mondale's "inevitability" before he came crashing down, and whether the cover of *Time* should be considered the kiss of death. We all laughed. A week later the Gennifer Flowers story broke, and it was *deja vu* all over again. Clinton recovered, because he was as experienced as you get, and had all the advantages of the front-runner in a front-loaded system created just for him.

Howard Dean was ahead in the polls, but he was never the establishment front-runner.[36] That was the whole point of his campaign. He was the insurgent who peaked too early, but according to his campaign manager, Joe Trippi, he would never have survived anyway. Something happened the very moment Howard Dean became the front-runner at the end of 2003: He began making mistakes. (Trippi started counting them, but by then the two of them weren't even speaking.) Of course, the press buried him too. The level of scrutiny changed. He was viewed through a different lens, and he didn't hold up. And it wasn't just the talking heads who were gunning for him—although my friends in the crew would tell me that he talked back to us, not happily, when he heard us criticizing him, as if we were making up something that wasn't really happening. He was ready to put Osama bin Laden on trial. He quoted a terrorist. He got the Jewish community up in arms by calling for something like evenhandedness in the Middle East. Howard Dean had been the longest-serving Democratic governor in the country at that point, and he'd been running for president almost nonstop for nearly as long as Jimmy Carter did. But like so many people running for president for the first time, he made mistakes, and when the spotlight came on strong, they were there for everyone to see. Winning the endorsement of former Vice President Al Gore confused the message of the campaign, while only ratcheting up the scrutiny.

Between 1984 and 2004, the process of front-loading accelerated, with more and bigger states moving up, in the hope of having some influence on the selection of the nominee.[37] After 2000, the party rules said that Iowa and New Hampshire could both move to January, and allowed other states to move to February (in rules lingo, the "window" now opens in February instead of March), causing a major jump forward. Kerry locked up the nomination in New Hampshire, and sealed the deal on the first of two Tuesdays in which fourteen states were holding primaries in February within two weeks of New Hampshire, before we even got to the "real" Super Tuesday on March 2, which used to be considered the beginning of the action. You have to already be set up in those fourteen states, even before you win New Hampshire; you have to be set up and ready to go in the ten that come after that. Meanwhile, you're in do-or-die land in Iowa or New Hampshire. Under-funded candidates on the run may have a hard time running twenty statewide campaigns at the same time . . . which cynics would say is the point. Then again, there's the Web.

★ ★ ★

There is currently a new commission meeting to determine the schedule for 2008.[38] The concern is not that the process has given too great an advantage to front-runners, but that with the exception of Carter (whose victory we have tried to undo) and Clinton, it has failed to produce a winner. Now, almost anyone outside the Democratic National Committee might think that such a track record has less to do with the process than with the candidates themselves, and of course they'd be right. And most of the proposals being offered would actually make it even more difficult for outsiders or insurgents to mount an effort. In fact, you'd think they were still trying to stop Carter.

The latest commission, like the Hunt Commission, is aimed at Iowa and New Hampshire. Nothing is new under the sun. It is an outgrowth of a promise former DNC chairman Terry McAuliffe made to Michigan senator Carl Levin and Debbie Dingell, the wife of the powerful Michigan congressman, who were supposedly so mad that Iowa and New Hampshire had a "lock" on going first that they were going to try to move Michigan up in 2004. Instead, Terry promised—guess what?—another review of the rules. The argument against Iowa and New Hampshire that you hear in Democratic circles is that they aren't really "representative"— which means that you're giving power to a bunch of white people who live in states that usually vote Republican. In other words, that what's missing are base Democratic constituencies like African Americans, trade unions, and poor people. Of course, the base is not the problem for Democrats in a general election; it's white people who often vote Republican, in states like Iowa and New Hampshire, both of which are now considered swing states. The way the Michigan caucuses have traditionally worked is that whoever has the support of the UAW and the machine wins, which doesn't necessarily prove anything about strength in a general election. In 1988, Jesse Jackson won Michigan, although we were fairly clear that many of his voters weren't registered, and some of them voted twice, since our polling told us that we were ahead among Michigan Democrats by at least 15 points. (Of course, it would have been extremely bad form to point that out.) Having Michigan go first that year would have been nothing but an embarrassment for the party. Nothing against Michigan, but this is the least of the problems.

There are other problems with Iowa and New Hampshire that are far more serious, that Democrats don't mention as often. There is real concern about just how far left and just how far right Iowa skews, because of the investment it takes to go to a caucus. As we say in politics, the difference between being involved and being committed is like the difference between the contribution of the chicken and the pig to that ham and egg breakfast: The chicken is involved, but the pig is committed. You have to be committed to go to a caucus. It means going out on a cold night in January to stand in a room with a bunch of your fellow citizens, and after listening to some speeches by people who want to be delegates representing the different candidates, you stand in different corners of the room, which is how you vote. If one candidate doesn't have enough people in his corner to make a whole delegate, those people regroup and go to a different candidate. If you think it's hard getting people to vote, this is a whole different level of participation. While Iowa has been using caucuses since the 1800s, the thinking behind including them in the rules for selecting delegates was that they would bring new people into the party and be a "party building" experience. "Party building" was a big theme of the rules commissions, code for taking the party away from the Big Boys.

So who goes to caucuses? People who are organized. People who have buses they can use to bring other people to the caucus site at the appointed time.

One of the other pieces of great lore about Iowa is how Jimmy Carter in 1976, and Pat Robertson and Ralph Reed in 1988, discovered the buses of Iowa. The 1976 story is about the group on the Democratic side who are most organized, most accustomed to going to meetings, and have the easiest access to buses: teachers, of course. Jimmy Carter went after teachers full bore, winning the support of the National Education Association, and the school buses came out for him on caucus night. But that was nothing compared to the church buses that hit the roads of Iowa on caucus night 1988 for the first time. Across Iowa, there were church suppers being held (early) that Monday, so that afterward everybody could pile on the buses that were parked outside and already warm and head straight to the caucus. You knew something was up just by the yellow buses with church names on them rolling down every street.

These days, everybody imports out-of-staters for the last few weeks to canvass in Iowa, which makes for a good show, although their effectiveness is open to question. My favorite story out of Iowa in 2004 is of a confrontation between a union group working for Gephardt and some longhaired scruffy kids in colored T-shirts working for Dean. The Gephardt guys turned to the Dean kids and said menacingly, "We don't do meet-ups. We do beat-ups."

Real votes still take work. The truth told year after year: A reporter asks an Iowa farmer after he has listened to the candidate whether he's going to vote for him. The farmer looks shocked and says, "How do I know? I've only met him once." Iowans will argue that they take the measure of a candidate in a way that voters in later states, who make their decisions based on television ads, do not. But the skills that are tested in Iowa and New Hampshire are not the ones that a national campaign requires. You can be pretty horrible on television and win Iowa. You can win New Hampshire even if you don't believe in negative advertising. You can come out believing that it's totally unnecessary to have a message or a vision or a presence. You can be as liberal as you want to be; in fact, you better be. On the Republican side, not only do you have to contend with the Christian conservatives' control of the caucuses, but New Hampshire's Manchester *Union Leader,* which requires a no-tax pledge and punishes those who refuse to curry its favor. In many respects, it is more like running for governor than president— and, while that makes it easier for some candidates, it doesn't necessarily help ferret out the most qualified presidential candidate.

The proposals currently being floated aim to give some juice to more or other states. There's the idea of regional primaries, which has been around for a long time, and is likely to go nowhere;[39] there is also the idea of a Western primary day early in the process.[40] Dotty Lynch points out that Harold Ickes is there this time as well, obviously ensuring that Hillary's interests will be vigorously represented.

Those commission fights can get pretty brutal—especially when Harold Ickes is involved. In 1980, I recall, there was a rules problem relating to a vote on the abortion plank. At the time, I was working for Ted Kennedy; we were technically neutral on the question, and the Carter people, including the chair, were opposed. Suddenly I found myself on the phone with Bella Abzug, screaming at me. I turned to Harold: "What do we do? How can I save this?" Harold grabbed the phone, and he and Bella started yelling. I heard Harold's half, and the language I heard I have never heard equaled in the twenty-five years I have worked in politics. At the time, Bella Abzug was the most prominent and outspoken feminist member of Congress. But to Harold—and you might want to skip this line if you're easily offended—she was "Bella, you runny c—t."

With that, he handed the phone back to me. "Everything is fine," he said. "We figured it out."

So you can see why I don't expect anything very substantial to happen in this latest set of talks, although there will be plenty of noise made in the process. As party chairman, Howard Dean has already told the *Des Moines Register*, which has a major vested interest in the Iowa caucus (because the entire national press corps reads it for months before the race begins), that "I don't believe that the system's going to be changed or that the order is going to be changed. You're going to have to show me a reason to change. I'm just not going to change it for change's sake."[41]

While the Supreme Court has held that a political party takes precedence over the state in setting the rules for the selection of delegates to its convention, the party can't force a state to pass legislation to hold or move a primary.[42] So if the state doesn't want to do that, all the party can do to force such changes is to have its own caucus on a date different than the Republican primary. If the Republicans are holding a hotly contested primary on a certain date, what's the point of the Democrats holding a low-profile caucus on a different date— particularly if it's likely to be later? Which state is going to be interested in alleviating front-loading, or facilitating a regional primary, or giving the West a day of its own, by agreeing to move its primary back or hold a caucus instead? It's easy to talk theory, and I couldn't help but laugh at all the clever guys rediscovering the wheel, but the reality is that most of this requires Republicans and state legislatures; other than reports that Alabama may move up and California may move back (because state candidates want it later), there's little reason to expect much change.

Besides, everything's begun anyway, at least on the Republican side, where Iowa and New Hampshire are going to be huge. There will be intense interest, debates and mini-debates; advertising time will be clogged beyond imagining; a few candidates will think they are the only ones to decide to begin advertising early, so it will begin in September 2007, and it will feel like it's never going to end . . .

These days, everybody who's spoiling for the fight in 2008 is already out there. Hillary hasn't hit Iowa, but she's circling it, and courting Iowans in DC. She recently traveled to Cleveland and Minnesota and Wisconsin. And all of those stops are a bus ride away from Iowa. The people she visits can go canvass every weekend. They can sign up to be part of the largest land invasion in Democratic caucus history. They can go to Iowa and win it for Hillary. Who goes with her on these trips? Her chief political adviser, Ann Lewis. Who else? Organizers, fund-raisers—the usual. What do they do when they get there? Raise money, sign people up, put together the team that will put the state in Hillary's column three years from now. She raises money for the local congresswoman. Does a dinner for Legal Aid. A private reception. Even a book signing. Hundreds of people wait in line to have their pictures taken with her; they bring their copies of *Living History* for her to sign. In three years, just watch—those people will be working phone banks for her. Anybody who bets two dollars on a horse is going to root for that horse to win. If you bought a copy of Hillary's book, much less stood in line for her to autograph it for you, are you really that likely to root for someone else? Why would you, when later you can have the pleasure of telling everyone how you knew—of course you knew!—back then.

Hillary enjoys a freedom that no other candidate does. In the old days, the challenge in Iowa was to see if you could get out of there without being pushed so far to the left that you fell off the charts. Every four years, the Democrats would pledge our souls to save the family farmers—regardless of whether, in the process, we ended up rewarding corporate farmers, or those who farmed the government, allowing agriculture policy to be dictated and distorted by the political calendar. And we would come out frozen—that is, committed to some form or another of nuclear freeze, from which we would spend months getting unfrozen enough to not be attacked as soft.

Hillary's love affair with core Democrats, and theirs with her, is strong enough that she's been able to move toward the center without ever shaking the confidence of her base. Committed women are not going to desert her for reaching out to the other side on the abortion issue; she is the one candidate who has license to do that. Right now, she is scoring 70 percent or higher among African Americans, and this is before Bill Clinton has even set foot to campaign with her in a single black church. The Democratic National Committee may have elected Howard Dean as its new chairman, but Hillary didn't have a horse in that race. Under the rules, half the members of that committee are women; I served with most of them, and believe me, those are strong, tough women, the kind most likely to be in Hillary's corner.

★ ★ ★

The easiest way for Hillary to win the Democratic nomination is to smash everyone in Iowa and New Hampshire, and then lock it up in South Carolina, and the other early states. In the meantime, have major organizations all over the place. Look big. Look daunting. Done.

By smash everyone, I mean meet or beat expectations, whatever they turn out to be—not just win, but win convincingly.

The easy way to win is the way Al Gore and John Kerry did it. The key to this secret strategy, known only to a handful of us insiders, is . . .

. . . *to win Iowa and New Hampshire.*

Win the early primaries: Simple as that.

And the groundswell's already beginning:[43]

CLINTON WINS S.C. STRAW POLL

Richland County Democrats held the nation's first straw poll for the 2008 presidential race Wednesday and the surprise winner was U.S. Sen. Hillary Clinton of New York.

Clinton's victory at the sparsely attended event was a mild upset. Former U.S. Sen. John Edwards of North Carolina, a native South Carolinian and last year's Democratic vice presidential candidate, had been considered the favorite.

Clinton got 44 votes to 34 for Edwards. Virginia Gov. John Warner [sic] came in third with 32 votes and U.S. Sen. Joe Biden of Delaware got 24 votes.

Everyone else scored in the single digits.

The straw poll was conducted by the Democratic Party of Richland County, the most Democratic county in South Carolina and the state's second-most populous.

—LEE BANDY,
The State (South Carolina), June 16, 2005

What was John Kerry's strategy for winning New Hampshire? Winning Iowa.

What was Mike Dukakis's strategy for Super Tuesday? Winning New Hampshire.

Think about it for about thirty seconds: If you know you can win the nomination by winning cleanly there, are you going to focus on getting it done?

Particularly if history tells you that the longer it takes to win the nomination, the less it's worth, and you know the other side will be shooting at you the whole time, hoping to weaken or even to eliminate you . . . and you have those spending limits staring at you . . .

I laughed when I read an item in Robert Novak's column claiming that Hillary insiders were considering skipping Iowa because the state was too liberal.[44] Think of how stupid that is: First of all, why would you repeat the mistake made by Ed Muskie, Scoop Jackson, and Ronald Reagan, that cost the first two the nomination, and almost cost Reagan the sure thing in 1980, and give someone else the chance to take off and get unlimited media attention, when all you have to do is go in and win a third of the vote, keep up the steam and win New Hampshire, and basically you're done? The only thing sillier is the notion that anyone who was even remotely a Hillary insider would be leaking strategy to the "Darth Vader" of Democratic campaigns, conservative fire-breather Bob Novak.

The easiest way to win New Hampshire is to win Iowa.

What makes this strategy all the more imperative is the contrary point: not losing early, or failing to meet expectations.

Everything gets overblown.

Put thousands of reporters in a place with only a hundred thousand voters, and everything *has* to mean something.

Sometimes, what it means is disaster. The terrifying thing about Iowa, from the point of view of a candidate running for president, is that a stunningly small number of people control your destiny. "Thirty-three percent of the citizens of Iowa couldn't be wrong," Ted Kennedy famously said on the night he lost the Iowa caucus in 1980, which promptly pushed him to lose New Hampshire, before he came back and won in big states like New York, Pennsylvania, New Jersey, and California, when it didn't matter any more. We were dead after Iowa. Seventeen percent of the people in Iowa that year killed us.

There were fewer than two million registered voters in Iowa in

2004. With enormous attention being paid, about a hundred thousand Iowans participated in the Democratic caucus. Six thousand votes separated Kerry and Edwards. Nearly that many people vote in my neighborhood alone.

There was much talk in 2004 about how Howard Dean was using the Internet to revolutionize primary politics.[45] For all his efforts, though, it was George W. Bush who mastered the Internet, harnessing its power as an amazingly successful fund-raising and organizing tool, and by far had the best and most sophisticated list operation. (Hillary's people had a very good one in her 2000 Senate race, and presumably will have one again this time.) But so far no one has really captured the potential of the Internet in politics. We keep trying to adapt it to our old way of doing things, rather than doing things differently. That's a fact that should make even the most secure front-runner a little nervous.

The great advantage of conventional organizing strength should be on Hillary's side. But how hard is it to identify and communicate with a few thousand people on the Internet? In the old days, that was a big job: finding them, ID-ing them, keeping in touch with them—it was all labor-intensive work, which required a fair amount of up-front support and money to do. Not anymore. Find some groups with people who share your cause. Create them. Use the Web to find your audience. Offer blind dates. Then find a way to bring them to a caucus. Howard Dean meet-ups, my students told me, were the hot place to meet people before his candidacy collapsed. Someone is going to take all of this to the next step and make it translate into votes. The question is who.

Remember, you don't have to beat Hillary; that would be tantamount to killing the Gorilla. You just set the expectation bar, and campaign as the alternative.

Second, the old rule—that everything in a front-loaded system happens too fast for a third tier candidate to take advantage of momentum—ignores the instantaneous nature of all communications and transactions on the Internet. The world of getting checks into banks and waiting days for them to clear so you can get the ad on the air is gone. Hello, PayPal. Instant access. There are no delays.

Mondale won in a marathon after he got upended in Iowa and New Hampshire. At the time, Hart literally couldn't get the money he was raising in the bank fast enough to transfer it out to the states to put it on television. Do you know how long that would take today? Ninety seconds. Hart wasn't slated everywhere because meeting slating requirements was a big deal. Smart kids with a good website could have recruited delegates and filled slates. If Dean hadn't fallen apart, I certainly don't think he could have been "stopped" by Congressional leaders certain of impending doom.

What would you do if you were running Hillary, I ask a friend (who isn't, but might want to work for her some day, so I won't use names)?

Easy, comes the answer. Big show of strength. Come on with everything and win early. Get it down before anything can go wrong.

What would you do if you were running against Hillary?

Now he laughs. Why? This is the fun one, the challenge.

"Give me a candidate I can move to Iowa. Ex-governor. Put him to work charming people, he meets everyone, she meets no one . . .

"Then turn her into Ann Richards. Do to her what George W. did. Nice old lady, but old ideas. Mumbo jumbo. Part of the past. Nothing personal. Still hasn't gotten over health care. Still talking about the Clinton administration. He looks old. She sounds old. My guy is the next generation.

"P.S.: We need a winner. Can we really go through *that* again—the debacle of Kerry and Gore? Get an independent group to do the tough stuff. Keep it gender-free. Use a woman's voice. Sell my guy as the future. The real thing. The Bill Clinton for the next generation.

"Then push just a little, and the press will do the rest, and they won't mean to kill her. But they will. And she'll fall so fast you won't believe it, and people will be unbelievably relieved."

There's no such thing as a sure thing, of course. We're not talking about millions of people. Just some folks who the candidates are actually going to meet in Iowa. In a sense, Iowa thus puts them all on a more equal footing than they really are, increasing the chance of an upset, or of giving "someone" a chance to "emerge." And then you let the "media effects" and the press and the Internet exaggerate their judgment about a thousandfold: *Are Americans Taking a Second Look at Hillary? Hillary Heading Down? Is Whatshisname the Hillary Slayer? Who is the Next Bill Clinton? Who Will Go One-on-One with Hillary?*

He who slays her becomes an instant giant. A few thousand votes could do it. He becomes a superstar going into New Hampshire. Win those two and he's on the way to the presidency of the United States . . . from Keokuk to 1600 Pennsylvania in less than 365 days. That's the idea that has them on the shuttle, up at dawn, crammed in the small planes.

Why am I telling you this? Many of you might not want to hear it. You want to hear that she'll go through this process without a nick. Maybe she will. That's the ideal way to do it. Or go through it triumphantly, getting stronger in the process, dispensing early with whatever laundry she must get out of the way.

But I don't view the men Hillary is running against as junior varsity. They may not as be qualified, or experienced, or appealing as she is. But a number of them could certainly take off, command attention, turn her subtly into something she's not, and at least prolong the process if not even take the nomination away. I have too much experience with every aspect of this process not to worry greatly about how smart people can work it. If you understand history enough to know that any event is predictable in retrospect, you know that complacency is the most foolish mistake of all. This is particularly true in the election to come, when the Republicans will be simultaneously picking their own candidate and trying to pick off Hillary. Why would they do such a thing? Why not? They know she can win, even if some Democrats don't.

★ ★ ★

Jim Barnes describes the Democratic field as a three-layer cake, with you-know-who at the top, the 2004 ticket as the next layer, and then the rest.[46] Here's how I see the chances for the other layers.

John Kerry, the Massachusetts senator, who almost won despite himself, was trailing Hillary Clinton as of election night 2004 by almost 2–1 in the polls. That tells you where he stands in the hearts of Democrats: way behind her. Before the body was dead, they had abandoned him. Actually, they would have left him at any point up to the convention if she'd tossed in her hat.

Kerry could not have a cleaner shot than he did last time, and there is no reason to think Democrats will ever give him another chance. John Kerry got the nomination in 2004 because he was supposed to be electable, but he didn't turn out to be quite as easy a sell as Democrats hoped. *He's a Vietnam vet—who could object to that?* Remember when that sounded like a real argument? Meet the Swift Boat Vets. Electability is not an argument you can make twice.

Fool me once, shame on you. Fool me twice . . .

Nothing is worse than the enmity in the Democratic Party toward the nominee who runs and loses; it generally takes about three conventions to receive redemption. Not since Adlai Stevenson has a nominee been given a second chance, and there was little personal fondness for Kerry even when he was the choice of the party. (There was even less for his wife, who could not find a nice word to say for her own husband at the Democratic convention.)

After Teresa Heinz Kerry's speech, I asked Vickie Rideout, the woman who was running the speeches operation in Boston, what happened. I was asking half in jest, because I knew exactly what happened. Vickie is a brilliant woman; Jack Corrigan, the 2004 convention manager, had recruited her from the Kaiser Family Foundation to review every speech before it was given, to ensure that it conformed to the themes the Kerry campaign had selected, and I've worked with her on umpteen campaigns. There was no way in you-know-where that she could have had anything to do with the speech Teresa gave in Boston that Tuesday night—a speech that led Fox's Chris Wallace to call Mrs. Heinz Kerry the Evita Peron of the Democratic Party. The purpose of having a candidate's wife speak at a national convention is to fill in blanks that the candidate can't. Laura Bush does this rather brilliantly: Her convention speech was all about how long and hard George Bush had thought about the war in Iraq, about how difficult a decision it was, which comforted people who might have felt he was a little bit too eager to attack Saddam.[47] She also spoke about what a devoted husband and father he is—as she did again at the Correspondents' Dinner in mid-2005, when she launched a charm offensive to combat his plunging ratings.

Not Teresa.[48] She insisted on talking only about herself. And no one, and I mean no one, could have stopped her.

Of course, everyone knew ahead of time that it was going to be a terrible speech. But Teresa was never going to listen to staff. After all, she's rich. Doesn't that mean that she is the smartest person in the room? She's been known to describe those who would presume to give her direction as "too bossy." Big people take advice from those who might have more experience, or a fresh perspective. Candidates exist in a bubble, which is an easy place to lose perspective. Bill Clinton is a truly great listener—sometimes too great. Little people impose their will, and by that standard John Kerry's wife is among the smallest.

Indeed, there is so much built-up bad feeling toward Mrs. Heinz (yes, she's going by Heinz again) among big-league Democrats, that there's an effort under way to trade her back to the Republicans. If she wants to be a Heinz, one major Democrat recently said to me, let her be 100 percent Heinz. He's not the only one who feels that way. I know, Hillary was hardly Miss Congeniality in 1992; indeed, many thought that the flak she took may have helped her husband in a way, deflecting it from him. If people don't vote for vice president, they certainly don't vote for first lady. But what does matter is what the wife says about the man himself. It hardly reflected negatively on Bill Clinton that he chose to marry the smartest girl in the class. Teresa is a different matter. In New Hampshire, she was charming; by the convention, she was an arrogant loose cannon. Their relationship no longer looked like a love match, but something else, something much less attractive—a man whose wife wouldn't listen to common sense, because she had the checkbook.

It takes a long time to recover from losing the presidency. For some men, it takes a long time even to face it. As recently as this winter, I'm told, John Kerry was still bragging about how many votes he had gotten, about how he had gotten more than Clinton in either 1992 or 1996, as if that means anything at all. None of which bodes very well for John Kerry's political future.

According to a Zogby poll taken in the spring of 2005, when support for the war in Iraq was hitting new lows, Kerry would still have lost to Bush by a margin of about five percentage points—46 to 41 percent.[49] So much for how many votes he got; he would get fewer now. On the Democratic side, the energy was anti-Bush, not pro-Kerry. Kerry's presidential team has disbanded; at the top levels, at least, it was mostly Kennedy people anyway. The state chairs in both Iowa and New Hampshire are saying publicly that voters are looking for someone new. It doesn't get much clearer than that, even if the candidate himself doesn't want to hear it, and isn't listening, and can't face it.

Consider the following quotes from the April 30 issue of the *National Journal*:[50] "I think there's just a general belief that [Kerry] had a shot and that the nation is looking for a different kind of leader in '08," said Iowa Democratic chairwoman Sheila McGuire Riggs. "He had his shot, came close, but I don't think people would be inclined to do that again," echoed New Hampshire House Democratic Leader Jim Craig.

Even so, it is not in Hillary's interests to have John Kerry disappear. Quite the contrary, having Kerry in the race for as long as possible would give more than a few advantages.

First, it would make the field look and feel crowded, blocking potentially more attractive and electable alternatives. Kerry would take up space and time, with news crews, reporters, and newscasts, not to mention party leaders, organizers, and donors. How many Democrats can you cover, when the Republican race is bound to be even more interesting? How many top-notch Democratic organizers are there in Iowa and New Hampshire? How many storefronts, phone banks, buses, rental cars, not to mention television availabilities for advertisements can you find, with a dozen Republicans already there taking up huge amounts of space?

Second, defeating Kerry would look like a serious accomplishment, even if it isn't. So what if the only argument for Kerry in the first place was his supposed electability, an argument that has now been conclusively disproved? Beating the Massachusetts senator in New Hampshire would certainly look like a significant victory. The other great advantage, for Hillary, is that he would run to her left—making her look more conservative, and legitimately so.

In 1988, the best thing that happened to Michael Dukakis after he clinched the nomination was that he got to beat Jesse Jackson every Tuesday for weeks on end. All spring long, Jackson would attack us from the left, and in the wake of his rhetoric we would win. Like clockwork. No wonder that, by the end of the cycle, the country thought Dukakis was more moderate than he was. It was only because Jesse had enough convention delegates to make real trouble on the floor with minority reports (the way I did in 1980) that we couldn't keep letting him attack us—or create the attack, as Bill Clinton did four years later when he went after the rap artist Sister Souljah. We had to create peace, because the only thing worse than being too liberal (for a Democrat) or too conservative (for a Republican) is having an unruly convention. If you can't control your convention, most people wonder, how are you ever going to run the country? Ask George H.W. Bush about that little get-together in Houston in 1992 and how much it helped him.

So of course Kerry thinks he's running, and maybe no one will ever tell him otherwise. The people around a would-be candidate rarely tell him the truth; they generally have no interest in doing so. If John Kerry doesn't want to spend the rest of his life in the Senate, do you think his aides do? Have you ever walked into the back offices of Senate staffers, particularly those who work for a senator in the minority? It's like walking into a maze, where mice run. It is not anything at all like the West Wing of the White House. Doing foreign policy for a senator is nothing like being national security advisor. Ditto for being a Senate press aide versus White House press secretary. Every Senate staffer wants his or her boss to run for president, because it makes them more important—which is one of the problems with the entire structure of advice in politics. (Don't even ask about political consultants, who generally make their money off a percentage of the advertising buy— meaning that the more of those terrible commercials they put on the air, the more they make.)

Very few people ever tell candidates the truth. Saying no to power is tough. You need to have guts, or nothing to lose, or both. Imagine telling John Kerry that his chances for higher office are over, plain and simple. That he was picked because he was supposed to be electable, but he wasn't, so now he's finished, and he should go off and form a mega-think tank. That a second loss, in Iowa no less, which he won once before, would be devastating and make him look very small. That you should never finish worse the second time than you do the first. However delicately you might try to phrase it, believe me, he doesn't want to hear it.

Do you know what his response would be? I'm willing to predict: He would cough, look at his watch, say "We have a PAC that's doing a lot of interesting things that you may be interested in" (assuming you got in to see him because you're rich), and have you escorted away, never to see him again. More likely, by the time you got to him, you wouldn't say it. I once heard David Gergen, an aide to both Ford and Clinton, tell the story as Ike's aide Sherman Adams told it: that the person who wants to scold a president starts by unloading on an aide, revealing everything he's going to tell the boss that he's doing wrong. Then, the minute he's ushered into the office and shakes hands with the boss, the first words out of his mouth are: "You're doing a great job. The country loves you. Don't believe those polls." I can't begin to tell you how often this happened with Dukakis.

There is a story that John Kerry recently had a run-in with Mark Dayton, the Minnesota senator, after Dayton introduced Hillary as the next great Democratic president, and Kerry called him on it. What are you doing helping my 2008 rival? Kerry supposedly asked him, not entirely in jest. As we speak, Kerry is apparently traveling through key swing states, rallying the troops, trying to turn his 2004 mailing list into a grassroots operation. Do you think anyone is telling him it's a waste of time? I promise you: No. He wouldn't believe them if they did.

The very best thing Kerry could do for his reputation is elevate himself, pronto, to elder statesman status. Take on a few projects with Bob Dole—big ones. Leave the little fights to the little people. It would suit him, after all. Why go back to farm breakfasts in Iowa and take the risk of doing less well this time—almost a certainty—and give up the chance of becoming the elder statesman, in favor of being just another loser.

There's just no storyline that has the party turning to Kerry again. The fact that he's running second in the national polls will disappear the minute those who aren't for Hillary find someone else they like. It's the fact that 80 percent of all Democrats *aren't* supporting the last nominee that should be sending him a message. If Hillary should stumble, if there should be a move to the future, to a younger generation, to an outsider, to a non-senator—whatever it could be, it won't be John Kerry. That dog don't hunt.

The question is whether he'll figure it out or not. I say, he won't run.

John Edwards used to be seen as a moderate (he represented North Carolina, after all), and that was certainly how he ran as senator. I was certainly interested to see him listed that way in the most recent roundup in the *National Journal*.[51] But in 2004, when he ran for the Democratic presidential nomination, the fact is that he ran to John Kerry's left. For a while, I thought he could be a young Bill Clinton. If he were to beat Hillary Clinton in Iowa, or finish a surprisingly strong second, that's who he would become overnight. Then people would say, "Maybe he *is* better than Clinton. His personal story is certainly better.[52] He and his wife have a wonderful marriage. They have suffered much. They lost their teenage son in a car accident. They were blessed with two more children, and now she is fighting serious breast cancer. They are a strong family." When Al Gore was looking for a running mate, Clinton was very high on Edwards. (He told me that Edwards was his first choice for VP for Gore, but that there were a number of good choices—so long as he didn't go with Joe Lieberman.)

John Edwards was a very successful trial lawyer, and the first time you see him on the stump, it's hard not to be entranced. I saw him in New Hampshire in 2004, and I was blown away. From what I understand about Iowa, he was especially strong in the rural areas; had it gone a few days longer, some say he could have pulled off a caucus victory.

But his momentum didn't keep growing, and while he enjoyed another moment of sunshine with the vice presidential selection, it didn't last very long. During the last cycle, he was never really able to get beyond his "Two Americas" stump speech theme, and his unbelievably boyish good looks, coupled with the fact that he had only served one term in the Senate, raised the obvious gravitas question, particularly when compared with Dick Cheney. People started to ask whether there was enough there. Did he have a bigger vision? After the election, his wife Elizabeth Edwards (the polar opposite of Teresa Heinz), one of the best liked political spouses to come down the pike in recent memory, was diagnosed with breast cancer, which obviously became his first priority.

Since that time, Edwards has established a center on Law and Poverty at the University of North Carolina Law School, continuing to focus on the country's obligation to those who have the least. While some analysts (perhaps seeking employment) have tried to compare that focus to Bill Clinton's emphasis on welfare reform, both the words and the melody strike a different chord. Frankly, Clinton was heard and understood not as calling for the country to do more for those on welfare, but calling on those on welfare to do more (and for the country to do less, *a la* Reagan). Edwards sounds more like Bobby Kennedy, telling the rest of us that we aren't doing enough to help. Poverty is not the only issue where Edwards is positioned to the left; in 2004, he also went left on trade, which didn't help him much in the primaries, and could be deadly in a general election.

Not long ago, the *Des Moines Register* was reporting that Edwards had no clear plans for 2008.[53] But he now seems to be back in action with his "One America" campaign, which I'm sorry to say has been the subject of a lot of joking among my cynical political friends. Here's the problem: Most of us have seen too many losing campaigns based on populist slogans to believe for one minute that this kind of message ever gets you past 46 percent. The debate is about how to reach voters when they've stopped worrying about doing more for the poor, and started worrying about themselves. That's how we got Reagan Democrats.

Does that make it a losing message? No, not for the Iowa caucus. That's the whole point about this process. That's why no one asks about Willie Horton in the primaries. That's why being against the death penalty is good in the primaries and potentially deathly in the generally. Poverty won't cost Edwards in Iowa. He has the only organization left over from 2004, especially in rural areas. Iowa Democrats are solidly liberal, and this is the sort of message that will win him votes in the Democratic caucus. It will compare favorably with whatever Hillary has to say about being a moderate who spends a lot of time working with Republicans. It's just in a general election that Edwards's message leads middle class voters to contemplate becoming Republicans.

In a debate, John Edwards could do very well against Hillary. As a trial lawyer, he is better on his feet than she is; people forget that she is no Bill Clinton. In fact, Edwards is more Clinton than Clinton. Nobody is better talking about religion than he is. It was Edwards who pulled out that Abe Lincoln quote (which John Kerry later appropriated) at a New York television debate—about us being on God's side, not God being on ours. Edwards can talk about faith, and about bad things happening, and going on with life, with a clarity and meaning that nobody is going to touch, Hillary included . . .

Is this guy dangerous doing retail politics in a small state where he came in second, given that he's running as a liberal, which is fine there, and he's essentially unemployed, so he can go there whenever he wants, and he still has something of an organization, and is a former trial lawyer?

Yes. He's dangerous. The reason I choose that adjective is that while many of my friends are also friends with the Edwardses, and while I have liked him and especially Elizabeth every time I've met them, I'm worried about the Gravitas/One America/Trial Lawyer/One-Two-Three attack in a presidential election, aimed at a guy who is vulnerable on those counts. At least in 2008, I think the Republicans would love to have him.

As a matter of fact, if I were a troublemaking group of independent Republicans, do you know what I might think of doing? Just what Gray Davis did in California a few years ago, when he jumped into the Republican primary to eliminate his strongest opponent, Dick Riordan.[54] Of course, there would be no fingerprints. Beat Hillary in Iowa and spend the general election running against a guy who wants Americans to spend more to stop poverty. Spend a few million now, save a few hundred million later. It worked for Davis, to a point. The problem, in the end, was that voters ultimately recalled him—and one of the things they held against him, in some analyses, was that he tampered with the Republican primary to force his own reelection.

There's a problem in this scenario, and I don't just mean the danger for Hillary. The problem is that Edwards, whom I happen to like enormously, is the set-up in the story. He has the potential to be president, but he really isn't getting gravitas on the permanent campaign selling One America and himself across key states. Other than his wife's health crisis, he has not gotten out of campaign mode. It's too bad he can't do something totally different: go to Israel for a year and work on terrorism, or go to Saudi Arabia and push for reforms. So much better than two more years of pancake breakfasts in the hope that Hillary stumbles, in the hope that you catch fire at the end, in the hope that you do better than expected, or can make her look old and insincere and irrelevant, and grab the nomination and the big win.

It could happen, of course. Did George W. Bush have gravitas?

The upside on this one is hard to resist, telling the truth and nothing but. He clearly doesn't have any deal to step aside if Kerry decides to run, as Al Gore and Joe Lieberman did in 2004. The result was that Lieberman was forced to wait and wait, until Gore finally decided not to run, forcing Joe to a late start, which was the least of his problems. But the analogy doesn't apply here. From Edwards's perspective, it doesn't matter if Kerry runs. Then the giant for him to slay—or the first one anyway—is his former ticket-topper, which he can do faster than you can say Iowa. John Edwards is someone everybody likes. John Kerry is an acquired taste. Do I have to go on? Edwards could take off early as a real answer to Hillary: more electable (Southern) and more liberal (at least for now) and more likable. The problem will be that he isn't more qualified. He could make up for that by doing more events and being more passionate in debates. That will get you through Iowa and New Hampshire, and in that scenario whoever wins those two, probably wins a couple of the next five, before Hillary regroups.

(Which, in this fast moving environment, she may not be able to do—the dark underside of front-loading.)

John Edwards isn't the only one who could pose a problem for Hillary in the early stages of this process. My other most likely "other" candidate is Virginia governor Mark Warner. I saw one of his classmates and supporters the other night, who laughed at the recent filing that had Hillary raising $7 million. He said, "For Mark, that's nothing. He just takes out his checkbook." That's another way to win the money primary: Show up ahead of the game, as Warner already can. And the most "qualified" Democrat considering a race is almost certainly Delaware senator Joe Biden, who has been sounding more like a candidate lately.

THE SENATORS

Every member of the Senate thinks he's a future president. The old joke is that every alderman sees a president in the morning when he shaves; if that's true for an alderman, how much truer for a senator. The problem is that being a senator is, practically and traditionally, a terrible place to start if you're running for president. The last person to pull it off successfully was John Kennedy, and he was never really a man of the Senate. If you're wondering what's wrong with being a senator, look no further than John Kerry, and think about his explanation of his position on the war. Or go back and check out some of the Republican attacks on his defense record, where they compiled how many times he had voted against defense bills, and people like me had to go figure out how to defend him on hundreds of votes we'd never heard of and had to scramble to research.

My favorite example happened just recently. The Senate met in an all-day session on the same day that the National Governors Association began its conference.[55] The senators were fighting about Karl Rove, the president's top aide; the Democrats were introducing legislation saying that he should be stripped of his security clearance, and the Republicans countered by suggesting stripping top Democrats of theirs. *Cross-fire* may have been canceled by CNN, but it's alive and well on the Senate floor. This is precisely what Americans hate most. Meanwhile, the governors were on their convenient little junket to Des Moines, to discuss Public Education and the American Family . . .

So is it any wonder that George W., Bill Clinton, Reagan, and Carter were all governors?

Hillary is a senator, but at this writing she has been in the Senate only four years; most of the people who have run since JFK were lifers. Having said that, I must admit that being in the Senate doesn't seem to be doing her speaking skills much good. I've read every one of Hillary's major speeches, and I was not hypnotized. There were some very nice moments, but Hillary has a tendency—and believe me, as someone forced by circumstance to write speeches much too often, I respect the profession—to speak in that particular language that senators have long mistaken for English. She is wonderful at mastering the details of who sponsored what bill, and how many cosponsors there are, and who is cutting what bill, and all of that. Okay, it's more than a tendency. She *loves* it. She loves every act she's ever co-sponsored, and she loves telling her audiences that the greatest challenge we share is the cuts the other side wants to make in this program, because of changes in formulas that would come from some allocation of this and that . . .

She's caught the disease, but she can still be cured. One of the things that's true of Hillary—and not of all candidates, or all senators—is that you can play back an answer and tell her *This won't do,* and she will listen and get better. No one who saw her at the beginning of her New York campaign and at the end saw the same person. I talked to a few people who saw her at Renaissance Weekend who thought her answers were too long. That's the sort of stuff that's easy to fix with a candidate who is as smart and disciplined as Hillary. That is where all of her assets work to her advantage.

Among the most respected senators on the Democratic side considering a run for the White House is **Joe Biden** of Delaware, who last ran for the presidency in 1988. He's been in the Senate going on thirty years. Right from the start, Joe has a fire-in-his-belly problem: People will ask, rightly, whether he has it. Without it, as Fritz Mondale once remarked (and never lived down), you're facing a long road of Holiday Inns. Biden has already gone on television last spring saying how tough Hillary will be:[56]

> Oh, I think she'd be incredibly difficult to beat. I think she is the most difficult obstacle for anyone being the nominee. And by the way, I am one—I shouldn't be saying this, admission against interest—I am one who doesn't believe that she is incapable of being elected. I think she is likely to be the nominee. She'd be the toughest person. And I think Hillary Clinton is able to be elected president.

A few months later, Biden goes back on TV again to say that he's thinking maybe he will run, and of course everyone notes that he has already pointed out how tough Hillary will be.[57] How is he going to explain that comment on his fundraising calls? That kind of uncertainty in candidates is about as attractive as neediness and desperation on a first date.

Running is a horrible strain, and those with long memories will recall that Biden survived two aneurysms more than a decade ago. Racing to Iowa every spare second to go to farm breakfasts at 5:30 A.M., making calls every minute begging for money, flying commercial (coach, no less) day after day, gets old awfully fast if you don't have that fire in your belly. With the Secret Service at least clearing her path, Hillary will always travel better than Biden. For him, being a senior senator—and future Secretary of State if a Democrat wins—may be a lot more appealing.

Besides, Biden doesn't have a case. He's qualified, but so is Hillary. He's always wanted to be president, but so have lots of little boys. He's already said he thinks she's electable and qualified. He can't exactly do a generational attack on someone of his own generation. Their positions on issues will be difficult to distinguish. So what's his argument for being in the race? What does he say, *I'm standing by in case she stumbles— so give up your life for the next year, or go out and start raising money, and calling every friend you have, because you never know what might happen . . .*

Insurance is not an inspiring political message.

Evan Bayh is the Republicans' top choice for a Democratic nominee, according to Frank Luntz.[58] That makes sense. The former governor and now senator from Indiana, a big red state, son of a former liberal senator and presidential candidate, he is young, earnest, and a leading champion of the school of thought that says that Democrats must move to the middle, abandon harsh rhetoric, pursue a moderate agenda, work with Bush, etc.

You know the drill: He's the conservative candidate. He has the centrist calling card: He has won in a very red state. He knows how to win in places Democrats don't. But you know the problem, too: Where is he going to find supporters in Iowa?

Perhaps Joe Lieberman could lend Bayh his list. Of course, some of the people who were on that list, quite frankly, were there because Joe was Jewish, so they'd have to come off. And Joe, after all, was the Democratic nominee for vice president. And even so, I don't think it's really necessary to rub salt in the wounds by pointing how many votes Joe got anywhere, or how long he lasted in the race.

Let's just put it this way: There is no base for conservatives in the Democratic Party. If you don't believe me, ask yourself: Who was the last conservative to win the nomination?

Okay, what about the last one to play a major role at a convention?

Conservative Democrats stand a very good chance of winning the vice president's slot. Think Bentsen. Think Gore, a DLC'er back then, before he became a Howard Dean man.

Besides, when you meet Evan, he looks young, earnest, and young. *Gravitas.* He keeps telling you his resume, but he still seems young to be president. I had dinner with him and a group of "friendlies" one night, and their sense was that he wasn't ready. He is Gore in '88. Will a race do him good? It depends. I don't think 1988 helped Gore, frankly. I think *not* running in 1992—putting family first and writing a book— helped him much more. But others might disagree . . .

What's Bayh's case?

In the best version, it's this: *If you want to win, you've got to move the party to the middle. So you should pick a candidate from a red state. (And don't pick a Clinton.) I'm the only candidate who's been both a senator and a governor, who's won three times in a row in a red state, and I happen to have a great wife . . .*

What Bayh is really running for, many people think, is vice president. Clinton/Bayh '08 would be fine. So would Clinton/Warner.

You will hear the names of other senators. Just the other day, I heard that Russ Feingold of Wisconsin, now that he has taken the late Paul Wellstone's place among the most liberal senators, has been testing the waters. But even in the small towns of Wisconsin, where he spends time, the waters are murky.

THE GOVERNORS

The best hunting ground for presidential candidates is generally considered to be among the nation's governors, because they have the advantage of being chief executives (which sells) and having no voting records (which doesn't hurt). Governors also generally have an easy time raising money, since major players in their home states have no choice but to give. I remember looking around in June 1987 at Michael Dukakis's first million-dollar fund-raiser and realizing that no one in the room, with the possible exception of me and one or two others, thought there was a chance in the world that the governor would be the Democratic nominee for president fourteen months later. So what were they all doing there? Or more to the point, why had each of them not only paid a thousand dollars to be there themselves, but in most cases raised at least ten or twenty times that for the candidate? Simple: Because they *expected* him to lose, and continue to be governor of Massachusetts. Looking around me, I realized that I was surrounded, as best as I could tell, by every single developer in the state.

The problem with being a governor these days, as even the Terminator is discovering, is that it's virtually impossible to balance your own books—which, unlike the way they do it in Washington, is generally required at the state level. Other than in Texas, where the lieutenant governor actually holds the power and the governor is relatively weak, governors have both power and responsibility; they have to cut programs or raise taxes, and often both. They also have real jobs, which get in the way of campaigning. If you're a governor who wants to run for president, you'd better be out of office already, or have both houses of your state legislature in your control. Otherwise, those houses can make campaigning hell. That was one reason California governor Pete Wilson ran into a brick wall with his presidential effort. (And you can't always count on your candidate to make the best of a good situation: Dukakis had both houses, and a Democratic lieutenant governor, but he still felt pressure to go home whenever he could.)

A number of current governors have been mentioned as presidential possibilities, including **Ed Rendell** of Pennsylvania, **Tom Vilsack** of Iowa, and **Bill Richardson** of New Mexico, the Hispanic with the least Hispanic-sounding name in America. The problem with most sitting governors is that they may still be governors in 2008, and there's no predicting what disaster might befall them between now and then. Just last week, Bill Richardson was stuck in a speeding snafu, apparently not his first; governors get much more attention from the local press than senators who live in faraway Washington, D.C.

My friend Bert's candidate is **Mark Warner** of Virginia, because at least he doesn't share the incumbent governor's problem. His term is about to end, and he can't succeed himself. He's the perfect candidate for a Jewish mother: Nothing else can go wrong.

But he's not entirely perfect.

He did have to raise t—

What? Shhh . . . (*Taxes*, I whisper.)

Washington consultant Michael Powell sees Warner as the un-Hillary. But Republican pollster Frank Luntz hasn't been able to poll him effectively, because he doesn't show up.

Can he beat John Edwards to emerge as the young, Southern alternative to Hillary? And where?

This is the great game in primaries. You get to play so long as you can say: Here is where I am going to do it (in this case, beat Hillary). The South moved up to give guys like Mark Warner, and Evan Bayh, an answer: March 14. Unfortunately, by March 14, everyone but the winner will be dead. You have to have a strategy that gets you there much, much sooner than that. By then, you have to have done better than expected (Iowa?), and built on it (South Carolina), and then gone on to score (Maryland and Georgia). Then you can say that Super Tuesday has your name on it. That has clearly got to be Warner's strategy.

Warner is a fifty-year-old first-term governor.[59] He's also a self-made multimillionaire. Harvard Law, class of 1980. I have one friend, a classmate of his, and a supporter and fan, who tells this story: When he graduated, my friend recalls, Warner didn't have a job—not an easy thing at Harvard. All his classmates flew off to their new jobs. He moved into his car. He was last in our class, my friend jokes. That can't be, I say. I started teaching there in 1981. We didn't even *rank* last. We didn't rank at all past cum laude. Very Harvard.

Warner didn't want to be a lawyer. That will no doubt be a strong selling point. After he made his fortune in venture capital (which allows one to boast about how many good private sector jobs you created), he turned to politics. He ran against John Warner (no relation) for senate, lost, regrouped, then ran for governor and won. Facing a Republican legislature and a budget crisis, he managed to find enough Republicans to work with him to put together a budget package that raised taxes and balanced the budget, got lots of attention for governing from the center, and is barred by state law from succeeding himself.

There'd been some talk about his running for the senate against George Allen, but even more about his running for president. That's certainly how it's looking. How else to explain hiring a top operative with national experience to guide him through his lame-duck days in Virginia? Raising taxes is like furloughing Willie Horton: You get a de-layed reaction. Attacking you for it is not necessarily a good thing in places like New York.

Now, here's an interesting Mark Warner question: If you talk to Re-publicans, many of them see a "dark horse front-runner" (to quote the *Hotline*'s Chuck Todd) in **George Allen,** the former governor and now senator from Virginia, not to mention son of the legendary Washington Redskins coach by the same name. But what does that do to Warner's stock? We can't have two Virginians, can we? Then again, what about two New Yorkers? As I write, no less dedicated a Christian conservative than Pat Robertson himself said he wouldn't stand in the way of Rudy Giuliani running as the Republican candidate for president (did some-body say *Roe v. Wade?*). As Frank Luntz has observed, that would leave the poor people of Alabama forced to confront a choice between two New Yorkers. (At least Frank is finally giving Hillary credit for being a New Yorker . . .)

Mark Warner has a case, the skill to make it, and the money to back it up. He takes his "disadvantage"—one term as governor, not exactly a gravitas festival—and turns it to his advantage by posing as a young, sane, experienced Ross Perot, who'll promise to clear out all that fool political talk. Of course he never wanted to be a lawyer. He wanted to do something productive. Sorry, friends. And when he took office in Virginia, and found out that everybody was downgrading the state—which was going to cost the state, and the schools were going to face severe cuts—instead of playing silly political games he found Republicans in the legislature who had the courage to work with him, and he and his fellow Democrats balanced the books (raising taxes along the way, though no doubt on a select few), improved our ratings, and created jobs.

People are sick and tired of the old Washington games of gotcha, he'll tell you. *That's why I got into politics. I couldn't believe what I was seeing. I still can't. You look at what they do in the Senate . . .*

And meanwhile, people in this country . . .

With all due respect, I don't want to re-fight the last war. I think I know where we need to go, and what we're going to have to do to get there . . .

Government is more important than ever to provide for our basic needs: security for our nation, education for our children, a climate for jobs and growing businesses for the twenty-first century . . .

I'm Mark Warner, and I'm running for president . . .

Good morning, Iowa.

I'm just making this up, but something like that.

Of course, none of these folks have made any decisions yet.

★ ★ ★

And what of the Republicans?

In 1992, I landed at the Houston airport for the Republican convention where I was working for ABC. I was three months pregnant with my second, very-much wanted child; I was carrying needles and hormones with me to keep my levels high to reduce the chance of miscarriage, just in case; I had checked my baggage, something I don't do if I'm traveling for two weeks, so I wouldn't have to lift it; not to mention the fact that I was already on my way to being a future diet-book author. As I stood at baggage claim, a couple approached me; the woman stared, and said loudly, "I know you." I smiled and said,

"Yes," and before I could say another word, she said, "You're the baby killer." Apparently I'd become a pro-choice poster child to the right-to-life set.

That night I caught up with my friend Tom, who told me about the platform hearings, where they wanted to strike out a Lincoln reference as too secular. I wore my baseball cap for the rest of the convention, and told my friends in Arkansas even before it began not to worry about getting attacked as the big-government high-tax governor.

After their 1988 adventures on the buses, the right figured out what the left already knew, though they did it with far more efficiency and precision. The nominating process lends itself to takeover by small groups of organized ideologues.[60] This is even more true of the Republican side, which never got rid of all its slots for town committee members and state committee members, and all the other honorifics that go to people who show up at meetings that mainstream middle-of-the-road Republicans stopped attending years ago. Caucuses are made for the religious right. It is a closed system. Even if the state holds a primary, there is often still a caucus to slate the delegates, and that still requires people to show up and do the sides of the room business.

Moreover, as the Democratic system has evolved, it's brought the Republicans along with it. The effort by the DLC to create Super Tuesday for the South has brought the South much more to the forefront of the Republican process as well; once you get past Iowa and New Hampshire, that's part of what saved George W. Bush from John McCain (South Carolina moved even further up, and that gave W. his backup)—that and the front-loaded system, which allows the rich candidate to be ready to roll in eighteen states even if he loses two big ones.

Thus, the conventional wisdom on the Republican side is that the right wing picks the candidate. That's certainly what they did the last time John McCain ran, and they picked George W. Bush.

2000 Republican Presidential Primary Results[61]

	Candidate	Home State	Popular Vote		Delegates	
■	George W. Bush	Texas	11,676,689	60.22%	1,597*	84.8%
■	John McCain	Arizona	6,314,800	37.57%	252	13.4%
■	Alan Keyes	Maryland	1,003,070	5.17%	22	1.2%
■	Other	—	396,654	2.05%	13	0.7%

Clinched Nomination

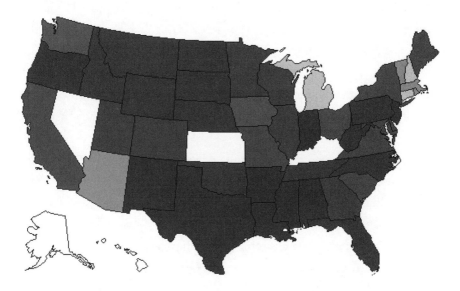

The summary doesn't tell the whole story, of course. John McCain had George W. Bush on the run after New Hampshire;[62] in South Carolina, Bush beat him 53–42 in one of the uglier campaigns in recent memory, featuring the worst kind of push polling ("Have you heard. . . . ?"), a controversial visit by Bush to Bob Jones University, which bans interracial dating, and even an Internet newsletter to tens of thousands of people claiming McCain had an illegitimate child, which he didn't. There was much more, attempting to malign McCain's patriotism and service.

But McCain came back on February 22 in Arizona and Michigan, winning not just in his home state, but also in Michigan. That victory helped him stay alive, which pushed the contest to March 7—which has now become the mini-Super Tuesday, where McCain was knocked out, as Edwards was four years later.

Of course, in 2004 the Republicans coalesced around a front-runner in George W. Bush well before the process began. This time, unless his brother runs, there is no equivalent establishment front-runner on the Republican side. Returning from his tsunami trip with Bill Clinton, George H. W. Bush said he thought Hillary would run in 2008 and Jeb would not. But after Bush ordered a continued investigation of Michael Schiavo, Terri's husband, after the autopsy results had convinced most Republicans to drop the issue, even some of the Florida governor's closest advisers admitted that Jeb had made no final decision about running. Could there be another Clinton–Bush contest? The right would certainly rally round him: He's from the right state; his wife is Hispanic, and he would instantly become the candidate to beat. But no one's betting on it yet. Maybe in 2012 . . .

Beyond the next Bush, the candidates who lead in the polls of Republican primary voters are the most moderate: John McCain and Rudolph Giuliani. But "Republican primary voters" doesn't really refer to the people who vote in the early primaries, go to caucuses, control the buses—not if half of them say they're for the two most moderate candidates.

Who really wins, then? (I don't know. Go ask a Republican.)

Dick Morris has been touting **Condoleezza Rice**[63]—an African American woman who has never run for office, has no domestic policy experience, no known views on domestic issues, and no known personal life. I like Condi, but the *Republican* candidate for president? Get real, Dick. Chief executive, when she's always been number two? When every study shows that people don't credit women with outside experience? Beyond selling books (certainly nothing to scoff at) and scoring clever points (my friend Dick is nothing if not very, very clever), the selling of Condi's candidacy only underscores the admitted weakness of the Republican field, and the strength and logic of Hillary's candidacy. Poor Dick; nobody wants to beat Hillary as badly as he does, and he knows that the boys who are out there can't do it. His fictional candidate reflects the real power of the urge to see a woman step forward. Is that urge strong enough to fuel Ms. Rice's VP nomination?

Tell me which one of them would do it, and whether he has any chance of ending up at the top of the ticket.

I don't think any of them would: they'll pick one of the other of them. Senators pick governors; governors pick senators. Within that, like everyone else, they seem to pick people who look like them, and think they're the most qualified. How else to explain George Bush preferring Dan Quayle over then Justice Sandra Day O'Connor in 1988? Think of it: He could have made history, instead of an embarrassing mess. Bill Clinton explained his choice of Al Gore as seeking to duplicate his best features—young, smart, Southern, moderate. Who is going to look at Condi Rice and identify in any way with her? Of course, that won't be it. Not to get into the details of foreign policy here, but the mistakes of the Bush administration on Iraq alone should keep Rice off the short list. It'll have nothing to do with gender. Or race.

Indeed, would she be on your short list, Dick, if she were a white man? Of course sex has *nothing* to do with it.

John McCain is the Evan Bayh of the Republican Party (though somehow I don't think he would like being called that).[64] When Democrats are asked to name a Republican they like, they think first of McCain. He is refreshingly straightforward and un-partisan. Unlike George W. Bush, he is a real hero whose life story is one of genuine service and bravery. He came to Kerry's defense when his war record was attacked. He is largely responsible for campaign finance reform. He has carved out a role for himself in the Republican Party, as with the latest filibuster compromise, as someone who is not afraid to work across party lines. He stood up to the right in the 2000 campaign.

For all these reasons, most Republicans think he cannot win the nomination.

McCain is the perfect example of the difference the process makes. If there were a national primary, he could win; he could even carry the day with a system of four regional primaries, particularly if you began with all the Western states on the same day. But we don't do it that way. We begin with Iowa, where McCain didn't even compete in 2000. Then you have New Hampshire, where he would be expected to win. Then you go to the same series of states listed above, assuming all those moderates and Democrats who love McCain are now voting for Hillary or Edwards or Warner or whoever in the Democratic process, and we're on buses now: South Carolina, Michigan, Massachusetts, New York, even New Hampshire. Tell me what happens in a multi-candidate field, and the answer is: No one knows. That's the charmer here.

Republicans really don't have much experience with a mess like this one, and their winner-take-all-system creates the potential for a bit of mischief. It means that they—whoever "they" are—don't necessarily control the process anymore than the "theys" within the Democratic party do. If the electorate divides among a wide variety of candidates, then the candidate with the most votes gets all the delegates.

One interesting question at this point: Who is more worried about McCain, Democrats or Republicans? Based on my entirely non-scientific survey, I would say Republicans. Republicans find the prospect of his being their nominee far more unacceptable than the Democrats find the idea of facing him in November '08. The GOP *machers* I know sputter at the idea. McCain is not seen as a team player. There will be substantial forces arrayed against him.

What Democrats point out about McCain:

He's more conservative than you think he is. He's as anti-abortion as the next guy. He will be with them on the Supreme Court and vote for whoever Bush nominates. By the time the election rolls around, his conservative stripes will be clear. The reason he led the charge on campaign finance reform was that he was one of the Keating Five.

For them, it's all about loyalty. Sure, he supported Bush in the end.

But before he did, he flirted for just a little too long, in a lot of Republicans' judgment, with the idea of being Kerry's vice president.

He has had skin cancer twice. His wife, Cindy, who is twenty years younger, has had a stroke. They have young children. While everyone says he is running—that the odds are that he will—it is not clear to those who know her that she wants it.

The Democrats will use his age and health against him. One smart Dem tells me: "He will be a seventy-two-year-old man who has had cancer twice and is known to be erratic, running against the most disciplined sixty-year-old woman in the country." My advice: Be careful talking about health issues. But I heard it. From Republicans too.

Have I noticed that Bill has developed a warm relationship with the senior Bushes lately? Well, yes. I have. Who on the globe hasn't? Some people might think that the dominant political genius of the western world might be hoping to persuade the Bushes to take four years off and not help nominee McCain quite so much if he should run against you-know-who—their daughter-in-law, practically, after the way Bill has become a member of the family. Maybe in the back of their minds they're thinking Jeb could always run in four years . . .

Former New York mayor **Rudy Giuliani** is a hero to many people in America. If he runs, some in the party may see him as a savior, from the bland troupe of governors and the maverick senator from Arizona. There are just a few little tiny problems, which have even his own people a little bit nervous. Rudy became a big pro-choice man when he became mayor, going so far as to support public funding for abortions. How do you flip on that? When I talk to Frank Luntz, who is close to Giuliani, he is careful to talk about Rudy's *perceived* positions—and I think, Here we go. In fact, Rudy wasn't always pro-choice; it was a position he adopted to be mayor. So is he John Kerry? How do conservatives eat that?

And what about gay rights? When he moved out of Gracie Mansion (which wasn't pretty either—am I the only one who remembers when he sent out his lawyer on Mothers' Day to complain about his wife squealing like a stuffed pig, and how he sued to force his reluctant children to stay over with his then-girlfriend?), he moved in with a gay couple who were friends of his. Didn't bother anybody in New York. In South Carolina, on the other hand, Republican primary voters are still defending that ban on interracial dating at Bob Jones University. How do they deal with a pro-choice, pro-funding, pro-gay rights candidate?

Compared with whom?

There's Dr. Excitement, **Bill Frist,** whose blood runs as blue as it can for a red state guy. He's a Princeton legacy, Harvard Med School man, hardly the norm in the religious right crowd. But they do understand gratitude. Fellow Republicans describe Frist as being more effective one-on-one. If that isn't a way of saying he can't work a room, I don't know what is. He has devoted himself to winning the hearts and minds of right-wing primary and caucus voters with the Terry Schiavo melodrama and the *pas-de-deux* on judges, and he's very smart about it, and they keep score. He has money from his share of HCA, the for-profit hospital chain founded by his father and brother; blame them if your uncle died there, he just takes his share. He leaves the Senate in 2006, and will have two years to spend eating breakfast in Iowa with maple syrup from New Hampshire.

George Allen, noted above, was the top choice in the Hotline poll; his favorite place to have his picture taken is seated on a horse, and he is therefore described by some as Reaganesque. "Allen is W," according to the Hotline's Todd, which would make him George III. Who does this sound like: "Wins more on style points than on candle wattage"? It's a *National Journal* description of Allen, but couldn't it just as easily be you-know-who? That's probably why so many Republicans are enthusiastic about Allen. I think he's the logical choice: former governor, name is George, likes to be photographed on a horse. What else does he need? Turn the Democratic Party on its head, and see if you can answer the question: Can the insiders put it together for this guy with everyone watching?

Mark Sanford, the governor of South Carolina, was chosen as the Most Conservative Governor in America in 2003 by the American Conservative Union. Now, imagine how hard that is to win. He is big on tax cuts, and will be competing for the support of the right. Who won't?

Chuck Hagel is the kind of Republican people like me like (which is probably the kiss of death): while he's an anti-abortion, pro-prayer Nebraska conservative, he isn't an intolerant born-again Christian. He's a former POW who came to Kerry's defense on his military record. He's already said he won't take the pledge never to raise taxes, and he's been critical of the war in Iraq. If McCain says no, maybe he'd run with Hillary.

Mitt Romney is the Mormon governor of Massachusetts, whose father, Michigan governor George Romney, is best known for losing his chance at the nomination by suggesting that he might have been "brainwashed." Mitt ran against a woman for governor and won. It pains me to say it, but how else could a Romney have beaten an O'Reilly in Massachusetts? The polls show that people in Massachusetts don't want Romney to run for president, but there's no particular reason to think he's paying much attention, given his recent travel schedule. He just released a statement showing that his mother, Lenore Romney, was prochoice back when she ran for governor of Michigan in 1970. I'm not sure how this plays into his race for the presidency, but Mitt Romney is a very talented politician who is much hated in Massachusetts on that account.

Haley Barbour is a brilliant political operative and former party chair who went home and ran successfully for governor of Mississippi—then woke up, looked at the current field of presidential contenders, thought about the primary calendar, and saw the mismatch. The strong guys in this field are not the guys who can win the game.

The guys who could win the game aren't the guys who have the juice. That suggested an opening for a guy with juice who knows the game. And being a governor is the ticket you need to play. Haley Barbour could be the Republican Jimmy Carter (circa 1976), from the inside.

If Rudy asks his friend Bernie Kerik to do for him what Bernie should have done for himself—vet him, that is—and turns up anything even remotely like what Bernie should have come up with on himself, there's always **George Pataki,** the governor of New York, to step in for Rudy. Never underestimate George Pataki, everybody always says . . . perhaps because one's instinct, inevitably, is to do so. Another Jimmy Carter? Suddenly everybody is Jimmy Carter, even if the rules have changed to make that particular move a little more difficult and a lot more expensive.

There are also many more, so stay tuned for late additions.

★ ★ ★

Two more points to make at this early stage:

One is that the length of the current list of candidates makes it difficult for lesser-known contenders among both the Republicans and Democrats to get attention. There are only so many crews, so many producers and reporters, so many minutes of news for politics. Imagine you're a TV news producer: You start by assigning someone to Hillary and Rudy and McCain, that's three; add Kerry and Edwards, and before long you're running out of camera crews. Aspiring candidates had better jump out of this pack soon, or they'll be dead. That makes the "money primary" that comes first, along with Iowa and New Hampshire, all the more important as well. The less celebrated candidates will look like midgets in this crowd—not because they're unworthy, but they're governors no one has heard of and majority leaders who are the epitome of bland.

The second point is how difficult it is to control the process once it begins. Any one of these men might look just fine if the light shined on him very brightly for five minutes. Whether he would hold up for twenty-five, who knows? But five, yes. So if any one of them should take off in Iowa or New Hampshire, the question would then become whether they're able to back it up—at least for long enough to start getting ads on the air.

Because, as everyone knows, *somebody* is going to have to run against her.

6.

IT ISN'T JUST ABOUT
(HER) SEX

★

We need a chapter, my editor reminds me, on Hillary's positions, on what she stands for and against, lest we leave readers wondering whether the only reason to be for Hillary Clinton is that she's a woman. It's the platform chapter, and he must know he is sticking it to me, Madame Platform.

My editor is extremely smart and he sees right through me. It is the one chapter I'd been wary of trying to write. I thought a review of the political terrain was much more practical, and figured maybe it would satisfy my readers' needs . . . but ultimately I know that explaining how she can win doesn't tell the whole story of why she *should* win.

I could rehearse all the obvious excuses: How could anyone presume, so early on, to predict the particular issues the nation will face three years from now? Who knows if we'll be out of Iraq in three years? Who knows how many Supreme Court vacancies there will be? For that matter, how could I pretend to come up with the exact campaign slogans that each candidate will spend countless painful hours working out with the help of advisers, polls, focus groups, and behind-the-scenes infighting? If I told you I'd come up with that perfect phrase—one that includes the word "family" and implies both "listening" and "acting"—would you believe me?

But the basic positions are out there. They're the foundation—they don't change with time. I know this because I used to write the issue papers, and platforms, and Senate reports, and floor speeches where they're captured for posterity. That's how I started in politics. Everyone has some kind of radar—something they can see coming a mile away. I have radar for BS in policy documents. And there's plenty of it out there to find. It's the consequence of the endless games of gotcha that both sides and the media have perfected, to the point that no one dares to say anything, because any new idea or proposal might subject them to some form of attack. I discovered early on that I could clip a summary page to almost anything, and all the press would do is repeat the one or two most quotable bullet points from the summary page, and then analyze the political impact of the whole thing, no matter what the "white paper"—the document itself—actually said. Once I realized that, no one turned them out faster than I did. I was a veritable white paper factory.

All those years of experience crafting policy papers may help explain my reluctance to do this chapter. I have a virtual allergy to the language of policyese, the cousin of legalese, a particular campaign style that involves not saying anything while appearing to be deeply troubled and taking substantial steps and offering incentives as well as public- and private-sector solutions. Recognizing, of course, that government can't solve all these problems, but it can be a leader . . .

What is truly unbelievable is how little things have changed from my day. The buzzwords may have changed a bit. But the fundamental principles—where the real stuff dwells—remain the same.

Here's the short version: The Democrats agree with one another on almost everything. The Republicans (except Giuliani, who is a product of New York City politics, which defined his positions on social issues, and does anyone think he'd take the same ones today?) agree with one another too, and they disagree with the Democrats. Everybody is against terrorism and for God and country. Everybody is for families, a strong economy, work, equality, peace, security, fairness, justice, against crime, and for the troops. The Democrats are all pro-choice, against discrimination against gays, but also against gay marriage. The Republicans are all against abortion (except Giuliani when he's in New York) and against the gay lifestyle (ditto). The Democrats are against tax cuts for the wealthy. The Republicans are against tax hikes—or they will be, as soon as they get to New Hampshire. McCain seems to be very different, but he's still a Republican. My Democratic friends have taken to pointing that out regularly to me. I wonder why.

We know what they'll say about Hillary.

They'll say: LIBERAL, LIBERAL, LIBERAL. *Kennedy! Mondale! Dukakis! Kerry!* Whoever said names could never hurt you wasn't doing politics.

We'll say: MODERATE, MODERATE, MODERATE. And while we're at it, we'll say *Clinton! Clinton! Clinton!*

Hillary Clinton is a moderate Democrat. She is as unliberal as you can be and still retain your Democratic Party membership. But she still wins the nomination, because she is Hillary Clinton, and because her genuine commitment to women and children, and her support among racial minorities and union members, is strong and unyielding. It is so strong that she has the flexibility to move to the middle, support the military, be a budget hawk, insist on welfare reform, support teacher testing, and bring about real education reform.

The "vast right-wing conspiracy"—that is, the guys who imitate Rush and Sean, the ones with less talent but the same lines, and all those blonde Republican talking heads who have never been victims of discrimination, but would never be where they are today if not for those of us who demanded that women be present—will run around calling her an ultra-liberal, and saying she isn't really a moderate, and that she's really more liberal than Ted Kennedy and Mike Dukakis . . .

Ridiculous. Ted Kennedy doesn't care about deficits nearly as much as Hillary, and he'd go for a broader health care plan in a New York minute. He is definitely more liberal on the war, hands down. And Mike Dukakis? Again, no contest. He's against the death penalty. He always wanted to spend less on defense. Hillary was for welfare reform, and for budget cuts in the Clinton administration. Don't believe me? Ask Dick Morris. In his anti-Hillary book, he says she was a moderate in her husband's administration.

When their name-calling doesn't work, of course, you know what they'll do next.

They'll scream: *Makeover!*

Makeover, that great sexist code word that allows them to sneer at all the hairdos, to make their veiled reminder of the former first lady's insecurities. (Even now, when we know what she had—or, more precisely, what her husband had—to be insecure about.)

The charge of "makeover" is intended to make you think that positions that Hillary has taken her whole life long were adopted cynically for this campaign. It comes with a subliminal question: Does she change what she says as fast as she changes how she looks? Hillary Clinton promises step-by-step change, and the announcer muses, *Hillary Clinton proposed the most massive government health care program in history in 1993. Oh, well. Guess she's had a makeover . . .*

How's that for an issues debate? Well, that's all the conservatives have.

We say Armed Services, and they say Makeover.

We say budget hawk, and they say Makeover.

We say tough on crime, and they say Makeover.

The problem is, she's held most of these positions for most of her life. You notice that they never mention the Clinton administration on that list with Kennedy and Dukakis?

But that's the level of discourse that passes for debate in politics today.

There's more, to be sure. Even as we speak, Hillary and some of her smartest issues people are thinking about what book would be right for her to publish right after the 2006 election; what innovative new ideas out there are likely to catch fire with the voters; what the themes for the campaign should be. They have people in all the think tanks; they're looking at all the polls. I hope they bring brilliant new ideas to the table—both campaign strategies and policy innovations.

In the meantime, it isn't too hard to predict what the basic themes are going to be. After the horrendous 1980 election, Carl Wagner and I spent months reviewing Senator Kennedy's campaign, trying to understand what had happened. We studied all the polls and the returns, interviewing everyone we could; I probably learned more doing that study then in any course I ever took or taught. I wrote a section of our report on themes, which argued that Democrats weren't hearing what Americans were worried about. The theme that I believed would define the 1980s was—are you ready?—*security*. I remember it very well, because I actually took some heat for it inside Kennedy's office. Some people thought the piece—and thus its writer—was racist: Security included national security, economic security, and personal security, and personal security included crime. The senator himself, to his credit, understood the importance of crime: The victims, he saw, usually looked exactly like the perpetrators, only more vulnerable. He thought security sounded right. It still does.

If you ask me what the first plank in Hillary's platform will be, it's got to be security. As she has already proven she understands, her credibility as a leader depends on her credibility on matters of defense.[1]

SECURITY: Hillary Clinton is tough enough to stand up to terrorism and smart enough to understand that America is stronger when we are part of the world community than when we go it alone.

What's next? Bread and butter. Remember the Clinton years—the *first* Clinton years. Remember the greatest peacetime expansion in history. I know, it seems like a lifetime ago. As I write this, it was only five years— and more than $400 billion in federal deficit dollars.

PROSPERITY: Hillary Clinton will restore the economic prosperity the Republicans squandered when they gave tax cuts to the wealthy and built up huge deficits. She will promote job growth for working people, support small businesses, and increase our investment in our most valuable resource—our human capital.

No surprise there: Working people have always been the Democrats' greatest passion.

INDIVIDUAL FREEDOM: Hillary Clinton will make sure that individuals are able to live their lives free from the intrusion of government into their most personal decisions. She will appoint Justices to the Supreme Court who are committed to respecting individual liberties.

And here's the clever part: We don't stop there . . .

REAL FAMILY VALUES: Hillary Clinton understands the demands on families today, the challenges faced by working mothers, the hardships faced by so many children, the struggle to raise children in an atmosphere of increasingly violent video games and an overly sexualized culture. She is ready to stand up to Hollywood and stand up for the children; she understands the importance of faith in our lives; she believes parents need the tools to allow them to do their jobs.

And then someone will say, *Should we stop there? That sounds good.* And someone else will say, *But what about the environment, and health care, and education?* And of course they'll be right, and Hillary will keep speaking out the way she has all along. And then there's the Middle East, and she'll remind us that she has always been a strong supporter of Israel. And for goodness' sake Social Security gets its own category.

And if this starts to sound like a laundry list, isn't that what platforms are?

That's what always happens. That's why they have all these eager young issues staffers, and people send them questionnaires in the hope that someone will get an answer and force a candidate to take a position that will drive a campaign. For instance, sooner not later, there will be a position paper on farm subsidies and how to save the family farm, in which Hillary confronts the reality of corporate farming and farming the government—for she, too, is a believer in what Senator Kennedy used to call the "farmily fam."

As of now, though, this is mostly me talking, not Hillary. She's hardly begun the work it takes to find the right way forward on all the issues, and the younger versions of me haven't started converting her positions into white papers. They will be much, much more careful than I am being here. They have real jobs, after all, from which they can be fired, and there are fact checkers working for opposing campaigns. By contrast, I'm free.

But she is the only candidate who would say the things I'm about to say. And she is certainly the only one who could accomplish them.

This is really the first point:

None of the other candidates are going to change the way people see government. That's not their passion.

No one else is going to call on the Baby Boom generation to remember the idealism of their youth, renew their pledge to make a difference in their lives, and give up their six- and seven-figure salaries to take positions as teachers and case workers in poor communities, or as bureaucrats in Washington. Mark Warner wasn't part of that generation of youthful idealists. He was a business guy.

No one else is going to sit down with the national heads of the

Teachers Unions and decide that something has to be done about public education, and say that if we're recruiting more teachers, and paying them better, they're going to have to be better, and be willing to take some risks. The teachers wouldn't trust anyone else, and no one else would have the clout to force them to the table. Put the big-city mayors at the table with them, and the smartest people in education, and you have the beginning of change. But there has to be a national pact, not just a national expansion.

No one else is going to consider it her personal mission to deal with the nation's health care crises. No one else understands it the way she does, much less feels what is at stake the way she does.

When asked in the NBC/*Wall Street Journal* poll last summer which of a series of everyday issues preoccupies them the most, 44 percent of those adults surveyed said the cost of health care and prescription drugs; 37 percent said teaching children good values; and 32 percent said the quality of public education, followed by other issues.[2]

Those are Hillary's preoccupations, too.

Hillary Clinton isn't just qualified, she is uniquely qualified. If she's elected, it will be electrifying.

It will be a unique moment in history, and that will give her an unmatched moment to challenge the nation.

She will be able to do things, with that mandate and status, that no one else could. And she will be able to do those things because she is who she is.

She's the most experienced candidate.

It's a big claim, but it's an important point. If you've been at a job for a while, you know that from time to time things come up that you've been through before, and the experience of having seen them through gives you the benefit of better judgment the second time around. Few people have the benefit of direct experience when they come into the presidency, but Hillary would have just that, in all but name. Not only has she spent the last thirty years deeply involved in issues of public policy, but she was intimately involved in the major decisions of the Clinton presidency—well beyond health care. Among all the plausible candidates, she quite simply has the most experience dealing with national and international issues. Yes, her status as a moderate Democrat makes her best positioned to pull together a winning coalition. But experience isn't just about the right positions.

It's about the mistakes you didn't have to make: things like the Bay of Pigs, because you accepted bad advice when you should have been asking more questions, or the Travel Office bungle, because you're green in dealing with Washington, or picking Bert Lance as your budget director, because you didn't know your way around, or trying to take Waco by force, because your attorney general didn't ask the hard questions she should have.

Vice presidents are always claiming that they can hit the ground running, but it's never true because vice presidents were never really there. Hillary was, and she can hit the ground running. There is simply no overstating the advantage involved. No, she wasn't co-president, and the suggestion that her election would violate the Constitution turns sexism into a rule of law. But she certainly was as close as any of the president's advisors, closer than any senator, or governor, or general.

The fact that she will also be, pound for pound, the smartest, most thoughtful, most policy-oriented candidate in the race—as well as the best fundraiser, the most charismatic, and the most committed to public service—makes the case easier still.

She has been through a transition. She knows what not to do. She is, by this point, an old Washington hand, with a very, very experienced team. There is just no comparing her to the greenhorn who moved to town all those years ago and scoffed at attending the obligatory dinner parties, when she was a kid (and so were the rest of us).

President Clinton was once telling me how much his golf game improved while he was president. I have to confess I was surprised; being president, I thought, would hardly leave you a lot of time to get better at golf. He explained that it wasn't that he played so much, but that every time he did play, he played with one of the great players. "When you play with great players, your game gets better," he said. A mutual friend confirms that this is what has happened for Hillary: "There is no book, no course, no job that could teach what she knows," he says, describing the obvious but true benefits of living history at Bill Clinton's side for eight years. If you think of the Clinton administration as John Harris portrays it in *The Survivor*—as a course in being president—then the person who reaches the end could only go on to be a good president.

And *that*, at the end of the day, is what will prepare her for everything she wants to accomplish.

She really will be the Education President.

I know, they all say that. They all mouth this stuff about how schools are the future, and we need the best human capital. And then you check the figures on math and science scores, and everybody says *Oh, no*. But then nothing improves; depending upon where you live, things may stay the same or get much worse, or you may get lucky and get your kids into the right private schools and save or borrow enough for college.

But then what? The Republicans have trouble right away, because they are for a smaller federal role in education and low property taxes at the local level, and you can only rant and rave about evolution and sex education for so long. The voucher answer, which worked so well for so long on talk television, doesn't work at all in real life. Forget about the constitutional issues, which I actually think might be manageable. Most of the time, it hasn't gotten that far. For one thing, the one place where public schools still work is the suburbs, where Republicans live, and they don't want vouchers. Vouchers were overwhelmingly voted down in California. In the inner cities, where vouchers should be popular, teachers unions are more powerful, and nonprivate and Catholic alternatives are already bursting at the seams without vouchers. So much for that horse.

Testing and everything that goes with it—no promotion, no graduation, no passing go—has been the big draw for Republicans, along with campaigning against incompetent teachers. The problem for the Republicans is that they won. They got the testing. Everybody agrees: *Let's test.* At best, schools take a little extra time to get the kids ready for the test; some don't even go that far. In any case, it still doesn't work. There are too many kids, and too many of them are failing the tests anyway, and no matter how much you rant about teachers, there just aren't enough of them. Once everyone agrees to measure failure, they have no plan for what comes next. Lower salaries? Mandatory expulsions?

For Democrats, the question always comes around to the teachers unions. You have to understand that teachers formed unions, as opposed to the polite professional associations of old, so they'd get paid as much as janitors, and have protection against the arbitrariness of unfair administrators, which they needed. Ask anyone who organized teachers in the old days, and they'll tell you that in many places it was extremely difficult to convince teachers, who thought of themselves as professionals, to affiliate with a union, and think of themselves in collective terms.

In many cases, the districts have no one to blame but themselves if their hands are tied now. If they had treated teachers better, many of them might not have joined the unions or demanded the kind of protections that now are bones of contention. Individual teachers needed the protection of the union to deal with a system that was often arbitrary—and, for all the nice talk about the important work they do, the pay stank—and in many cases still does.

So what you get is frustration. You get success stories, and smart people coming together to talk about what works, but politicians generally remain paralyzed by a lack of funds and a lack of will. Voters set aside money for education, and budget-strapped legislators fight with teachers unions about whether to take it away . . .

But Hillary has been at the forefront of this question for years.[3] Here are just some of the positions that make up her policy on education, drawn from her record of public statements:

* She believes in providing schools with funding to recruit teachers and principals, including loan forgiveness programs, especially for high-need school districts and subjects.

* She believes in keeping class sizes small.

* She believes in improving student access to books and advanced technology, and co-sponsored the Improving Literacy Through School Libraries Act, which did just that.

* She introduced the Healthy and High Performance Schools Act of 2001, to create programs to provide grants to states to help districts make schools healthier and more energy-efficient.

* She proposed bills for funding vocational training for adults, an issue she has fought for since her days in Arkansas.

* She has fought to end our nation's teacher shortage. In her words, "This crisis in our classrooms requires a serious, coordinated response. A virtual army of teachers is needed to fill our classrooms. That's why I am working with my colleagues in Congress to tackle the shortage head on. The first step, I believe, is creating a National Teacher Corps. That is why I have introduced the National Teacher and Principal Recruitment Act. Under my bill, we can bring as many as 75,000 new teachers each year into our highest-need school districts and give communities the resources they need to support them."

★ She has also "worked to expand opportunities for women to
enter non-traditional occupations that pay a self-sufficient
wage by requiring states to disaggregate their performance
data to show how women are faring and to take special steps
to prepare women for careers that are traditionally
categorized as 'male' careers."

She's against school vouchers. As the *Women's Quarterly* reported in
2002, "Clinton agrees with the AAUW and the National Organization for Women: She doesn't like [vouchers]. But Clinton is smarter
than NOW and the AAUW. 'Public school choice should be expanded
as broadly as possible,' Clinton insisted. 'There should not be any obstacle to providing single-sex choice within the public school system.' That
is Hillary's key insight."

★ She has also fought to help non-traditional students receive
an education: "These students not only grapple with daily-
life challenges," she says, "but many also are intimidated by
the college experience and afraid to ask for help if they
struggle academically or don't understand something."

★ The first challenge she took on in Arkansas was the schools.
That was nearly thirty years ago. For a Midwestern girl
educated in the northeast to come to Arkansas and take on
one of the worst public school systems in the country, deal
with the issue of teacher competency, understand the
importance of a Democrat standing up to the unions at the
same time as increasing teacher salaries, gives me more
confidence than copying every position paper every Democrat has ever written, or telling me ten times that your
opponent was against the Department of Education, or
voted to deny funding to such and such a bill, or whatever
the Republican case may be . . .

Hillary has had the guts to stand up to her own friends on education.

She cares more about kids than anyone who has ever sat in that chair in the Oval Office. Because she understands the role education plays in their lives.

Hillary will have the best experts in the world working for her, but you don't need them to tell you that there are no three-thousand-kid private schools out there, in which the parents never set foot. Smaller schools, parental involvement, accountability on a per-school basis: When people are paying money, that's what they demand, that's what they get, and it works. The tragedy is not that nothing works, but that we still do nothing for so many kids, even though we know what does. Bureaucracy, ideology, indifference, and inertia—take your pick, it almost doesn't matter. The kids pay.

During her campaign, Hillary will get on school buses, ride with the kids, talk with the parents at the bus stops. She will embrace a political revolution that begins in the school, with education as the fundamental right of kids, participation as the duty of parents, competent teaching as the obligation of the teachers and their union, and accountability for failure from the principal.

I have a friend named Steve Barr, who was one of the cofounders of Rock the Vote, and then worked with me in the Dukakis campaign before he decided that there was a smarter, more productive way to do politics than standing around waiting for candidates who might or might not show up (more on that later). So he turned to education, and used his background as a political organizer to create one of the most successful groups of charter schools in California (the Green Dot schools), as well as a political organization (the Small Schools Alliance) to support reform. Our schools (I serve on his board) have unions, but they exist within each school, and the pay is better than in LA Unified. Parents sign contracts agreeing to volunteer time and supervise their kids. Everybody wears uniforms. None of our schools have more than five hundred kids. All of them send 90 to 95 percent of their graduates to college, though they come from areas where most kids can't read at a ninth-grade level. When we open a new school, Steve gives one speech at a local church or community center and the applications to fill it up come in overnight; then there's a lottery, and a waiting list that lasts forever. Parents want better, but they can't find it. They're looking for someone who understands that they're ready to do their part, given a place to do it. That is as true of the poor inner-city parents as the wealthier suburban mothers.

Hillary will be the first president to have begun her career in public service in educational reform, dealing with one of the poorest systems in America, with teachers as many as half of whom could not have passed a stricter test.

It is her issue to finish. She has the stature and the brain trust to make the necessary moves. She will have the support of the big-city mayors who have to be part of any solution on education, and of the teachers unions, who have to be at the table if the country is to change the way we think about public schools and the role they play in all our lives.

That's not BS, either. I know people who search for places to volunteer when there's a school on the corner. Schools should be the social center of a community. Today, that doesn't exist—not yet. Hillary will call a national summit on education, and out of that will come a commitment to a teacher corps, a commitment to smaller classes and smaller schools, a commitment to accountability for both teachers and administrators, and a new social compact for public education.

Who could argue with that?

If anyone can solve the ongoing health care crisis . . .

Don't take my word for it. Ask Newt Gingrich. He says she's the only one who understands it. She also understands what went wrong last time, and how to get it right this time.

What's amazing, in retrospect, is not that Hillary's efforts to revolutionize health care failed, but that she came as close to passing legislation as she did. She almost moved a mountain. Everything she was accused of—remember the Harry-and-Louise commercials, the couple worrying about losing their doctor, and having all the decisions taken out of their doctors' hands?—all that happened, of course, without HillaryCare, or any government protections. She should have cut a deal when she could; what she could have is, in retrospect, a miracle we didn't see at the time. It turned out that you had to co-opt the private insurers, not try to eliminate them; that the problems of the (mostly) insured and the chronically uninsured are different, substantively and politically; that passing legislation to provide programs for uninsured children was often easier than getting their parents to apply for it.

I don't think there is anyone who has spent more time thinking about what went wrong and why, and how to right it, than Hillary.

It was the first time she, personally, out front, hit the wall head on.

She had asked for what she wanted, did it her way, went way out front, took control, led the charge, and failed royally.

Most people go through that at a young age, and get used to it. It's not easy when you go through it the first time in your forties, on national television, on every network, and even if you try, you can't really blame anyone else.

Hillary blew it on health care. She did the public part brilliantly—the congressional testimony, the television appearances, all of that. Had the people who worked for her done as well, she would have solved the most difficult and intractable problem in the American economy.

But it isn't right to place the blame on the people around her. It was hers; she chose whom to listen to and whom to ignore. Ultimately, one of the big steps in her road to political maturity has been accepting responsibility for the failure of health care, and moving on.

But you only move so far. You don't stop caring about the problem just because you failed to solve it on the first go-round.

Hillary Clinton not only knows how to deal with the health care crisis, understands it better than anyone on the planet; she is the one person running for president with an enormous piece of unfinished business that requires her to succeed in the area where she has suffered her biggest defeat.

All the best parts of her ambition demand that she fix this one, that her legacy include the last chapter. Would you bet against it? I wouldn't. She has a great deal to prove on health care, and like her or not, you know I'm right when I say that she will prove it.

She even has a sense of humor about it. Here is Hillary on Health Care:

I know what you're thinking.[4] Hillary Clinton and health care? Been there. Didn't do that!

The failure of government to help contain health costs for employers has led to a fraying of the implicit social contract in which a good job came with affordable coverage.

As a whole, our ailing health care system is plagued with underuse, overuse and misuse. In a fundamental way, we pay far more for less than citizens in other advanced economies get.

There is no "one size fits all" solution to our health care problems, but there are common-sense solutions that call for aggressive, creative, and effective strategies as bold in their approach as they are practical in their effect.

First, the way we deliver health care must change. For too long our model of health care delivery has been based on the provider, the payer, anyone but the patient. Think about the fact that our medical records are still owned by a physician or a hospital, in bits and pieces, with no reasonable way to connect the dots of our conditions and our care over the years.

We should adopt the model of a "personal health record" controlled by the patient, who could use it not only to access the latest reliable health information on the Internet, but also to record weight and blood sugar and to receive daily reminders to take asthma or cholesterol medication. Moreover, our current system revolves around "cases" rather than patients. Reimbursements are based on "episodes of treatment" rather than on a broader consideration of a patient's well-being. Thus it rewards the treatment of discrete diseases and injuries rather than keeping the patient alive and healthy.

Our system rewards clinicians for providing more services, but not for keeping patients healthier. The structure of the health care system should shift toward rewarding doctors and health plans that treat patients with their long-term health needs in mind and rewarding patients who make sensible decisions about maintaining their own health.

I strongly believe that savings from information technology should not just be diffused throughout the system, never to be recaptured, but should be used to make substantial progress toward real universal coverage. By better using technology, we can lower health care costs throughout the system and thereby lower the exorbitant premiums that are placing a financial squeeze on businesses, individuals, and the government. At the same time, some of those savings should be used to make substantial progress toward real universal coverage. (I may have just lost Newt Gingrich.)

Our neglect of public health also contributes to spiraling health costs . . . Public health programs can help stop preventable disease and control dangerous behaviors . . . It comes down to individual responsibility reinforced by national policy. The public health system also needs to be brought up to date. The current public health tools were developed when the major threats to health were infectious diseases like malaria and tuberculosis. . . .

We need to be concerned not just about pathogens but also about carcinogens. Over the last three years, I have introduced legislation to increase investment in tracking and correlating environmental and health conditions.

We should also be looking at sprawl—talking about the way we design our neighborhoods and schools and about our shrinking supply of safe, usable outdoor space—and how that contributes to asthma, stress, and obesity. We should follow the example of the European Union and start testing the chemicals we use every day and not wait until we have a rash of birth defects or cancers on our hands before taking action. And we should look at factors in our society that lead to youth violence, substance abuse, depression, and suicide and ultimately require insurance and treatment for mental health.

Finally, as a society, we need greater emphasis on preventive care, an investment in people and their health that saves us money, because when families can't get preventive care, they often end up in the emergency room—getting the most expensive care possible.

All that we have learned in the last decade confirms that our goal should continue to be what every other industrialized nation has achieved—health care that's always there for every citizen.

It will, as I have been known to say, take the whole village to finance an affordable and accountable health system. Employers and individuals would share in its financing, and individuals would have to assume more responsibility for improving their own health and lifestyles. Private insurers and public programs would work together, playing complementary roles in ensuring that all Americans have the health care they need.

Insurance should be about sharing risk and responsibility—pooling resources and risk to protect ourselves from the devastating cost of illness or injury. It should not be about further dividing us. Competition should reward health plans for quality and cost savings, not for how many bad risks they can exclude—especially as we enter the genomic age, when all of us could have uninsurable risks written into our genes.

So achieving comprehensive health care reform is no simple feat, as I learned a decade ago. None of these ideas mean anything if the political will to ensure that they happen doesn't exist. . . .

As someone who tried to promote comprehensive health care reform a decade ago and decided to push for incremental changes in the years since, I still believe America needs sensible, wide-ranging reform that leads to quality health care coverage available to all Americans at an affordable cost. The present system is unsustainable.

Anyone who's a part of the American health care system knows that she's right about that. And anyone who's tracked her actions on health care since she became a senator knows that she's taking it on the right way—with passion, yes, but also discipline and maturity.

She will bring the best people to government.

George W. Bush did not promise to bring the best people to government. Why? Because, in his worldview, the best people don't really *belong* in government. It's just not the most important place, not the spot where the most vital work gets done. That would be the private sector. So why would you want the most talented people in government? You need them where things really count—making money.

I'm not being facetious. Think about it: If you believe, as conservatives do, that the private sector is more important than the public; that government should take less, do less, decide less; that it is full of inefficient people who want to take your money but don't know how to spend it, whose only approach to problem-solving is to throw money at problems and at unions, and to waste and abuse their big budgets (except for the military)—if you believe all this, then why would you want to fill it with all your best people?

Hillary Clinton has always understood the importance of government. She has always believed in public service. She was part of the generation where, as one person put it, "the smart people went to law school, and the dumb ones like George W. went to Harvard Business School . . . which explains everything." Well, maybe not everything.

Political science was the most popular major at Wellesley, in Hillary's day and in mine. Taking law boards and going to law school was the most popular post-graduate pursuit. Washington was the place for a generation raised on the possibility that government could change a century of discrimination by enforcing the rule of law, that participation by citizens could shape the foreign policy of a nation. That generation is already middle-aged, facing retirement. It's last-hurrah time. The best and the brightest of the baby boom aren't babies anymore; they know it's now or never. Hillary is "the bridge for the baby boom," my friend Doug Wilson put it, "the bridge that connects the baby boom to the next generation." She is also their last chance to get it right, to prove that government can make the positive difference, albeit in ways different from what we might once have expected.

The morning after I wrote this, the *Boston Globe*, faithful chronicler of baby boom angst, carried an article reporting the latest trend: boomers starting second careers in public service, seeking to recapture that lost spirit of doing something "more" after retiring from successful private sector careers.[5] Why not make it a national spirit that bridges generations, by electing a president who embodies the trend?

I hoped that 9/11 might inspire a new commitment to public service and a new belief in the importance of government—the sense that we're all in this together, and if we don't get the fundamental stuff right, nothing else matters. Alas, I teach young people today, and I can tell you this: Political science is not their favorite major, law school is not their most popular graduate training, and public service is hardly the choice destination of the smartest students. Not much did change after 9/11; the people in power didn't make the connection between national security and public service, so why should others?

Hillary Clinton can, and she will. Do you doubt that? There really would be people standing in line to work in a government with her at the helm. Of course, in part, that's because her party has been out of power for eight years. But it's also because this would be seen as a time to do something, to make some change happen.

There would be a new spirit of environmentalism at the EPA, a fresh sense of opportunity.

There would be a new sense of possibility at the Department of Education; at OSHA, which regulates workplace safety and health; at the Labor Department; the Food and Drug Administration; Health and Human Services; the National Institutes of Health.

Is there a difference between working in the Interior Department for Robert Kennedy Jr., as opposed to a guy who used to be a lobbyist for a mining company?

Is there a difference between the vision of Marian Wright Edelman and a businessman trying to cut entitlements?

If Christine Todd Whitman, the former governor of New Jersey, couldn't make it in this administration, and Paul O'Neill, the former treasury secretary, was ostracized for honesty, consider the difference between those who have been accepted and the people who will come with Hillary—people like Madeleine Albright, Joe Biden, Maggie Williams, her former chief of staff. I'll take Richard Holbrooke any day over the warmongers who got us into this mess without ever thinking about the peace, thank you.

She will take on the Right, and bring back family values.

People keep asking: Where is the liberal side of the Christian church? The answer is Hillary Clinton. I don't want to antagonize anyone, but the Reagans were not churchgoers. Hillary really prays. She and Bill met at Yale, but unlike so many of their friends there, they were not part of the East Coast liberal Jewish intelligentsia. She is, at her core, not a wild lesbian—what a joke, Ed Klein!—but a Methodist, a Stone-Davis girl, a Midwesterner; she IS square, and it's real, thank God. She does pray every day, she does stay in touch with her high school minister, she never left the church, it has always been part of who she was, she was never wild and crazy, she only had a few boyfriends.

The reasons the right hates her have very little to do with her.

There is a stunning gap between the icon of Hillary Clinton and the reality of a slightly dumpy middle-class (even if she is now rich) married woman, who has made her peace with a long marriage, raised an adult daughter she is incredibly proud of, and deals with an aging mother who still gets to her.

The icon you know—that beyond-ambitious, ruthless, stopping at nothing, craven, money hungry, power mad, immoral woman of Dick Morris's nightmares—is a figment.

The real woman is someone you're more likely to find upstate somewhere, in a basic black pant suit—not Armani, which wouldn't be cut for her anyway. She is more comfortable there than she is with some of the high rollers and fancy ladies who call themselves her "friends."

She's really "Midwestern," says one old friend, trying to think of a way to describe her appeal. That's the secret. She's upstate, which is why people will relate to her in Florida and Ohio. She's conservative in all kinds of Midwestern ways, including style and taste. She brought Kaki Hockersmith, her Arkansas decorator, with her to the White House, and the fancy ladies from New York and Los Angeles guffawed; the rooms looked like Cleveland, someone once told me. Indeed. That's good. She also used the White House chapel frequently to pray.

The ironic message of all this: The right is hating the wrong person. They should see Hillary as an affirmative opportunity, just as the Democrats do.

Taking back family values is more than a rhetorical challenge. You have to be pretty comfortable with your own faith, to take it to the Right for their abuse of religion and faith to hurt people, for turning the words of the Bible into the sword that has hurt teenage girls who have been raped, and punished gay and lesbian teenagers for feelings they can't help.

Take just one example:

The latest way to frame the abortion issue is to say of Hillary that she's against parental consent. How ridiculous. Who could be against the principle of parental consent? Certainly not a mother who raised a daughter. In most cases the best thing for a young girl is to tell her parents, and that is the goal of having laws about parental consent. No one is against that.

But surely you cannot do without an exception for girls who have been raped or abused by one of their parents—which unfortunately happens more often than people would like to think—or girls whose parents are likely to abuse or hurt them if they should reveal what happened to them. In other words, exceptions for cases where it would be dangerous for the girl to tell her parents. As a matter of fact, you have to have such exceptions—or the bill isn't constitutional.

But the political right has no interest in passing constitutional bills. So instead of building in such exceptions—or, better yet, leaving it to doctors and hospitals to set up their own procedures, the way they do for every other procedure they perform on minors, where parental consent is also required—the right insists on unconstitutional bills. They prefer laws with no exceptions. They make up procedures that don't even exist, like "partial birth abortion," which isn't a medical procedure but the invention of a Congressional staffer, and they say *Let's ban it,* and not even provide an exception. So what if doctors become afraid to perform lifesaving procedures on women in late-term pregnancies, even where the fetus has died?

Do you think the right is working to create alternatives for teenage girls? Do you think they're focusing on protecting teenagers from unwanted pregnancies? I respect the individuals who disagree with us on moral grounds. But the political leadership of the right in this country is about politics, about tallying up who's with who, and showing off for the stands, and putting people up to votes that will make them look bad back home, not reducing the number of abortions. They'd rather pass unconstitutional show off bills than help anybody.

In Florida, the state literally went to court to claim that a thirteen-year-old who had been the victim of statutory rape while living in a state orphanage was not mature enough to make the decision to have an abortion and should therefore be required to become a mother.[6] Read that again: Not mature enough to make the decision to have an abortion, so she should have a child instead . . .

The judge ordered a delay to perform further psychological evaluation of the girl.

Under state policy, the state is barred from consenting to an abortion, so unless the girl was declared to be a mature minor and exempt from the consent law, she would not be allowed to have an abortion.

By the time the judge issued the order allowing her to have an abortion, she was in her second trimester.

That happens all the time, advocates report. Why not make abortion more traumatic for the girls? More expensive? Higher risk of complications? That'll make the decision a lot easier, won't it?

Most of the time, we Democrats just defend our position on parental consent, instead of going on the attack on the cynical use of the most vulnerable among us to score political points. Maybe it's time for that to stop.

Try this one for size: The House passed a bill that would punish anyone who takes a girl across state lines to get an abortion without the consent of both parents.[7] No exceptions for a grandparent or a minister—those were proposed and rejected. No exceptions for victims of rape or incest. No exceptions for states like North Dakota or Oklahoma, where you can't find a doctor who will perform a legal abortion, *Roe v. Wade* or not.

What are we doing?

In Whose name?

Remind people of what was done in the name of Terri Schiavo, whose husband was investigated even after an autopsy affirmed him on every score—except the one that tallies points for the religious right. How else to explain Jeb Bush's order to keep investigating? What year will it all wrap up—2008? 2012?

How can these people exploit tragedy for political gain?

Where is the concern for life and dignity?

Shame on George Bush for flying back from vacation to score

points over a woman's dead body. A president should be better than that.

Here is the sad part: Nominate Hillary Clinton, and we will mobilize the religious right.

Amy Sullivan isn't the only one who would shrink from this threat. In a much-quoted column in *Time*, Joe Klein argued that Hillary shouldn't even run because there are so many haters out there and they won't go away.[8] Surrender without a fight, he said.

But there is a better way. Flush them out, isolate them, take them on. Let decent people see them for what they are, and show them that the other side is not what they've been told it is.

The real way to deal with Hillary hatred is for the woman herself to stand up to it. She is better positioned than anyone else in the country to bring us past the simple-minded hatemongering and show us that we're all closer on the issues than we think we are.

Most people are against abortion; who wouldn't be? Most people are also against the government making private decisions about our own lives. The balance struck by the Supreme Court in *Roe v. Wade*—a balance based on the stage of the pregnancy, as well as the health of the mother—is the one that determines whether a doctor will perform the procedure, and under what regulations. Most people favor parental consent, until you ask them if the victims of parental rape or beatings should have to tell their parents. Then they realize the importance of exceptions. When Hillary Clinton runs for president, she should do so with the support of a new Christian Coalition—a generous and inclusive one, based on an inclusive Judeo-Christian morality that restores family values without punishing those who are different.

John Danforth is a conservative Republican, as well as a former Republican senator and an Episcopal minister.[9] He recently wrote:

> Many conservative Christians approach politics with a certainty that they know God's truth, and that they can advance the kingdom of God through governmental action.
>
> Moderate Christians are less certain about when and how our beliefs

can be translated into statutory form, not because of a lack of faith in God but because of a healthy acknowledgment of the limitations of human beings. Like conservative Christians, we attend church, read the Bible and say our prayers.

But for us, the only absolute standard of behavior is the commandment to love our neighbors as ourselves. Repeatedly in the Gospels, we find that the Love Commandment takes precedence when it conflicts with laws. We struggle to follow that commandment as we face the realities of everyday living, and we do not agree that our responsibility to live as Christians can be codified by legislators.

Clearly there's more to the Christian electorate than Senators Frist and Santorum.

Imagine how powerful that could be, if she can tap into it.

She will get (more—and better) things done.

Hillary is in her prime. Her colleagues in the Senate love her. With the exception of her brief time at Yale, it is the first time in her life that she has been in a place where the men around her enjoy and respect her and even flirt with her. This is part of maturity, too.

Hillary understands something very fundamental that most people on the left don't (Howard Dean, for instance). If you're going to govern effectively in this country, you have to do it from the middle; you may on occasion be able to win an election coming from one side, as Reagan did, but you must get hold of the center if you're going to make things happen. Ultimately, you have to be the embodiment of the majority.

Hillary gets this. And she's working with Republicans because she wants to be the one to break the partisan logjam.

She will "forgive her transgressors," or his, for impeachment, and start a new day for America in her inauguration. She's already started to do that explicitly, reaching out in particular to some of those who prosecuted her husband to co-sponsor legislation. Hillary and Lindsay Graham? Of course. It's exactly what people want: they hate all the fighting. They want politicians to work together. Besides, if that doesn't say "maturity," what does?

Hillary will put a couple of her Republican Senate friends in her Cabinet and her White House. She will build a fusion team. She will do it differently from the way Bill did—her way, reaching out to Republicans from day one, showing the country and the world a different way of governing. It wouldn't even surprise me if she put another respected senator on the ticket, emphasizing experience, and the ability to work with Republicans and get things done.

She will build a nationwide coalition by starting one in her own Washington backyard.

She is tough enough to restore America's place in the world and fight terrorism without having to start a war to prove it.

Hillary has probably seen more of the world than anyone who has ever assumed the office of the presidency. She knows what it used to be like to be an American in this world, and what it's like now; and how much more dangerous it has become.

America, are you safer today than you were four years ago?

She will bring back Madeleine Albright. Biden and Holbrooke will duke it out for the key positions. The world should be big enough for all of them.

She will send Bill to the Middle East. That should keep him out of trouble.

And she will continue to set a tone of peace, cooperation, and human rights throughout the world, as she has been doing for almost two decades:

> Israel is our strongest ally in the Middle East.[10] Now, more than ever, all
> democratic nations must stand behind Israel as it fights against terrorism
> and for the principles all democracies share. Democratic nations through-

out the world must understand that turning their backs on Israel at this time would hurt all freedom loving nations.

—SENATOR HILLARY CLINTON,
Letter to Colin Powell, April 9, 2002

Events in the Middle East are absolutely critical to our hope for a safer, more secure world, a world in which every nation is free from the threat of global terrorism.[11] And a strong, lasting relationship between the United States and Israel is essential to our efforts to build that world of peace and security.

Now, Israel is not only, however, a friend and ally for us, it is a beacon of what democracy can and should mean.

First, no matter what one thinks about events that have unfolded in Iraq, there is no doubt that the American military has performed admirably, with professionalism, and that every young man and woman who wears the uniform of our country deserves our support, whether they be active duty, guard, or reserve troop.

I believe it is our obligation as friends and supporters and allies of Israel to support Israel's efforts for peace, stability and security. Now, this means doing more than providing Israel with economic aid so that it can remain strong in the face of ongoing threats. We must also demand that President Abbas dismantle the structures of terror that the Palestinian leadership has employed for so long.

And of course, one of the areas I am deeply concerned about is Iran, and its pursuit of nuclear weapons, because a nuclear-armed Iran would shake the foundation of global security to its very core.

So let us be unequivocally clear. A nuclear-armed Iran is unacceptable, but it is not just unacceptable to Israel and to the United States. It must be unacceptable to the entire world, starting with the European governments and people.

—SENATOR HILLARY CLINTON,
*American Israel Public
Affairs Committee Policy Conference, May 24, 2005*

She will restore respect for the United Nations:

My first observation is simple but it must govern all that we do: The United Nations is an indispensable organization to all of us—despite its flaws and inefficiencies.[12] This means quite simply, that everyone here today, and governments everywhere, must decide that our global interests are best served by strengthening the U.N., by reforming it, by cleaning up its obvious bureaucratic and managerial shortcomings, and by improving its responsiveness to crises, from humanitarian to political.

My second point is equally simple, but directed primarily at my own nation: The U.S. benefits from a stronger, more effective U.N. As the founding nation, the host nation, and the largest contributor, the United States has far more to gain than to lose by insisting on reform, transparency, and performance. In the humanitarian and peacekeeping fields, we pay roughly one quarter of the overall costs, and we pay 22 percent of the regular budget. Thus, if the U.N. is effective, our investment is highly leveraged. If it is weak, our money—along with yours—is worth less, and more of the burden will fall directly on us, the richer nations represented here today. Thus, I fully support the Secretary General's reform efforts, and urge him to do even more.

I have elsewhere deplored people in my own nation who have sought to weaken, undermine and underfund the U.N. There are many in the U.S. who feel the U.N. is too strong, but the truth is quite the opposite: It is far too weak to serve the great causes that are its calling: fighting poverty, conflicts and disease, and promoting equal human rights for all.

In the post-Cold War world, NATO, and other multi-national military forces, can and should play important roles in peacekeeping operations in support of U.N. mandates.

For me, the first lesson is [that] the U.N. Security Council must meet its obligations. It did not do so, for example, in Rwanda. The second is that it cannot succeed through the old, failed system of slowly assembling peacekeeping forces from around the world. These are often weak, poorly equipped, and poorly led. This is where NATO—the best peacetime military alliance in history—can play a role.

I am not advocating that NATO do all things in all places, but we should learn from the past and keep an open mind on future NATO assignments in implementation of Security Council mandates.

—SENATOR HILLARY CLINTON,
Munich Conference on Security Policy,
February 13, 2005

She brings America back into the world community.

We stand at a point in time where we are now in the process of redefining both American internationalism and American interests.[13] That probably would have been inevitable, because the process of adjusting to the changes at the end of the Cold War, the extraordinary advances in technology and globalization, the spread of so many problems globally, most prominently terrorism, would certainly have brought that about. But it is also true that given our reaction to the events of September the 11th and to our missions in Afghanistan and Iraq and other problems that we face around the world . . .

For more than a half a century, we know that we prospered because of a bipartisan consensus on defense and foreign policy. We must do more than return to that sensible, cooperative approach. I think we should be in the midst of working to reform the institutions and alliances that we historically have been part of, revamping agreements that we reached in the past that may no longer be as timely and effective as we would hope, working and examining relationships around the world not because it's a good thing to do, not because it worked in the 20th century, but because it remains as essential today as it was in the past in order to meet the 21st [century] challenges of terror and the proliferation of weapons of mass destruction. We obviously need to build a world with more friends and fewer terrorists.

—SENATOR HILLARY CLINTON,
Council on Foreign Relations, December 15, 2003

Her vote to give President Bush authority to go to war gives her the ability to criticize how it has been waged. That's how politics works. She is a member of the Senate Armed Services Committee. She has been an unequivocally strong supporter of the troops. No voting for and against for Hillary. Only hawks can criticize wars.

> I was one who supported giving President Bush the authority, if necessary, to use force against Saddam Hussein.[14] I believe that that was the right vote. I have had many disputes and disagreements with the administration over how that authority has been used, but I stand by the vote to provide the authority because I think it was a necessary step in order to maximize the outcome that did occur in the Security Council with the unanimous vote to send in inspectors.

> —SENATOR HILLARY CLINTON,
> *Council on Foreign Relations, December 15, 2003*

What she didn't sign up for was bad intelligence, no plan for peace, and Gitmo. She didn't sign up to make Americans pariahs in the world community.

> We need a tough-minded, muscular foreign and defense policy, one that not only respects our allies and seeks new friends as it strikes at known enemies, but which is understood and supported by the majority of the American people.[15] The consequences of unilateralism, isolationism and overtly expressed preemptive defense, I think, are severe. We will end up with fewer nations, fewer intelligence services and fewer law enforcement personnel internationally helping to protect us against attacks, fewer nations helping to counterattack when we are struck, and less leverage in advancing democracy, freedom, open markets and other values that we believe elevate the people of the world even as they protect our people here at home.

This is not to propound some golden rule of international affairs, be-cause I think it's rooted in the intelligence and the success of the 20th century. The more we throw our weight around, the more we encourage other nations to join with each other as a counterweight. We have a lot of problems besides Iraq and Afghanistan on the horizon. The number one problem remains the spread of weapons of mass destruction and those falling into the hands of either rogue nations or borderless terrorists.

—SENATOR HILLARY CLINTON,
Council on Foreign Relations, December 15, 2003

And, oh yes, she changes the lives of women and girls around the world, like no president of the United States ever before . . .

Ten years ago, women from one hundred and eighty-nine countries came together in Beijing.[16] Some of you were there. Some of you were still in school. Some of you watched from afar. It was a gathering that lasted only a few days, but it changed the world. Women of all colors and races, eth-nicities, languages, religions, knew that although there were differences among us, what we shared in common was so much greater.

And in Beijing, after years, decades, indeed centuries . . . we broke our silence. Together we spoke up. And we spoke out.

And we did so not just for ourselves, but on behalf of all women. And our daughters, our mothers, and our sisters. Women who were un-derpaid, under-educated, undervalued. Women who were deprived of the right to go to school, earn a living, see a doctor, own property, get a loan, cast a vote, run for office. Women who were persecuted, abused, violated, even killed—because there were no laws to protect them or no enforce-ment of the laws that were on the books.

Although there were many who doubted that a United Nations con-ference on women could have an impact, or should have an impact, what transpired in Beijing was the beginning of a global movement—a global movement focusing attention on the issues that matter most in our lives: access to education and health care, jobs and credit, the opportunity to enjoy the full range of political, legal, and human rights.

We called on governments around the world to promote and protect women's rights unequivocally . . . and to act on the ideal that "women's rights" are human rights and human rights are women's rights.

We made our case—that global progress depends on the progress of women and girls. That democratic institutions cannot thrive and survive without the participation of women. That market economies cannot grow and prosper without the inclusion of women. That societies are not truly free and just without legal protections and rights for women. That a nation cannot advance into the 21st century, into the Information Age, without educated, literate women.

As we made this case, there were the naysayers. There were the critics. Those who do not believe that women are equal or that women are entitled to the full range of rights available to them. I remember coming back from Beijing and appearing on a radio program that was broadcast by the Voice of America, and it was a call-in program. So after talking about the conference, I got a call from a man in the Middle East who asked me, What on earth did I mean that women's rights were human rights. And I said, "Well, sir, if you would for a moment, shut your eyes and imagine all the rights that you, as a man, take for granted. We want the same rights." And there was a pause. And he said, "That's impossible!" Well, it is not only not impossible, it must be made possible and real.

I believe we have learned that our nation, the United States, any nation, and the world as a whole cannot be secure or at peace if women are denied the right to fulfill their God-given potential.

It is unfair for governments and people in developed countries who have access to the full range of reproductive and family health services to deny those to women in other countries around the world. When women and girls are healthy, we all benefit from lower rates of maternal and child mortality, improved public health, a decline in unwanted and uncontrolled population growth, a more productive work force and more stable families.

—SENATOR HILLARY CLINTON,
Vital Voices Global Partnership

and NYU's Center for Global Affairs Public Forum:

Women's Rights are Human Rights, March 6, 2005

And what else?

She will protect gay rights,
help the cities,
protect the rights of unionized workers,
preserve the environment,
strictly enforce health and safety laws,
provide greater opportunities to small business, especially those
    owned by minorities and women,
cut gas prices,
enforce laws protecting Americans with disabilities,
reduce the deficit.

This is why I eventually got out of the platform-writing business. I kept waking up in the middle of the night thinking of things. Like stricter regulation of airline safety. And food safety. Increased medical research. Poverty and hunger. Did someone say Family Farms? Agriculture? Dairy for Wisconsin?

This is why Hillary Clinton got into public service. Because she stays up at night thinking of them, too. And she will make them happen.

7.

MOMENTS OF TRUTH

★

Presidential politics is amazing. You can spend hundreds of millions of dollars and it doesn't necessarily matter. Or it can matter, but only to a point. Once upon a time—before "spin" was a word everyone knew—it was how we played the game. Then came the word, and then came the "spin room," and now it's just a joke, no longer even worth the trouble. There's so much attention, so much focus and coverage, that I believe the voters just figure things out for themselves. I have never seen a campaign that did not, at some point, in an important way, reveal the man at the center of it.

How does someone win? George W. won because Kerry played his hand wrong (Vietnam vet), and Rove handled his voter lists brilliantly—so that, even though he lost all three debates, in the midst of an increasingly unpopular war, Bush still won Ohio.

Not exactly something you could have predicted three years in advance—I don't care how smart you are. So that kind of prediction I'm not even going to attempt.

But clearly that's not stopping everyone else from trying. Every morning, I wake up to read some new prediction about 2008. So far, they all seem to have Hillary carrying the day on the Democratic side. So far, so good. But the Republican side changes, and how we get there changes, and anyone who thinks they can predict an outcome three years out is frankly nuts.

What is involved is both art and science: a combination of taking the measure of the candidate, and the arithmetic of the Electoral College. The measure of the candidate isn't simply a creation of his—or her—handlers. Amid all the glossy sugarcoating of scripted messages and well-produced TV ads, every presidential campaign offers the public a few windows of direct access, where we get to see the candidate firsthand. The early debates in the race for each nomination, and those telling moments in each debate where some candidates reveal their inexperience and others show promising command. The decisions about what a candidate's message is going to be—the moment when John Kerry decides to run on Vietnam, or Al Gore decides not to run on Bill Clinton's record. The gaffes, minor (John Kerry windsailing in blue trunks, Bob Dole falling off the platform) or major (the Muskie tear, the Dean scream). The conventions, the nomination acceptance speeches, then the debates, which show us two candidates (or three), alone on stage, forced to think on their feet. Traditionally, debates can give us make-or-break moments that can shape the closing days of the campaign: Nixon's sweaty jowls, Reagan's "Are you better off now?", Dukakis's perceived frostiness when confronted with the idea of his wife's rape and murder. (Then again, they aren't foolproof: See again George W. Bush's three debates in 2004.)

A week before the 2000 Democratic National Convention, I talked to President Clinton. It was a strange conversation. I was on my way downtown to meet a friend of mine who was running the convention. He told me to tell her I had this great idea, but to make sure I told her it was *my* idea.

We were talking about his convention speech, which was scheduled for Monday night. He told me he was going to make the case for what he and Al Gore had done for the economy over the last eight years, and for staying the course. Then, the next morning, he was scheduled to get up at five A.M., fly to some football field in Michigan, and pass the gauntlet to Gore in front of a hundred people or so . . .

He had a better idea.

Three quarters of the way through his speech—just as he was saying, *If you want to keep growing on this path of economic recovery and surpluses and growth, the way to do it is to elect Al Gore*—the backstage camera would show, to the audience's amazement, Al Gore himself walking toward the podium . . .

The hall would go wild, as Gore joined Clinton on the podium.

And Clinton would pass the gauntlet to him in person—in front of one hundred million people on television, instead of one hundred people on some football field.

I thought it was a great idea. This was supposed to be *my* idea?

I'd do it if I were him, the president said.

I ran downtown, idea in tow . . . and came face to face with a brick wall. *Gore has a fundraiser that day in St. Louis,* my friend said.

I rolled my eyes. *Reschedule it,* I said.

There isn't a hotel that can accommodate them in LA on Monday night, she said. *They have to wait until Clinton's out of town.*

I rolled my eyes again. She and I both know how to do this. Gore wouldn't have to overnight at the convention. Send him on to Phoenix, then San Francisco. Bring him back Wednesday.

You've been talking to Him, right? She said.

Right.

Gore won't do it, she told me. *We heard the same thing yesterday—but then it was Terry McAuliffe's idea. Gore's afraid Clinton will upstage him. Take up all the space.*

That was the problem: Running for president is a test of size, and ultimately Gore wasn't sure he was big enough. His turning down Clinton's offer was another of those moments of decision that reveal the man—and determine the fate of a candidacy. Sometimes you can predict them, and plan for them, and do everything you can, and they happen anyway. They just spring up on you, like a surprise quiz.

I used to get asked all the time if I was the adviser who put Dukakis in the tank with the helmet on, and I never knew what to say. The literal truth was that I didn't, not at all. He was in that tank in the first place because folks like Georgia's then-senator Sam Nunn thought he had to prove himself to conservatives who thought he wasn't strong enough on defense. And yet Mike Dukakis didn't really share their views on defense policy, and somehow the photo op just highlighted that: When he put on that helmet, it looked like a silly hat. Had he gone to a hospital or a school—the kind of place he cared about, where he very much belonged—I really believe that he could almost have put on a *nurse's* hat and there would have been no negative blowback. But a picture that captures a candidate's real weakness is worth more than a thousand words.

Dukakis was just that kind of man: His internal compass was calibrated to matters of policy, not politics. A year before, as Madeleine Albright and I were with him preparing for a debate in New Hampshire, I told him that if he got a left-field question on defense he should just say, "I'll spend what it takes to keep America secure." Dukakis nearly bit my head off; making that kind of unlimited commitment would be financially irresponsible, he shot back. Madeleine just looked at me in shock: Defending the country at all costs—what kind of crazy person *wouldn't* feel comfortable saying something like that? I could see the look in her eye: *What the heck was I getting her into this time?*

Sometimes you see the collision coming, but you just can't get out of the way. That's what happened with that rape-and-murder question in Dukakis's second debate. Did we know it was coming? Of course we did, in one form or another. Bill Clinton had rehearsed an answer for it, brilliantly, but it was a Clinton answer, not a Dukakis answer. Dukakis's furlough program had already made the first-degree murderer and rapist Willie Horton a near-household name, thanks to Bush's hired gun Lee Atwater.[1]

We had plenty of reason to be prepared for the rape-and-murder question; in many ways, we'd been preparing since Horton's story made tabloid headlines in Boston. I am the person who put Dukakis in the back seat of a police car when he was running for reelection as governor. By the time I worked for him, I'd been teaching criminal law for eight years, was tenured at Harvard, and had written two books about how the criminal justice system worked. All of us on his presidential campaign—Tom Kiley, Tubby Harrison, Kirk O'Donnell, Jack Corrigan, Leslie Dach, Scott Miller—worried about Willie Horton, and crime, and values constantly. And did I mention that Willie Horton was black and the woman he raped was white, thus playing out one of the oldest and ugliest symbols of racism in our history? (For too many years in America, that was a crime for which even innocence was often no defense.)

We wanted him to talk about his experience as a victim of crime in his acceptance speech at the Democratic convention—but he wouldn't do it. (Olympia Dukakis did, but it wasn't as effective as hearing it first-hand.) We wanted him to lead the pledge of allegiance at the convention, as a way of inoculating himself against Bush's ludicrous *Don't burn the flag* campaign. He wouldn't do it. We wanted him to do politics, of the sort most people thought was necessary, and he said no. He had a different vision, of a positive campaign; he didn't think the mudslinging would work, and he didn't like it.

Sixteen years later, people still stop me—sometimes in anger—and say, "Why didn't you fight back?"

Here's the other part of the answer: Michael didn't want to talk about crime in his acceptance speech because he didn't think his furlough policy was wrong, and he thought the Willie Horton issue was about furloughs. You could talk to him about values issues until you were blue in the face, and he just couldn't see it that way. Clinton wanted him to apologize for the furlough program, and he didn't buy that. He wanted us to do an ad about someone who was out on the *federal* furlough program and killed somebody, just to point out that Bush's government was running the same risks in its furloughs that he was in Massachusetts. We ran the ad—I had to call the victim's mother to warn her about seeing the body on television—but it didn't make a difference, because George Bush, who supported the death penalty, wasn't vulnerable on the issue of toughness on crime.

I disagreed with Dukakis. So did most Americans. Fair enough. He was the candidate. But that wasn't the only time we ran into vision problems.

At the end of the primaries, we were up ten points. Things were going well: We'd picked the right running mate. We pulled off the convention. And then our candidate stopped his campaign cold. He turned the airplane around on the second day of what was supposed to be at least a week-long post-convention trip, stranding advance people in cities all over the country. One of my friends still reminds me of it every time I see him. I'd just made it back to Los Angeles, to sleep for the first time since October, when I got the call that they were heading to Boston. I tried to get on the phone with Mike himself, but he wouldn't take the call. I took the redeye back to Boston to make a personal appeal. But by then he'd decided he needed to go back to running Massachusetts, and he wouldn't talk to us until after 5:00 P.M., at the earliest. Instead, he spent his time interviewing judges, working on the budget.

What to do? I let the word out that a crisis had forced us back to Boston. (True enough, though not the kind of crisis most people would have imagined.) People demanded to see him. I put them off. I sat with our communications director Kirk O'Donnell, one of the finest human beings I've been privileged to work with, and agonized: We had nothing to communicate. Dukakis had decided that we'd already taken too much time away from his governorship for the campaign, and now he was taking back the "State House time" he felt we owed him. I started calling people in Washington—Paul Kirk, the party chair, and Ron Brown, who later held that job—and asked for help. We couldn't do ads or hire people without his approval. All we could do was muddle along, trying to make the best of an impossible situation. The national press accompanied him to state events, where he made mistakes, while we sat in Boston and fumed.

But we couldn't fool everybody. James Baker, President Bush's top man, told me in confidence that I was being too loyal, taking too much heat for the candidate; clearly he knew what was going on. So did Evan Thomas of *Newsweek,* who told me the same thing. But I couldn't see what choice I had, so I covered for him. I remember going to Mass General to deal with my stomach, which my nerves had thrown into a state of havoc. Sometimes, to relax, I would pretend I was going up to see him in the middle of the day, and slip over to Filene's Basement instead. When the going gets tough, the tough go shopping.

It wasn't until later—a good fifteen years later, when I was older and wiser—that I finally figured out what I should have done. As soon as I stepped off that redeye the first day, I should have gathered my senior staff and asked them all to join me in quitting. Just like that. We would not lead a losing effort. Too much was at stake. We were ten points up; I was at the top of my game; it was ours for the taking, or the losing. We should have gone right up to the state house—in the middle of his interviewing a judge from Bridgewater, or whatever he thought was so damned important—barged right in, and threatened to quit en masse and go to the press unless he turned the state over to the lieutenant governor and went back on the road. I should have put my staff to work to organize the DNC to replace him if I had to. I could have *made* him get out of that State House and campaign. Literally. And then he might have won.

But I was fifty when I thought of the answer, and it would have taken the fifty-year-old I am now to pull that off, to have the guts to say no to power that way. There were no fifty-year-olds in that campaign.

There was no one who was bigger, or wiser, than the candidate; there was no one who could save him when he needed to be saved. The first George Bush had Jim Baker, as his son did a dozen years later. Bill Clinton had Mickey Kantor. Who did Michael Dukakis have? There was a wonderful man named Paul Brountas, a lawyer and a good friend to the governor—but he wasn't a man whose views on politics could not be ignored, and he wasn't a man Dukakis needed more than Brountas needed him.

Something similar was true of John Kerry. Kerry was big enough, but his lodestar was missing. His old nickname was JFK: Just For Kerry. There was a kind of selfishness that got in the way of his good judgment. I don't mean to suggest that the things he chose were bad for others—just that he took a little too good care of himself. I'd known that for twenty-something years because (this is public knowledge, but not something I was advertising, for obvious reasons) he used to date a friend of mine, and he was a total "scumbag"—strung her along forever; he got elected to the Senate, and then told her it wasn't "fair to his constituents" (a line you don't forget) for her to move with him to D.C. Then he started dating Morgan Fairchild and Catherine Oxenberg. (Well, JFK, we used to say.) This was the kind of behavior that cost him loyalty among his own: When I went to one event and ducked in the back way—saying *I'm one of the senator's old staffers, like everyone else here*—they all knew I was talking about Senator Kennedy. Senator Kerry's old staffers weren't clamoring to see him.

So, at one level, presidential politics is a test of size, and a window on your soul, or some piece of it. When it comes to Hillary, I have no doubt on the matter of size. She is big enough for the job. I ask a Republican I know what one question he would like to see Katie Couric ask Hillary in a debate. He barely pauses before he asks: "What message does it send to young women that you don't seem to care at all about your husband openly having relationships with other women?" (Doesn't that sound just like Katie?) No. Of course, that's the one torch Republicans can't throw; if they try, they'll get burnt.

But are we really scared of it? Will anyone ask it? Does anyone care? Is it a hard question? Why doesn't a sixty-year-old woman care anymore? *After thirty years,* I laugh, *why would she?* How about the serenity prayer: God grant me the serenity to accept the things I cannot change, the courage to change the things I cannot accept, and the wisdom to know the difference. (I know Rush will say they're going to put a doghouse on the White House lawn for Bill if he acts up. Hillary should borrow the line, and make a joke about it: Why didn't I think of that twenty years ago? The second term could've been a whole lot different!)

A grownup like Hillary will know how to get past that quickly.

There are more important things to think about.

★ ★ ★

That is not what I am worried about, this time around.

Here is my question—not for Hillary, but for us.

Is America really ready for a woman president? You know the true answer.

That's the real reason I'm writing this book three years out.

It's the reason the campaign needs to begin now. Let's not kid ourselves.

Not all of us may believe we're ready. But God knows we're overdue.

★ ★ ★

There has been a concerted effort this year to stress how receptive the American public would be to a woman chief executive—a picture that, in all honesty, may be more rosy than realistic.[2]

This is one of those issues that Hillary can't tackle head on, so others have rightly addressed it on her behalf. The support for Hillary to date has been, de facto, premised on the idea that America is ready for a woman president. That's all well and good, but the danger of pretending that the problem doesn't exist, or has mostly gone away, is that people get complacent, that they think this election can be won like any other . . . and you end up with the sort of "politically correct gap" that

Los Angeles mayor Tom Bradley faced in his bid to become governor of California. Bradley, who was African American, won in the in-person exit polls, but lost by ten points on the phones, and at the polls.

In February 2005, at a conference at Siena College entitled "THE WOMAN PRESIDENT" co-sponsored by Hearst and the Ms. Foundation's White House Project, the Research Institute released a poll finding that 81 percent of Americans said they would vote for a woman president. Sounds great, doesn't it? The poll got lots of attention, with headlines like "AMERICANS MAY FINALLY BE READY FOR A WOMAN PRESIDENT . . ." which was clearly what was supposed to happen.

Problem is, the devil is always in the details. And the details suggest that in this, as in all things, women have a tougher time than men— much tougher than the headlines would suggest. When asked whether they thought the country was "ready for" a woman president, it turns out, the number who answered yes dropped to 66 percent. Only 60 percent said they expected the Democrats to nominate a woman for president in 2008.

The troubling number, according to every pollster I talked to, is the two-thirds figure. The question "is the country ready?" amounts to a measure of what people think about their neighbors, and pollsters generally agree that that's more likely to be an honest answer. Everyone knows that the "politically correct" answer to whether you're willing to vote for a qualified woman is "yes," which is why it's so important to look for other ways to ascertain the true attitude of respondents, not the one they think you want to hear. Similarly, in *Anticipating Madam President,* a collection of academic essays edited by Professors Robert Watson and Ann Gordon, the editors quote a Gallup poll from 1999 in which 91 percent of the respondents said that if their party nominated a woman candidate and she were qualified, they would vote for her (note that essentially one in ten wouldn't, even in those circumstances), but in the same poll only 49 percent thought the country was ready for a woman president, compared to 48 percent who didn't.[3] That's higher than Hillary Clinton's negatives. It suggests that the very idea of a woman president may, secretly, still be more polarizing than people are willing to admit.

Willingness to Vote for a Woman Candidate for President, 1937–2003[4]

Total
Numbers shown in percentages

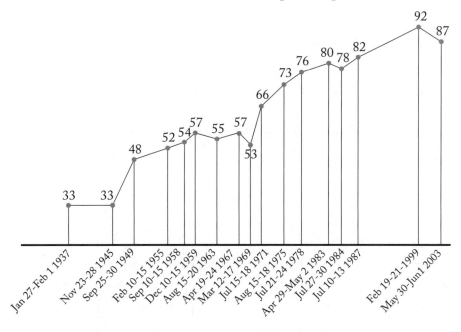

In their book *Madam President,* Eleanor Clift and Tom Brazaitis predict that there will be a woman president "soon."[5] But they offer the prediction at the end of a chapter in which all of the objective evidence is far more pessimistic: the polling information, the election statistics, the anecdotes all attest to the obstacles women face. The basis for their conclusion, as it turns out, is not their own research, but pop culture— everything from the Barbie President 2000 doll to the idea that screen-

Willingness to Vote for a Woman Candidate for President, by Gender 1949–2003

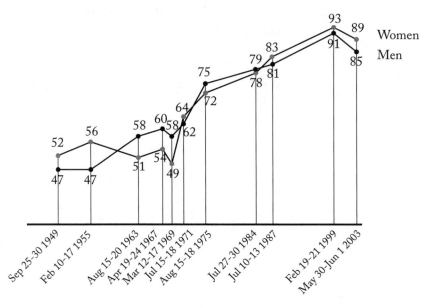

Willingness to Vote for a Woman Candidate for President 1949-2003

writers are making television shows or movies that will encourage girls to dream. They must certainly be encouraged to know that Geena Davis is going to play a president next fall on a prime-time television series. But the rest of the television schedule and the toy store are hardly as promising in their vision of the role of women. And the rest of society hardly provides too many role models for seeing a woman in the most powerful position in the world.

Tom Bradley's non-election was the first time people in the polling business really focused on what everyone now understands is a definite racial bias in polling that must be accounted for. The same thing happened a few years later to Douglas Wilder, the black Virginia governor who ran for the Senate. The line was that a black candidate had to be up by 5–10 points before Election Day in order to win. While some people have always maintained that the first woman president should be a conservative Republican, these statistics suggest some problems with that theory. If you're looking at some 20 percent of the electorate who won't vote for you and it comes from your own party, you're dead.

Among researchers, the problems facing women seeking executive positions are widely recognized. Women have done better getting elected to Congress than to governorships, with the result that there has been more study of women in legislative than executive positions.[6] In research funded by the Barbara Lee Foundation, pollsters Celinda Lake and Linda DiVall—Democrat and Republican respectively—found that women candidates face their most difficult challenges on questions of toughness and decisiveness, and among men and older voters.[7] And it's only to be expected that this would surface in a contest for the chief executive position rather than the legislature. Dianne Feinstein, California's senior senator, beats Arnold Schwarzenegger in state popularity polls, but she was soundly defeated in her one run for governor. No woman has yet held that job in California or New York, or held the mayorships of our two largest cities. Among the mayors of America's one hundred largest cities, only twelve are women.[8]

Much of this, no doubt, can be traced back to the unconscious stereotypes we all have about men and women—the same prejudices that garner women higher poll numbers on issues like health care and education and men on crime and defense. When you think about it, this is what makes Hillary all the more extraordinary. The current focus on issues of terrorism and security would normally spell doom for a candidate seeking to be America's first woman president. How many women are there in public life who could possibly meet the toughness threshold? And yet that is a question one never hears about Hillary Clinton. The issues that tend to plague women candidates—the traditional toughness/determination/fire in the belly trilogy—that would otherwise have every man running against her looking for his tank, just don't surface. She pays a small price for this toughness in the lesbian rumors—*If she's that tough*, the argument goes, *how could she possibly be a feminine woman?*—but even those don't really stick. Hillary is a unique woman, in this regard. In part because of the nature of the mud the right has thrown at her so relentlessly for so many years, no one in America today doubts her toughness.

In a 1998 study of six executive races, the White House Project found in each campaign that press coverage of female candidates focused more on their personal characteristics, whereas coverage of the men focused on their policy positions.[9] The messages of political campaign ads often reinforce these stereotypes, and in ways that aren't very subtle. I remember the discomfort of many of my friends on the Women's Campaign Fund board when liberal favorite Gary Hart mounted a military tank (more convincingly than my former boss, I should add) to defeat his rival for his Colorado Senate seat—who happened to be a Republican woman. Today, the urgency of issues of war and terrorism still works against women; in governors' and mayors' races, hard-core, black and white crime shots—the more violent the better—have become an efficient way to communicate the not-so-subtle message that it takes someone tough—read, *a man*—to fight back.

According to the work of the Lee foundation, voters tend to be especially wary of women outsiders (that is, women who come from the corporate or nonprofit world), often proving reluctant to give them credit for their experience. Among the greatest challenges for women running for executive positions, particularly in the wake of 9/11, is to be tough without appearing overly aggressive—to demonstrate expertise in matters of security and terrorism, so that people feel safe, while at the same time being able to connect with voters, which involves being an appealing woman. In the corporate world, it's called "the comfort zone." A man can be as masculine as he wants, but there's a narrow sphere—the overlap between the masculine and feminine circles—that the successful woman must aim for, if she's to succeed. Some people call it a vise.

Hillary herself at one point described it to Eleanor Clift by saying that women in politics must function within a "narrower range" than men when it comes to the emotional terrain of politics.

The difficulty people have with powerful, ambitious, tough women will of course prove an obstacle to Hillary, no matter how much we might want to wish it away. The first time I read Nick Kristof's column in praise of Hillary—followed by his conclusion that she would probably lose because "ambitious, high-achieving women are still a turnoff, particularly if they're liberal and feminist"[10]—I thought, *How dare he. Who is he to say?* But then I reconsidered. He's just stating the obvious. Of course it's true. She is trying to do the impossible, and we should not forget that for a minute.

My conservative friends, or at least some of them, would like to have it another way. They want this to be perceived as a debate about Hillary herself, not a judgment about tough, ambitious women. I can hear my buddy Sean Hannity now. (Yes, we really are buddies. People are always surprised when I tell them that. But in the end, when you work with people, it's all about how we treat one another. Sean and I watch out for each other; when I've seen him getting pulled in too many directions on a book tour, for instance, I've sat him down like the Jewish mother I am and told him, *Sean, you need a break, I don't want to see you get too tired and make a mistake.* Likewise, when I was totally exhausted at the 2004 convention, getting beaten up by my friends for working for Fox, finding myself twice forgotten by the motor pool and left stranded on street corners in the city where I'd been raped years before, it was Sean who immediately got operational and arranged for me to have a car on call twenty-four hours a day, on his tab. So don't yell at me for having conservative friends. Doesn't mean I'm going to start agreeing with them.) As I was saying, I can just hear Sean trying to argue that this isn't about women; that that's just the kind of posturing you should expect from a pseudo-liberal sexist institution like the *New York Times,* which points the finger at everyone but itself. *Susan,* I can hear him saying, *why can't you admit that there are great women like Condi Rice and Jeane Kirkpatrick who didn't ride on their husband's coattails? Why can't you see that being against Hillary Clinton has nothing to do with being against smart, ambitious women—even ones who are liberal and feminist . . .*

You know I love you, Susan, I can hear him saying. *You're smart and ambitious and liberal and feminist. But you're also honest and ethical and you don't use people, and don't lie . . .*

And then I'll laugh and say, *Sean, if I were running for president, you wouldn't like me either.*

For better or for worse, Hillary Rodham Clinton has become larger than herself, larger than any of us. She has become a symbol of all of us, of our generation of women.

She wins, we win. She loses, we lose. That's how it works.

Her husband was the first president of the baby boom generation. She may be the last.

He was forty-six and she was forty-five when they moved into the White House. This time she would be sixty when she was sworn in; he'd be seventy when she left office, if she served two terms. Her winning or losing defines what our generation, particularly our generation of women, accomplished or didn't.

Hillary is doing women a terrible disservice, Sean will say. *She's putting herself above the real interests of women. If she really cared about women, that would be one more reason she wouldn't take them down. Because if you're right, Susan—if it's true that, no matter what you do, her defeat will be taken as a defeat for women—then she shouldn't run.*

I love you, too, Sean. But you just don't get it.

Joe Klein, *Time*'s top political columnist—perhaps best known for writing the anonymous bestseller *Primary Colors*—has lately been saying the same thing about Hillary.[11] He was one of those who was totally charmed by Bill Clinton in 1992. But he's older now, and not so easily charmed. He wrote that he "like[s] her," and that she is "smart and solid," and that she "easily masters difficult issues—her newfound grasp of military matters has impressed colleagues of both parties on the Armed Services Committee." And he doesn't fall for some of the traditional arguments of Hillary haters: He recognizes that she is not a hardcore liberal, "she is not even vaguely the left-wing harridan portrayed by the Precambrian right," but rather a "judicious hawk on foreign policy" who "has learned her lessons on domestic policy overreach." He even quotes Newt Gingrich's paradigm-shattering line: "Hillary has become one of the very few people who know what to do about health care."

But still, he says, Hillary shouldn't even run.

Why not? The first reason he gives is that it would bring out the Haters. As if they would all disappear if we all just looked the other way, or as if giving in to them would diminish their power. Let's let the terrorists win.

His second reason explicitly embraces the double standard. Hillary shouldn't run because she's not a "brilliant" enough politician to create a "credible feminine presidential style, to deal with the 'toughness conundrum' any woman running for President will face. So far, Senator Clinton hasn't shown the ease or creativity necessary to break the ultimate glass ceiling." So says Joe.

This is just a taste of what's to come. Welcome to the world of arrogant men telling us what a "credible feminine presidential style" is.

Actually, Hillary is in far better shape to deal with the aforementioned "conundrum" than Joe gives her credit for; this is where all that respect for her Armed Services work, her deft handling of issues, her strong—even frosty—demeanor, helps her seem "tough." Not to mention her trips to Afghanistan with John McCain, and his endorsements of her toughness. Say what, Joe?

While women candidates generally face a gap of as much as ten points on leadership and decisiveness, the latest polls show Hillary scoring particularly strongly among New York voters on those measures. Seriously: Is there anyone in the world who doesn't think Hillary is strong enough, or decisive enough, to stand up to our enemies?

It gets worse, if you care. Joe goes on to pronounce her husband guilty until proven guilty in the matter of women—and then, in a dazzling move, in his next breath declares Hillary's move a Constitutional dodge to get her husband a third term. So which is it, Joe—is Bill Clinton living a separate bachelor's life, or running his wife's show as a matter of law? Apparently my friend Mr. Klein hasn't shaken that old notion of women as property, even when the woman in question is running for president.

And *nota bene:* Joe Klein doesn't say Hillary wouldn't make a good president. He doesn't say he's for someone else. *He simply says she shouldn't run.* No one goes around telling Bill Frist not to run. You don't want to vote for Hillary, you don't have to. But since when do columnists get off telling the candidate who is ahead in every poll, leading in fundraising, hiring organizers, leading in polls of insiders, that she's wrong to run? Say it ain't so, Joe.

Wonder why we need a woman president? Read Joe Klein.

But you can't ignore what they say. The larger message here is that there's work to be done that Hillary can't do alone. There is a bigger battle to be fought here, and it doesn't just have her name on it.

You have no idea what the e-mails are like on the days when I write about Hillary in my column. It's stunning—both pro and con. So can you imagine what it's like actually *being* Hillary? Sure, crowds applaud her wherever she goes. People stand in line to tell her how great she is. But there's also the other side—the people for whom Hillary Clinton is clearly the symbol of everything they are terrified of, every woman who has ever wronged them, every liberal they've ever fought with. Forget common courtesy or decency. When I get the anti-Hillary e-mails, I keep my finger poised on the delete key and my children far away from the screen. I can't even *guess* what her mail is like.

Joe Klein has described Mrs. Clinton as being surprised and troubled by the depth of the anger and hatred she encountered during the debate over her health care program. And I ask: Why wouldn't she be?

Wouldn't any decent person? She was trying to do something good, and there were people who came to hate her for it—or were incited to. The fact that she made mistakes didn't make her an evil person. The anger of the right wing did that, if only in their minds.

This is, and should be, a deeply troubling phenomenon. Some years ago, I was sitting in a PBS studio, waiting to go on the air with a radio personality, a man I didn't know at the time. We were having a perfectly civilized conversation about surrogate motherhood, since he owned an agency. All of a sudden the camera turned on, and the man was transformed before my eyes into something different—something approaching a demagogue, full of rage and resentment, shaking his figurative fist at the powerful. I almost jumped, I was so scared. That was when I realized who he was, and why he eventually became number one in the ratings. And what amazed me most was that he was able to turn it on for just a minute or two, like a spout, like an actor—except that, when it was on, I never doubted for a moment that it was real.

There is great power to the hatred out there, but that's hardly reason to run away from it. If Hillary isn't afraid to confront it, why is Joe Klein? If Hillary has the guts to face the haters, the least she should expect is that the Joe Kleins of the world should have the guts to cover it.

Here is the very good news, I think: The *true* haters are a small minority. The rest of the country, whatever their expectations, will wait to deal with the real person they see. And that real person will not be nearly as easy to hate as the caricature has been.

What Hillary Clinton has stood for, in caricature, is everything that everyone fears about professional women: that they are ball-busting, cold, demanding, ambitious, and fiendishly smart. Even women who see themselves as demanding and ambitious imagine that she has them licked. I'll never forget one woman—one of the most ambitious and successful I know—explaining to me that she didn't like Hillary because she was "too ambitious." I almost fell off my chair. It's as if, as long as Hillary is out there, you could always say, *Well, at least I'm not the worst . . .*

But that's the caricature, not the real person. And presidential races, as we've seen with Dukakis and Kerry, have a way of revealing the real person.

For all the flaws in our political process, and there are certainly many, the final stage of a presidential election comes as close to a meritocracy as any choice that we make in America. Is every moment, every snarky press leak, every negative ad, entirely fair? Of course not. But if you're a candidate who gets that far, chances are that you'll be judged on your merits—more so than in almost any other political system.

In part, this is ensured by those moments of truth I've mentioned— and most powerfully by the presidential debates. Ever since the modern system of debates was begun in 1960, and revived in 1976, armchair pundits have debated whether the televised debates ultimately clarify, or distort, our impressions of those who would be president. My belief is that these events, even at their most carefully stage-managed, give us the truest windows we can have into the candidates. Over the course of one, two, three, or four personal appearances together, we get to judge these figures by what they say, and how they say it, and who shows command. We see them act, and react, in real time. The handlers help, the ads help, the money helps, but in presidential campaigns, the contenders are ultimately judged on their own. After all, the reason Kerry truly had a shot against Bush was that Bush lost the first debate badly. Remember, the incumbent always has an advantage—and with his solid approval rating, all Bush needed to do was hold his own in the debates and he would have walked away with the race. Instead he fumbled, Kerry won handily, and the election almost fell into Kerry's lap.

In any two-candidate race, particularly where you have no incumbent, both sides go in with roughly 40–43 percent of the vote in their corner; that generally grows to 46 percent once each has secured his (or her!) base. The group we call "swing voters" makes up the difference.

In Hillary's case, the advantage is clear: It means she'll get a fair chance, which is all First Women ever can hope for. She gets to stand side by side with her opponent, and be compared in terms of the voters' lives.

No matter how people may complain about the choice they're being presented with, they will put the two candidates side by side and judge them on roughly equal footing And no matter who stands opposite her, that's a contest Hillary stands a strong chance to win.

At that point, the question is no longer whether Hillary would have been your first, second, or third choice; whether you were ready for a woman president; whether you approve of her husband, her marriage, or her ambition.

The question then becomes far simpler: Which of those two people will you trust with the future of your family and your country?

Frank Luntz, my Republican pollster friend, has compared Hillary Clinton to Ronald Reagan: She is beloved by the core of her own party, but sure to polarize the opposition. Did that polarizing effect ruin Reagan's chances? Of course not: In 1980, he won in a landslide.

I remember the moment in that election when the tide turned. I was in Florida, working for Carter. Carter had recently refused to debate with third-party candidate John Anderson, whom Reagan had insisted be included. (And don't think it was a matter of principle, on either side; having handled presidential debate negotiations myself, I can tell you that it's all about partisan calculations—in this case, that Anderson was taking votes from Carter.) As a result, there was only one debate between the two major-party nominees that year, and it was late in the campaign.

Until that point—people forget this today—the race was neck-and-neck. The economy, to be sure, was in terrible shape: The so-called "misery index" was in double digits, interest rates were as high as 15 percent[12] (I'd been collecting anti-Carter attack points for Ted Kennedy for nine months before switching to defending Carter, and I still remember these stats today). But Ronald Reagan was still the former actor, a man known for making offhand comments that suggested, among other things, that pollution was caused by trees. Every Democrat had a long list of these Reaganisms—stories he told about people who didn't exist, persistent reliance on facts that were demonstrably wrong. Somebody even released a record album of Reagan saying things that were either stupid or wrong with great conviction. The Kennedy for President campaign that year was the first time I'd ever done anything more advanced for a campaign than knocking on doors; I was told to go on the attack and I did. I had more fun than I've ever had in a campaign since—and I was still at it in August. I think Reagan would have won anyway, but it certainly didn't help Carter to have all of us shooting for nearly a year.

Years later, I asked some of my friends—who at the time were far more experienced than I—what the heck we were doing hammering away at Carter even as Reagan was nipping at his heels. They gave me two exactly conflicting explanations. Some said they didn't think what we were doing would seriously damage Carter, because Reagan could never win anyway. The rest said it didn't matter how hard we went after Carter, because *Carter* could never win anyway.

As for me, I remember believing the former—that Reagan, that polarizing ideologue, could never win.

I think that's how many Republicans view Hillary Clinton today.

Well, as Dubya might say, we misunderestimated Reagan—politically, at least.

In the one debate of the 1980 campaign, Reagan wasn't brilliant.[13] But he was fine. He didn't fumble lines. He didn't make any outrageous gaffes, as Ford had in 1976. Why would he? His team had negotiated a carefully controlled format; he looked great; and he answered questions he'd been asked a hundred times before, in a smooth and practiced way. He wasn't scary; in fact, he came across as a perfectly acceptable alternative to an unpopular president.

But his most brilliant move was the way he dealt with Carter's attempt to attack him as a dangerous ideologue. When Carter suggested that Reagan had tried to discontinue Medicare, he saw his chance to turn the tide—to paint Carter, for once, as the guy who kept getting things wrong. Turning from the camera, he looked directly at the president, and laughed, "There you go again . . ." That was it. Carter looked like a fool. And Reagan looked like an indulgent storeowner, wondering whether this fellow he'd hired was really up to the job after all.

And then, having effectively reduced Carter to a laugh line, Reagan turned his focus to the one place where it really mattered—the voter—and asked:

"Are you better off than you were four years ago?"

That was it.

That was all he had to do. He saw his chance, and he took it.

By the end of the debate, Ronald Reagan had erased the popular assumption that he was no more than a bumbling fool, a crazy risk to the country, the way we Democrats had been painting him for months. What's more, he was genuinely appealing, with a sense of humor, a twinkle in his eye, and a rare ability to connect to voters.

That night, the floor fell out from under Carter's reelection campaign. The next day, the Florida offices where I was working were almost empty. By the time Election Day rolled around, the only way I could drum up volunteers was to promise free bagels and plentiful bachelors to the hundreds of grandmothers I depended on every day.

In the general election of 2008, Hillary Clinton will have the chance to do just what Reagan did in that debate. Those who have believed in the caricature will, for the first time, see the person. And what they'll see is a woman who is smart and genuine, funny, knowledgeable, and appealing. If it becomes clear in the debates that Hillary has the better command of the facts, that she understands the problems of American families, that she will approach other countries with more experience and sophistication than her opponent, that she is tougher on terrorism, for a stronger defense, that she is well, different than a lot people thought she was . . . then she will win the debates, and likely the election.

I can't begin to tell you how grueling it is to run for president. Hillary is already spending her weekends traveling between key states and New York. She has to spend every spare moment fund-raising. When you get in the thick of it, you do four or five events every day, six or seven days a week. The rest of the time, you're on an airplane eating. The usual rule is that since you never know when you'll get your next meal, you should eat when you can. But since the people you meet at every stop assume you need your next meal—whatever time it is—there's always one waiting, usually involving buckets of the town's signature dish (fried chicken, ribs—never celery). So you eat—four or five meals a day is common—and do no regular exercise; and everyone starts getting fat. Farm breakfasts are at 6:00 A.M., and when you don't get in until midnight, no one goes running. Not to mention the fact that everybody gets sick, because the minute one person does, the germs circulate on the plane that everybody is on together every day.

Hillary's plane will be a circus from the day one. It will attract more reporters, more fans, more hecklers, more of everything. That won't make things easier. Her events will draw crowds, but they'll also draw protestors. She is not her husband on the stump; she does have to work on her stump speech, and even more on her answers, to make them sharp and crisp. From the start, the expectations for her will be impossible to meet. There are reporters out there waiting to write stories saying that she's disappointing, not as good a speaker as he was, and so on. They'll find people in the crowd who came hoping to like her and came away undecided. In a crowd that's freely assembled, you can find whoever you're looking for—which is why Bush's White House always carefully screens its crowds. Any flare-up inside her campaign—and there's no campaign without a few flare-ups—will become a screaming New York tabloid headline. Every mistake—and anyone who works eighteen hours a day makes an occasional mistake—will get the trumpet blare. And so it will go.

In the end, the press wants Hillary. Goodness knows, they need her. The presence of Hillary Clinton in a general election, regardless of her opponent, will make the election exciting. That means that people will watch more TV news, and read more newspapers, than they would otherwise. Even today, you can turn on the twenty-four-hour news networks and they're already talking about Hillary constantly for that very reason.

For the media, though, wanting Hillary to run isn't the same as giving her a free ride. They still need a contest. Hillary has never been known for getting great press. The anti-Hillary books will continue, the Hate Hillary websites will multiply like a virus. The far right's lifetime mission of taking her down will become a professional operation with a real reason for being at last, with new efforts to malign her on a daily basis.

You can call this operation what you will. "Right-wing conspiracy" is not a phrase I'd use, because "conspiracy" implies unlawful activity, and from what I've seen there's nothing unlawful about the right-wing attack machine. It's just incredibly efficient.

I can speak from experience. On the day the Swift Boat controversy broke last summer, for example, I was sitting in for Alan Colmes on *Hannity & Colmes*. As I said, Sean and I are friends; I think television is television, not a world war. So I asked him what kind of background material he'd gotten on the story from his side. He showed me what they were sending around that day—and it was a book. I don't mean *Unfit for Command,* the Swift Boat Veterans' book. I mean hundreds of pages of background information to use in attacking Kerry: old quotes, attack points on each issue, with backup and backup for the backup. It was the kind of stuff Gene Sperling in his youth would stay up for two days (literally) to produce.

And me? I had about three sheets of paper—literally—that I'd gotten from the Kerry campaign.

That wasn't the fault of the Kerry camp's issues team, by the way. They were great. The basic problem was that Kerry himself had held this one close to his own vest. Ultimately, though, it didn't matter how it happened: the preparation gap between the Republicans' output and ours was stunning. All I could do, as I sat there across from Sean on the *Hannity & Colmes* set, was cross-examine their guys like a defense lawyer, revealing the inconsistencies in their stories. That worked fine for one night, but it wasn't a strategy.

Sean Hannity had a strategy: *Attack Kerry.* And he kept at it for the next two months.

I don't believe in calling the other team names. They're not doing anything illegal. I believe in learning from what they do. And learning how to do it better.

The reason Hillary and others have characterized the right-wing attack machine as a conspiracy is that it shares the essential quality that distinguishes a criminal conspiracy from a simple crime committed by an individual: the obvious power of coordinated action. The reason conspiracy is granted special status in criminal law is that there is a special danger in coordinated group activity. It's one thing for one person to decide to commit a crime on his own. His chances of success are limited by his individual status. When a group gets together and commits to a course of action, however, the chances of success increase exponentially.

The group that wants to defeat Hillary Clinton has already committed to their course of action. They've been at it for years.

Those who support her will have to match them, block them, and push them back, so they cannot take advantage of a Senate race, or campaign finance rules, or the fact that it is, after all, three years out.

"It's going to be a hard sell," says one Washington woman, an old hand, when I tell her what my book is about. Most women have very complicated feelings about Hillary Clinton. Yes, indeed. Women's feelings about Hillary Clinton, particularly those women who wear black suits like her more days than not, tend to cover all shades of gray.

But is it hard for you to see that if we're to have a woman president in our lifetimes, I ask, she's it?

No.

Is it hard for you to see that if Hillary wins, the way smart, ambitious women and girls are seen in this country, and the world, will change for the better, in a way that nothing else we can do right now would accomplish?

No, it's not hard to see that.

And that would be a very good thing?

Yes.

Is it hard for you to see that if Hillary loses, it will inevitably be seen, understood, feel like a setback for women, a failure, a rejection not only of Hillary personally, but of everything the icon stands for?

No, it's not hard to see that.

And that would be a very bad thing?

Yes.

It's all very black and white, no matter how many shades of gray your feelings may be.

Which doesn't, I know, make it an easy sell. Just an urgent one.

The worst thing for women, for equality, for the progress of opportunity, would be for Hillary to win the nomination and lose the election. Sorry, Maureen, sorry, Sean, sorry Bert. There's just no way that such a loss isn't understood to be, at some level, about being a woman. Traditionally, you can survive a run for the presidency just fine, so long as you don't win the nomination. But if you win the nomination and lose, you—and your branch of the party—are toast.

That's what I worry about. Here we have this amazing opportunity and yet in the end, if she loses, we will almost certainly take steps back.

I run into people who keep saying: Surely there must be all these women behind her in line. That would lessen the impact. Let me point out that none of these people work in politics. If there were lots of people in line, I wouldn't be writing this book. My case would not be so urgent. Women would be in a different position. There would not be such a need for a new normal. If there were all these women, Republicans would be putting one on their ticket. They won't because they don't have one. Neither do Democrats.

★ ★ ★

If it were easy, it would not have taken this long.

It isn't. It won't be. It will take more than just a village. The flame throwing has already begun; it goes full force, even when they say it doesn't. For all the criticism of Ed Klein, his book was number two on the bestseller list.

It may be three years out, but August has begun.

If you don't want Hillary to be the nominee, pick another candidate and get to work. Because if she is the nominee, you can't afford for her to lose.

The person who will have to work the hardest, put up with the most, risk the most—and, make no mistake, she will literally risk her life in this process—is Hillary herself. She will be out in front of the campaign, every single second. She will be the leader and the target.

She can't do it alone.

The time for asking *What's wrong with Hillary?* is over.

So is the debate over whether she should be running.

Did anyone debate whether George W. Bush should run?

We need to stop worrying about whether she can win, and start helping her do it.

"Get over it," Marie Kaplan said, in the advertisement that closed Hillary Clinton's Senate campaign. You know whose side she is on. You know she will be there with you.

Where will you be?

Whose side will you be on?

This time, women have to do more than get over it. This time, women have to get to work. What does a president look like? What does a commander in chief sound like? Centuries of thinking have to change. It will take some doing for many Americans to get used to a completely different picture.

And then what a night it will be.

And, better yet, what a morning after . . .

NOTES

1. IMAGINE

[1] "You don't move thirty points . . ." Quinnipiac University, "Clinton Thumps Pataki, Edges Giuliani in Reelect Bid, Quinnipiac University Poll Finds," www.quinnipiac.edu/x11373.xml?ReleaseID=647, February 9, 2005.

[2] "I saw one poll, of political insiders . . ." James A. Barnes and Peter Bell, "Hillary in 2008?," *Atlantic Monthly*, July/August 2005.

[3] "The book could not have been criticized . . ." "Hannity Rejects New Hillary Clinton Book" www.newshounds.us/2005/06/22/hannity_rejects_new_hillary_clinton_book.php.

[4] "In the meantime . . ." "Klein's Hillary Book Hits #2 on *New York Times* List," *Newsmax.com*, June 29, 2005, www.newsmax.com/archives/ic/2005/6/29/184536.shtml

[5] "Two weeks after . . ." "Dem Leader Reid Says Clinton Not Necessarily Best Democratic Candidate for White House," *Drudge Report*, July 7, 2005, www.drudgereportarchives.com/data/2005/07/07/20050707_160000.htm.

[6] "Amy Sullivan, a wonderful writer . . ." Amy Sullivan, "Hillary in 2008?," *Washington Monthly*, July/August 2005.

[7] "A recent CNN poll has found . . ." CNN/*USA Today*/Gallup Poll May 20–22, 2005, www.cnn.com/2005/POLITICS/05/26/hillary.clinton/index.html, May 26, 2005.

[8] "It's in the Senate . . ." Quinnipiac University, February 9, 2005.

[9] "I never thought I would run for office . . ." Hillary Clinton, Remarks as Delivered

at the Wellesley College Reunion, June 5, 2004, www.friendsofhillary.com/speeches/20040605.php.

[10] "The sample they were looking at . . ." Andrew Sherry, "6:58 ET: The Early Leaders: Women," USAToday.com, www.usatoday.com/news/politicselections/vote2004/electionsBlog.htm, November 2, 2004.

[11] "She was already leading . . ." Hillary Clinton, Giuliani Early Favorites for 2008," www.gallup.com/poll/content/login.aspx?ci=14053, November 16, 2004.

[12] "The researchers are finally catching on . . ." Sylvia Ann Hewlett et al., "The Hidden Brain Drain: Off-Ramps and On-Ramps in Women's Careers," *Harvard Business Review*, March 2005.

[13] "According to the pollster Mark Penn . . ." Eleanor Clift and Tom Brazaitis, *Madam President* (Scribner, 2000), p. xiii.

[14] "When they went looking for potential choices . . ." ibid.

[15] "But there are 493 of them . . ." "Women in the Fortune 500," Catalyst, www.catalystwomen.org/pressroom/press_releases/2-10-05%20Catalyst%20Female%20CEOs%20Fact%20Sheet.pdf.

[16] ". . . and the number of women serving . . ." "California Women in Elective Office—Historical Summary," www.cawp.rutgers.edu/Facts/StbySt/CA.html.

[17] "Last spring, my students and I . . ." *The Tally*, www.latimesbias.org/talley.html.

2. IF NOT NOW, WHEN?

[1] "Gerry's was an exception" Ellen Goodman, "Yes, Ferraro Made a Difference," *Washington Post*, November 8, 1984.

[2] "We began having 'Years of the Woman' . . ." Judi Hasson, "Record number of women win," *USA Today*, November 4, 1992.

[3] "But women's progress has slowed . . ." "Women in State Legislatures," Center for American Women and Politics, Eagleton Institute of Politics, Rutgers University, www.cawp.rutgers.edu.

[4] "Women have done better getting elected . . ." "Municipal Offices," ibid.

[5] "These are some of the statistics . . ." Hillary Clinton, Remarks as Delivered at the Wellesley College Reunion, June 5, 2004, www.friendsofhillary.com/speeches/20040605.php.

[6] "As Sue Tolleson-Rinehart and Jeanie Stanley smartly point out . . ." Carol Lynn Bower, "Public Discourses and Female Presidential Candidates" in *Anticipating Madam President*, Robert P. Watson and Ann Gordon, eds. (Lynne Reinner Publishers, 2003) 110.

[7] "A 1999 survey by Deloitte & Touche . . ." Dianne Bystrom, "On the Way to the White House: Communication Strategies for Women Candidates" in *Anticipating Madam President*, Robert P. Watson and Ann Gordon, eds. (Lynne Reinner Publishers, 2003) 101.

8 "The idea that women are different . . ." *Reed v. Reed, 404 U.S. 71* (1971).

9 "It wasn't until then that the Supreme Court . . ." *Brown v. Board of Education, 347 U.S. 483* (1954).

10 "In 1971's *Reed v. Reed* . . ." *Reed v. Reed, 404 U.S. 71* (1971).

11 "Ten years earlier, a woman had lost . . ." *Hoyt v. Florida, 368 U.S. 57* (1961).

12 "Every university that has followed the lead of MIT . . ." Nancy Hopkins, "MIT and Gender Bias: Following Up on Victory," *Chronicle of Higher Education*, 1999, at: http://chronicle.com/colloquy/99/genderbias/background.htm.

13 "So what if we only have eight female CEOs . . ." "Women in the Fortune 500," Catalyst, www.catalystwomen.org/pressroom/press_releases/2-10-05%20Catalyst %20Female%20CEOs%20Fact%20Sheet.pdf.

14 ". . . or if 86 percent of congress is male . . ." "Women in the U.S. Congress 2005," Center for American Women and Politics, Eagleton Institute of Politics, Rutgers University, www.cawp.rutgers.edu/Facts/Officeholders/cong.pdf.

15 "After Anita Hill . . ." Jill Abramson, "Anita Hill and the Luster of Hindsight," *Miami Herald*, October 13, 1992.

16 "At an AARP lunch . . ." Liz Smith, SRO Brunch, Hotel Bel-Air, March 30, 2005.

17 "There's no way to predict substantively . . ." Hillary Clinton, Remarks as Delivered at the Wellesley College Reunion, June 5, 2004, www.friendsofhillary.com/ speeches/20040605.php.

18 "Andrew Sullivan described it as . . ." Andrew Sullivan, "New York warms to Hillary . . . next it could be America," *Sunday Times* (London), February 27, 2005 at: www.timesonline.co.uk/article/0,,2088=1502357,00.html.

19 "This decision, which is one of the most fundamental . . ." Hillary Clinton, Remarks to the NYS Family Planning Providers, January 24, 2005, http://clinton. senate.gov/news/statements/details.cfm?id=233748&&.

20 "Research shows . . ." Hillary Clinton, Remarks to the NYS Family Planning Providers, January 24, 2005, http://clinton.senate.gov/news/statements/details .cfm?id=233748&&.

21 "A few years ago, in an effort to understand . . ." John J. Donohue III & Steven D. Levitt, "The Impact of Legalized Abortion on Crime," 116 *Quarterly J. of Econ.* 379 (May 2001), http://ssrn.com/abstract=174508.

22 "And yet according to the Alan Guttmacher Institute . . ." "An Overview of Abortion in the United States," Physicians for Reproductive Choice and Health and the Guttmacher Institute, June 2005, www.guttmacher.org/presentations/ abort_slides.pdf.

23 "And how are those women ever to get access . . ." "An Overview of Abortion in the Unites States," Physicians for Reproductive Choice and Health and the Guttmacher Institute, June 2005, www.guttmacher.org/presentations/abort_ slides.pdf.

3. BUT CAN SHE WIN?

[1] "'She projects strength and the capacity . . .'" James A. Barnes, "The Rock Star and the Rest," *National Journal*, April 30, 2005 at: http://nationaljournal.com/about/njweekly/stories/2005/0429nj1.htm.

[2] "'I think she could win every state . . .'" Jennifer Senior, "The Once and Future President Clinton," *New York*, February 21, 2005 at: http://nymetro.com/nymetro/news/politics/national/features/11082.

[3] "'She can't win . . .'" Lloyd Grove, "Kanye Get $ To Do Mags?," *New York Daily News*, February 18, 2005 at: www.nydailynews.com/02-18-2005/news/gossip/story/281+26p-241603c.htm.

[4] "A majority are at least willing . . ." CNN/*USA Today*/Gallup Poll May 20–22, 2005, www.cnn.com/2005/POLITICS/05/26/hillary.clinton/index.html, May 26, 2005.

[5] "After senators Clinton and John McCain appeared . . ." "McCain: Hillary Would be Good President," *NewsMax*, February 20, 2005, www.newsmax.com/archives/ic/2005/2/20/112022.shtml.

[6] "In a Fox News poll . . ." "Fox News/Opinion Dynamics Poll December 16, 2004," www.foxnews.com/story/0,2933,141755,00.html.

[7] "In fact, as Dick Morris is warning . . ." Dick Morris, column, *The Hill*, February 9, 2005, www.hillnews.com/thehill/export/TheHill/Comment/DickMorris/020905.html.

[8] "A Marist Poll conducted in February 2005 . . ." "National Poll: Morning Line Campaign 2008," www.maristpoll.marist.edu/usapolls/hc050308.htm.

[9] "In New York, she has already proven . . ." Quinnipiac University, February 9, 2005.

[10] "At a Q&A session . . ." Lloyd Grove, "Kanye Get $ To Do Mags?," *New York Daily News*, February 18, 2005.

[11] "Don't believe it? Just ask . . ." Kathleen Hall Jamieson and Paul Waldman, eds., Electing the President (University of Pennsylvania Press, 2001); Richard Johnston et al.., *The 2000 Presidential Election and the Foundations of Party Politics* (Cambridge University Press, 2004).

[12] "'Southern Revolt on the Ascent of Hillary' . . ." Tony Allen-Mills, "Southern Revolt on the Ascent of Hillary," *The Times* (London), April 3, 2005 at: www.timesonline.co.uk/article/0,,2089-1552437,00.html.

[13] "Here's the delicious part . . ." Brad Schrade, "Bredesen: London paper misrepresented comments on Clinton," *The Tennessean*, April 6, 2005 at: www.tennessean.com/government/archives/05/03/6789274.shtml?element_10=678927.

[14] "The governor had himself . . ." Clay Risen, "Southern Man," *New Republic*, January 31, 2005, 18.

[15] "Charlie Cook, one of the most respected . . ." Charlie Cook, "In This Corner . . . ," *Cook Political Report*, March 8, 2005, www.cookpolitical.com/column/2004/030805.php.

16 "Ask Nick Kristof . . ." Nicholas D. Kristof, "Who Gets It? Hillary," *New York Times*, March 16, 2005.

17 "In May, for the first time . . ." CNN/*USA Today*/Gallup Poll May 20–22, 2005, www.cnn.com/2005/POLITICS/05/26/hillary.clinton/index.html, May 26, 2005.

18 "But, in the words of my favorite blogger . . ." Posting of Daniel Owen, "McCain, Giuliani, Clinton—Angus Reid Consultants," May 3, 2005, at www.ovaloffice 2008.com/2005/05/mccain-giuliani-clinton-angus-reid.html.

19 "As Mr. Owen points, out . . ." Rasmussen Reports Hillary Meter at www.rasmussenreports.com/2005/Hillary%20Meter.htm.

20 "Hillary's job approval ratings . . ." Raymond Hernandez, "Clinton's Popularity Up in State, Even Among Republicans," *New York Times*, February 22, 2005.

21 "Today, as conservative Thomas Galvin laments . . ." Posting of Thomas Galven, "New York Loves Hillary: Honest, Doing A Good Job According To Poll Hillary Clinton's 'Extreme Makeover' Project Is Working," February 9, 2005, at http://thomasgalvin.blogspot.com/2005_02_09_thomasgalvin_archive.html.

22 "In October 2000 . . ." Hernandez, *New York Times*, February 22, 2005.

23 "As you take a closer look at the numbers . . ." "Clinton Thumps Pataki, Edges Giuliani In Reelect Bid, Quinnipiac University Poll Finds; New York Voters Say 2–1 She's Honest," February 9, 2005, www.quinnipiac.edu/x11373.xml?ReleaseID=647

24 "One of the first and most important thinkers . . ." Andrew Sullivan, "New York warms to Hillary . . . next it could be America," *Sunday Times* (London), February 27, 2005.

25 "Or consider what Nick Kristof . . ." Nicholas D. Kristof, "Who Gets It? Hillary," *New York Times*, March 16, 2005.

26 "No less an observer than Peggy Noonan . . ." Peggy Noonan, "Riding the Waves: Why Hillary will be hard to beat," *Wall Street Journal*, March 31, 2005 at: www.opinionjournal.com/columnists/pnoonan/?id=110006487.

27 "2004 ELECTION RESULTS . . ." Election 2004, www.cnn.com/ELECTION/2004/pages/results/

28 "The numbers for white married women . . ." Lynn Sweet, "Did the women's vote count?," *Chicago Sun-Times*, November 10, 2004.

29 " 'In the election for president . . .' " *Los Angeles Times* National Exit Poll, www.pollingreport.com/2004.htm#Exit.

4. WHAT'S WRONG WITH HILLARY

1 "I wrote an article for *George* . . ." Susan Estrich, "Happily Ever After," *George*, October 2000, 26.

2 "In Living History . . ." Hillary Clinton, *Living History* (Scribner, 2003).

3 "The most important new book . . ." Posting of Matt Drudge, "New Clinton Book: The Lies, the Fights, the Insults," *Drudge Report*, May 30, 2005, at www.drudgereport.com/flash3jh.htm.

4 "In fact, *The Survivor*..." John Harris, *The Survivor* (Random House, 2005).

5 " 'I think now she's at least as good as I was...' " "Clinton: Hillary would be an 'excellent president', Separately, Biden says senator would be formidable candidate in 2008," February 28, 2005, *www.msnbc.msn.com/id/7041441/*.

6 "The pre-publication publicity..." Carol Memmott, "Hillary Gets Presses Humming," *USA Today*, June 13, 2005.

7 "Tina Brown, Klein's former boss..." Tina Brown, "Hillary Clinton Attacked by Man from Mars," *Washington Post*, June 23, 2005, C01.

8 "They could hardly say..." Christopher Anderson, *American Evita* (HarperCollins, 2004).

9 "Or *We don't like Klein*..." Dick Morris and Eileen McGann, *Condi vs. Hillary: The Next Great Presidential Race* (ReganBooks, 2005).

10 "It debuted at number one..." "Klein's Hillary Book Hits #2 on *New York Times* List," *NewsMax*, June 29, 2005, www.newsmax.com/archives/ic/2005/6/29/184536.shtml.

11 "If Klein is trash..." Edward Wyatt, "Biography of Senator Clinton Has a Few Unexpected Critics," *New York Times*, June 24, 2005, A16.

12 "Dick Morris has hinted..." "Author Says Hillary Will Run for President in 2004," NewsMax.com, July 29, 2003.

13 "Laura Ingraham's first book..." Laura Ingraham, *The Hillary Trap* (Encounter Books, 2002) 227.

14 "Peggy Noonan is the odds-on favorite..." Peggy Noonan, *The Case Against Hillary Clinton* (ReganBooks, 2000) xx, 8, 31, 103.

15 "In a clever moment of appropriation..." ibid, 10.

16 " 'The point is not that she had changed'..." ibid, 15.

17 "They are marked, too..." ibid, 27.

18 "... complete with Maureen Dowd's conclusion..." Katha Pollitt, "What Do They Want?" *The Nation*, November 6, 2000, also, Peggy Noonan, *The Case Against...*, 54.

19 "It is probably the single most commonly mentioned issue..." Hillary Clinton, Speech to Kaiser Family Foundation upon Release of Generation M: Media in the Lives of Kids 8 to 18, March 8, 2005, http://clinton.senate.gov/news/statements/details.cfm?id=233740&&.

20 "Dick Morris's anti-Hillary book..." Dick Morris, *Rewriting History* (ReganBooks, 2004).

21 " 'The larger lesson of the 1994 defeat...' " ibid, 97.

22 " 'I never thought of Hillary as...' " ibid, 112.

23 " 'Hillary was no stranger to the left...' " ibid, 132.

24 " 'With clear lines of authority'..." ibid, 101–103.

25 " 'Hillary's hold on a future...' " ibid, 261

26 " 'But as the decade unfolds...' " ibid, 265.

27 "'The praise for her staff . . .'" R. Emmett Tyrrell, Jr. with Mark Davis, *Madame Hillary: The Dark Road to the White House* (Washington, D.C.: Regnery Publishing, 2004.), 19.

28 "'She has demonstrated an extraordinary ability . . .'" ibid, 19.

29 "'Hilary steers clear . . .'" ibid.

30 "makes Bobby Fischer moves." ibid, 148.

31 "almost metaphysical . . ." ibid, 148.

32 "transcendent dreams of the feminist . . ." ibid, 148.

33 "modern suburban women . . ." ibid, 148.

34 "Limbacher begins his book . . ." Carl Limbacher, *Hillary's Scheme* (Crown Forum, 2003), xix.

35 "Amy Sullivan, the *Washington Monthly* editor . . ." Amy Sullivan, *Washington Monthly*, July/August 2005.

36 "It's too early for anyone to say . . ." ibid.

5. CAN SHE LOSE? THE ROCK STAR AND THE REST

1 "'How do you stack the lesser-knowns . . .'" James A. Barnes, "The Rock Star and the Rest," *National Journal*, April 30, 2005.

2 "So, despite columnist Ellen Goodman's plea . . ." Ellen Goodman, "The Trashing of Hillary," *Boston Globe*, April 21, 2005.

3 "I used to assign my undergraduate students . . ." Stephen Hess, "Why Great Men are Not Chosen Presidents: Lord Bryce Revisited," *Presidents and the Presidency* (The Brookings Institution, 1996, 33.)

4 "The other day, in a White House press conference . . ." Posting of Brian Stelter, July 12, 2005 at www.mediabistro.com/tvnewser/abc/abcs_terry_moran_calls_fox_news_a_friendly_channel_to_the_white_house_23525.asp.

5 "I just shook my head . . ." Byron York, "Lawyer: Cooper 'Burned' Karl Rove," *National Review Online*, July 12, 2005, www.nationalreview.com/york/york200507121626.asp.

6 ". . . save for Bill Richardson . . ." Bill Richardson, Governor of New Mexico Biography, www.governor.state.nm.us/governor.php.

7 "The minute I heard that Dean said . . ." Michelle Goldberg, "Howard Dean's Israel problem," *Salon*, September 9, 2003, www.salon.com/news/feature/2003/09/23/dean_israel/index_np.html.

8 "Agriculture policy in America . . ." Posting of Kevin Drum on Washington monthly.com, August 14, 2003, www.washingtonmonthly.com/archives/individual/2003_08/001900.php.

9 "In 1988, many people believed . . ." Tom Sherwood, "Campaign Has Bentsen's Star on the Rise; Surprise Popularity Enhances Reputation," *Washington Post*, November 6, 1988 at A24.

[10] "But when he did run . . ." David S. Broder, Thomas B. Edsall, "Protest Vote Cuts Bushs's N.H. Margin; Tsongas, Clinton Top Democratic Field; New Democratic Entry Seen Unlikely for Now," *Washington Post*, February 19, 1992, A1.

[11] "Jim Barnes of *The Atlantic*" Barnes and Bell, *Atlantic Monthly*, July/August 2005.

[12] "People talk about the Electoral College . . ." John Mark Hansen, "Even the best arguments for the Electoral College seem less a statement of principle than a defense of entrenched privilege," *Chicago Sun Times*, November 1, 2004, 43.

[13] "The nominating system was created . . ." The Primary System, 2004 Democratic Primaries, Online NewsHour, December 15, 2003, PBS, www.pbs.org/newshour/vote2004/primaries/sr_primary.html.

[14] "Then there was Scoop Jackson." Todd Crowell, " 'Maggie' out, 'Scoop' next for Northwest," *Christian Science Monitor*, November 21, 1980, 12.

[15] "Then there was Ronald Reagan . . ." Douglas E. Kneeland, *New York Times*, October 16, 1979, 10.

[16] "As for the first George Bush . . ." Geoffrey Barker, "Bush and Dole paper over their rivalry," *The Advertiser*, November 30, 1988.

[17] "In 1976, 'Uncommitted' beat Carter . . ." NelsonPolsby and Aaron Wildavsky, *Presidential Elections: Strategies and Structures of American Politics* (Rowman & Littlefield Publishers, Inc., 2003) 76.

[18] "Inside the Democratic Party . . ." Posting by Marko Moulitsas Zuniga on DailyKos at www.dailykos.com/story/2005/1/3/1343/67651.

[19] ". . . any modern insurgent who took off in the way Gary Hart did . . ." Against the Grain, "The 2nd (or 3rd) Coming of Gary Hart, May 1, 2003 at www.cbsnews.com/stories/2003/04/30/opinion/meyer/main551733.shtml.

[20] ". . . what academics call the 'media effects' . . ." Dhavan V. Shah; Mark D. Watts; David Domke; David P. Fan; Michael Fibison, "News Coverage, Economic Cues, and the Public's Presidential Preferences, 1984–1996," *The Journal of Politics*, Vol. 612, No. 4 (Nov. 1999), pp. 914–943 *also see* Nelson Polsby and Aaron Wildavsky, *Presidential Elections: Strategies and Structures of American Politics* (Rowman & Littlefield Publishers, Inc., 2003) 69–78.

[21] "The system that exists today . . ." Polsby and Wildavsky, *Presidential Elections . . .* , 89–136.

[22] "The revolution in party rules and platforms . . ." Ibid., *and* "Constitutional Safeguards in the Selection of Delegates to Presidential Nomination," *Yale Law Journal*, Vol. 78, No. 7 (June 1969), 1228–1252.

[23] "The McGovern Commission . . ." Polsby and Wildavsky, *Presidential Elections . . .* , 89–136, *and* Judith A. Center, "1972 Democratic Convention Reforms and Party Democracy," *Political Science Quarterly*, Vol. 89, No. 2 (June 1974), 325–350.

[24] ". . . but it wasn't until 1978" Polsby and Wildavsky, *Presidential Elections . . . ,* 89–136, *and* Susan Ann Kay, "Feminist Ideology, Race, and Political Participation: A Second Look," *The Western Political Quarterly*, Vol. 38, No. 3 (Spr. 1985), 476–484.

[25] "Before 1968, most states . . ." Polsby and Wildavsky, *Presidential Elections . . . ,* 89–136, *and* James R. Beniger, "Winning the Presidential Nomination: National Polls and State Primary Elections, 1936–1972," *Public Opinion Quarterly*, Vol. 40, No. 1 (Spring 1976), 22–38.

[26] "The 'Call' to the 1972 convention . . ." John R. Schmidt, Wayne W. Whalen, "Credentials Contests at the 1968—and 1972 Democratic National Conventions," *Harvard Law Review*, Vol. 82, No. 7 (May 1969), 1438–1470.

[27] ". . . until 1988 . . ." Polsby and Wildavsky, *Presidential Elections . . . ,* 89–136, *and* Larry M. Bartels, C. Anthony Broh, "A Review: The 1988 Presidential Primaries," *Public Opinion Quarterly*, Vol. 53, No. 4 (Winter, 1989), 563–589.

[28] "The idea, as political scientist . . ." John Haskell, "The Paradox of Plebiscitary Democracy in Presidential Nomination Campaigns," *Western Political Quarterly*, Vol. 45, No. 4 (Dec. 1992), 1001–1019.

[29] "George McGovern resigned as the chairman . . ." Judith A. Center, "1972 Democratic Convention Reforms and Party Democracy," *Political Science Quarterly*, Vol. 89, No. 2 (Jun. 1974), 325–350 and Dave Liep's Atlas of U.S. Presidential Elections, www.uselectionatlas.org/.

[30] "A new commission, chaired by Morley Winograd . . ." Gary D. Wekkin, "National-State Party Relations: The Democrats' New Federal Structure," *Political Science Quarterly*, Vol. 99, No. 1 (Spring, 1984), 45–72.

[31] " 'Former governor Jimmy Carter . . .' " R.W. Apple, Jr., *New York Times*, January 20, 1976, 1.

[32] "Why the changes?" Polsby and Wildavsky, *Presidential Elections . . . ,* 89–136.

[33] "Less dramatically, but no less significantly . . ." Martin Walker, "The US Presidential Election, 1996," *International Affairs*, Vol. 72, No. 4 (Oct. 1996), 657–674.

[34] "Joe Klein, then of *Newsweek* . . ." Joe Klein, "Clinton: The Survivor," *Newsweek*, July 20, 1992, 22.

[35] ". . . and Michael Kramer, of *Time* . . ." Michael Kramer, "Clinton's Second Chance," *Time*, July 20, 1992.

[36] "Howard Dean was ahead in the polls . . ." Michael Barone and Richard E. Cohen, *The Almanac of American Politics 2004* (National Journal Group, 2003), entry: Howard Dean.

[37] "Between 1984 and 2004 . . ." Anthony Corrado et al.., "The Parties Take the Lead: Political Parties and the Financing of the 2000 Presidential Election," in John C. Green & Rick Framer, eds., *The State of the Parties*, 4th ed. (Rowman & Littlefield, 2003).

38 "There is currently a new commission meeting . . ." The Democratic Party Commission on Presidential Nomination Timing and Scheduling, www.democrats.org/a/2005/06/commission_on_p.php, June 2005.

39 "There's the idea of regional primaries . . ." Mike Glover, "Democrats Considering Revamping Primaries," Associated Press, May 17, 2005, http://wtop.com/index.php?nid=213&sid=51516.

40 "there is also the idea of a Western . . ." "Democrats Launch Group to Build Strength, Majorities in West," http://www.democratsforthewest.com/.

41 "As party chairman, Howard Dean has already told . . ." Thomas Beaumont, "Dean says Iowa's caucus schedule is fine," *Des Moines Register*, January 14, 2005 at: http://desmoineregister.com/apps/pbcs.dll/article?AID=/20050114/NEWS09/501140416/1056&template=printart.

42 "While the Supreme Court has held . . ." *Cousins v. Wigoda, 419 U.S. 477* (1975).

43 "And the groundswell's already beginning . . ." Lee Bandy, "Clinton Wins S.C. Straw Poll," *The State*, June 16, 2005, www.thestate.com/mld/thestate/.

44 "I laughed when I read an item . . ." Robert Novak, "McCain's Headache May Go Away," *Chicago Sun-Times*, April 24, 2005, 37.

45 "There was much talk in 2004 . . ." Glen Justice, "Howard Dean's Internet Push: Where Will it Lead?," *New York Times*, November 2, 2003, 5.

46 "Jim Barnes describes the Democratic field . . ." Barnes, *National Journal*, April 30, 2005.

47 "Laura Bush does this rather brilliantly . . ." "Text: Remarks by First Lady Laura Bush to the Republican National Convention," *Washington Post*, August 31, 2004 at http://www.washingtonpost.com/wp-dyn/articles/A50438-2004Aug31.html.

48 "Not Teresa." "Transcript: Teresa Heinz Kerry," WashingtonPost.com, July 27, 2004 at www.washingtonpost.com/wp-dyn/articles/A19797-2004Jul27.html.

49 "According to a Zogby poll . . ." "Red/Blue Divide Still Evident: Red States Give Bush 50% Job Approval, 42% in Blues; War on Terror Bush's Strength—Low Marks on Other Facets of Job; Handling of Social Security Nets Lowest Score; Bush Would Still Beat Kerry Today (46% to 41%), New Zogby Poll Reveals," Zogby International, April 26, 2005, www.zogby.com/search/ReadNews.dbm?ID=989.

50 "Consider the following quotes . . ." Barnes, *National Journal*, April 30, 2005.

51 "I was certainly interested . . ." ibid.

52 "His personal story is certainly better." John Edwards Biography, One America Committee, http://www.oneamericacommittee.com/john-edwards.asp.

53 "Not long ago . . ." Mike Glover, "Edwards says 'Two Americas' theme still resonates," Associated Press, March 31, 2005.

54 "Just what Gray Davis did . . ." Franklin Foer, "Gray Davis and the Rise of the Staffer Mentality," *New Republic*, February 18, 2002.

[55] "The Senate met in an all-day session . . ." Ron Fournier, "Dems Call for Bill on Security Clearance," SFGate.com, July 14, 2005 at www.sfgate.com/cgi-bin/article.cgi?f=/n/a/2005/07/14/national/w093837D61.DT.

[56] "Biden has already gone on television . . ." Interview by Tim Russert with Senator Joe Biden, Meet the Press, Sunday, February 27, 2005.

[57] "A few months later . . ." Dan Balz, "Biden to Seek Presidential Nomination," *The Washington Post*, June 20, 2005, A3.

[58] "Evan Bayh is the top choice of Republicans . . ." Chris Suellentrop, "It's Never Too Early for a Wild Guess," *Los Angeles Times*, May 8, 2005, M2.

[59] "Warner is a fifty-year-old first-term governor." Governor Mark Warner at www.governor.virginia.gov/Governor/GovBioHome.html.

[60] "The nominating process lends itself . . ." Barbara Norrander, "Presidential Nomination Politics in the Post-Reform Era," *Political Research Quarterly*, Vol. 49, No. 4 (Dec. 1996), 875–915.

[61] "2000 Republican Presidential Primary Results" data culled from Federal Election Committee at www.fec.gov/pubrec/fe2000/2000presprim.htm.

[62] "John McCain had George W. Bush . . ." Associated Press, "Bush Handily Beats McCain in Virginia Primary," *St. Louis Post-Dispatch*, March 1, 2000.

[63] "Dick Morris has been touting Condoleezza Rice" Dick Morris, "To Stop Hillary, Draft Condi," *The Hill*, February 9, 2005, www.hillnews.com/thehill/export/TheHill/Comment/DickMorris/020905.html.

[64] "John McCain is the Evan Bayh . . ." Bill House and Jon Kamman, "2008: Will it be McCain?" *Arizona Republic*, June 12, 2005.

6. IT ISN'T JUST ABOUT (HER) SEX

[1] "As she's already proven she understands . . ." News: Statements and Releases, http://clinton.senate.gov/.

[2] "When asked in the NBC/Wall Street Journal poll . . ." NBC News/*Wall Street Journal* Poll, May 20, 2004, www.msnbc.com.

[3] "But Hillary has been at the forefront . . ." News: Statements and Releases, http://clinton.senate.gov/.

[4] " 'I know what you're thinking' " Hillary Clinton, "Now Can We Talk About Health Care," *New York Times Magazine*, April 18, 2004, 26.

[5] "The morning after I wrote this . . ." Diane E. Lewis, "As Retirement Looms, it's about Feeling Good," *Boston Globe*, July 10, 2005.

[6] "In Florida, the state literally went to court . . ." Abby Goodnough, "Florida Halts Fight to Bar Girl's Abortion," *New York Times*, May 4, 2005.

[7] "The House passed a bill that would punish . . ." *Child Interstate Abortion Notification Act, H.R. 748, 109th Cong.* (2005).

[8] "In a much-quoted column in *Time* . . ." Joe Klein, "Hillary in 2008? No Way! Why

the former First Lady should stay in the Senate," *Time*, May 8, 2005, www.time.com/time/columnist/klein/article/0,9565,1059000,00.html.

9   "John Danforth is a conservative Republican . . ." John C. Danforth, "Onward, Moderate Christian Soldiers," *New York Times*, June 17, 2005, A27.

10 "'Israel is our strongest ally . . ." Hillary Rodham Clinton, Senator Clinton Calls on Secretary of State Powell to Oppose EU Trade Sanctions Against Israel, April 9, 2002, http://clinton.senate.gov/news/statements/details.cfm?id=235375&&.

11 "Events in the Middle East . . ." Hillary Rodham Clinton, Remarks by Senator Hillary Rodham Clinton to the 2005 American Israel Public Affairs Committee Policy Conference, May 24, 2005, http://clinton.senate.gov/news/statements/details.cfm?id=23981.

12 "'My first observation is simple . . .'" Hillary Rodham Clinton, The Future Role of the United Nations Within the Framework of Global Security, February 13, 2005, http://clinton.senate.gov/news/statements/details.cfm?id=236353&&.

13 "'We stand at a point in time . . .'" Hillary Rodham Clinton, Remarks of Senator Hillary Rodham Clinton to the Council on Foreign Relations, December 15, 2003, http://clinton.senate.gov/news/statements/details.cfm?id=233760&&.

14 "'I was one who supported giving . . .'" ibid.

15 "'We need tough-minded . . .'" ibid.

16 "'Ten years ago . . .'" Hillary Rodham Clinton, Vital Voices Global Partnership and NYU's Center for Global Affairs Public Forum: Women's Rights are Human Rights, http://clinton.senate.gov/news/statements/details.cfm?id=233742&&.

7. MOMENTS OF TRUTH

1   "Dukakis's furlough program . . ." Owen Thomas, "Easy answer on prison furloughs eludes Dukakis," *Christian Science Monitor*, September 8, 1988, 3.

2   "There has been a concerted effort this year . . ." Sheryl McCarthy, "Are We Ready for a Woman President?," *Newsday*, February 24, 2005, A42.

3   "Similarly, in Anticipating Madam President . . ." Robert P. Watson & Ann Gordon, eds., *Anticipating Madam President* (Lynne Rienner Publishers, 2003).

4   "'Willingness to Vote for a Woman Candidate for President . . ." David Moore, "Little Prejudice Against a Woman, Jewish, Black or Catholic Presidential Candidate," The Gallup Organization, June 10, 2003, www.gallup.com/poll.

5   "In their book *Madam President* . . ." Clift and Brazaitis, *Madam President* (Scribner, 2000).

6   "Women have done better . . ." Vaishalee Mishra. "Guide Places Key Statehouses in Women's Reach," *Women's E-news* at: www.womensnews.org/article.cfm/dyn/aid/5T8/context/com.

7   "In research funded by . . ." "Keys to the Governor's Office," The Barbara Lee Foundation, 2001, www.barbaraleefoundation.org/usr_doc/governors_guide.pdf.

[8] "Among the mayors of America's . . ." "Women in Elective Office 2005," www.cawp.rutgers.edu/Facts/Officeholders/elective.pdf.

[9] "In a 1998 study of six executive races . . ." James Devitt, "Framing Gender on the Campaign Trail: Women's Executive Leadership and the Press," The White House Project, 1998, www.thewhitehouseproject.org/KnowTheFacts/Research/frame genderintro.html.

[10] "The first time I read Nick Kristof's column . . ." Kristof, *New York Times*, March 16, 2005.

[11] "Joe Klein, *Time*'s top political columnist . . ." Joe Klein, "Hillary in 2008? No Way! Why the former First Lady should stay in the Senate," *Time*, May 8, 2005, www.time.com/time/columnist/klein/article/0,9565,1059000,00.html.

[12] "The economy, to be sure . . ." CNN/*Time* Poll, January 17–18, 1996 at www.cnn.com/ALLPOLITICS/1996/polls/cnn.time/011796.shtml.

[13] "In the one debate of the 1980 campaign . . ." Adam Clymer, "Contradictions in the Debate," *New York Times*, October 30, 1980.

SELECTED RESOURCES

Polls: All major polls that everyone conducts for the 2008 race are collected in one place: www.pollingreport.com/2008.

BlogConnection: Links you to the daily news on the race with bipartisan English wit. www.ovaloffice2008.com

Insider Surveys are regularly conducted by James Barnes of the *National Journal.* www.theatlantic.com/doc/200507/hillarypoll has a summer insider survey www.nationaljournal.com has regular updates.

Excellent sources of information, research and action on women in elections include:

Center for American Women and Politics
www.rci-rutgers.edu~cawp.
(under the oversight of the brilliant Professor Ruth B. Mandel, who runs the Eagleton Institute of Politics at Rutgers)

The Barbara Lee Foundation, www.barbaraleefoundation.org/(formed by the self-named dynamo)

The White House Project, www.whitehouseproject.org (one of the brainchildren of Marie Wilson, the founder of the Ms. Foundation)

SELECTED BIBLIOGRAPHY

Albright, Madeleine. "Women and Foreign Policy: A Call to Action." Remarks at the Women's Conference, Los Angeles, October 5, 1999. *U.S. Department of State Dispatch* 10, no. 8 (October 1999).

Alexander, Herbert E. and Anthony Corrado. *Financing the 1992 Election.* Armonk: M.E. Sharpe Inc., 1995.

American Association of University Women. *Gender Gaps: Where Schools Still Fail Our Children.* Washington, DC: AAUW, 1998.

Barone, Michael, and Richard Cohen. *The Almanac of American Politics*, DC: National Journal, forthcoming, 2006.

Baumgardner, Jennifer, and Amelia Richards. "Why Not Elizabeth Dole?" *The Nation*, April 5, 1999, 6.

Broder, David. *The Party's Over: The Failure of Politics in America.* New York: Harper & Row, 1972.

Blumenthal, Sidney. *The Permanent Campaign*, rev. ed. New York: Simon & Schuster, 1982.

Bystron, Dianne G., Mary Christine Banwart, Lynda Lee Kaid, and Terry A. Robertson. *Gender and Candidate Communication.* New York: Routledge, 2002.

Clift, Eleanor and Tom Brazaitis. *Madam President: Shattering the Last Glass Ceiling.* New York: Scribner, 2000.

Corrado, Anthony, et al. *The New Campaign Finance Sourcebook*, Washington, DC: Brookings Institute, 2005.

Corrado, Anthony, *Campaign Finance Reform*, New York: The Century Foundation Press, 2005.

Cramer, Richard Ben. *What It Takes: The Way to the White House*. New York: Vintage Books, 1992.

Crigler, Ann, Marian Just, and Edward McCaffrey, eds. *Rethinking the Vote*. New York: Oxford University Press, 2004.

Cronin, Thomas E., and Michael A. Genovese. *The Paradoxes of the American Presidency*. New York: Oxford University Press, 1998.

Crotty, William, ed. *America's Choice 2000*. Boulder, CO: Westview Press, 2001.

Dershowitz, Alan M. *Sexual McCarthyism: Clinton, Starr, and the Emerging Constitutional Crisis*. New York: Basic Books, 1998.

Drew, Elizabeth. *The Corruption of American Politics: What Went Wrong and Why*. Woodstock, NY: The Overlook Press, 2000.

Ferraro, Geraldine, with Linda Bird Francke. *Ferraro: My Story*. New York: Bantam Books, 1985.

Fels, Anna. *Necessary Dreams: The Vital Role of Ambition in Women's Changing Lives*. New York: Pantheon Books, 2004.

Germond, Jack and Jules Witcover. *Mad as Hell: Revolt at the Ballot Box, 1992*. New York: Warner Books, 1993.

Goff, Michael J. *The Money Primary: The New Politics of the Early Presidential Nomination Process*. Oxford: Rowman & Littlefield, 2004.

Harris, John F. *The Survivor: Bill Clinton in the White House*. New York: Random House, 2005.

Iyengar, Shanto, and Donald Kiner. *Is Anyone Responsible? How Television Frames Political Issues*. Chicago: University of Chicago Press, 1991.

Jamieson, Kathleen Hall. *Beyond the Double Bind: Women and Leadership*. New York: Oxford University Press, 1995.

———. *Eloquence in an Electronic Age: The Transformation of Political Speechmaking*. New York: Oxford University Press, 1988.

Kaminer, Wendy. "Feminism's Identity Crisis." *The Atlantic Monthly*, October 1993, 51–68.

Klein, Ethel. *Gender Politics: From Consciousness to Mass Politics*. Cambridge, MA: Harvard University Press, 1984.

Mandel, Ruth B. *In the Running: The New Woman Candidate*. Boston: Beacon, 1991.

———. "Women's Leadership in American Politics: The Legacy and the Promise." In Cynthia B. Costello and Anne J. Stone, eds. *The American Woman 2001–2002*. New York: W.W. Norton & Co, 2001.

Mayer, William, ed. *In Pursuit of the White House 2000*. New York: Chatham House, 2000.

McGlen, Nancy E. *Women in Foreign Policy: The Insiders*. New York: Routledge, 1993.

Neustadt, Richard E. *Presidential Power: The Politics of Leadership*. New York: John Wiley & Sons, 1964.

Norris, Pippa. *Women, Media, and Politics*. New York: Oxford University Press, 1997.

Novak, Michael. *Choosing Presidents*. New Jersey: Transaction Publishers, 1992.

Patterson, Thomas E. *The Vanishing Voter*. New York: Vintage, 2003.

Polsby, Nelson. *Consequences of Party Reform*. New York: Oxford University Press, 1983.

———. "The Democratic Nomination and the Evolution of the Party System." In Austin Ranney, ed. *The American Elections of 1984*. Durham, NC: Duke University Press, 1985.

Popkin, Samuel. *The Reasoning Voter: Communication and Persuasion in Presidential Campaigns*. Chicago: University of Chicago Press, 1994.

Rhode, Deborah. *Theoretical Perspectives on Sexual Difference*. New Haven, CT: Yale, 1990.

Ross, Karen. *Women, Politics, Media: Uneasy Relations in Comparative Perspective*. Creskill, NJ: Hampton Press, 2002.

Schumaker, Paul D. and Burdett A. Loomis. *Choosing a President: The Electoral College and Beyond*. New York: Seven Bridges Press, 2002.

Sorensen, Theodore. *Decision Making in the White House: The Olive Branch or the Arrows*. New York: Columbia University, 1963.

Tilly, Louise and Patricia Gurin, eds. *Women, Politics, and Change*. New York: Russell Sage, 1992.

Wayne, Stephen J. *The Road to the White House 2000: The Politics of Presidential Elections*. New York: Bedford/St. Martin's, 2001.

Wolfinger, Raymond E. and Steven J. Rosenstone. *Who Votes?* New Haven, CT: Yale University Press, 1980.

INDEX